Dr Tom Bramble is Senior Lecturer in Industrial Relations at the University of Queensland. He has researched and published in the areas of Australasian trade unionism since the late 1980s and is an active unionist himself. He earned his doctorate from La Trobe University in Melbourne on the Australia Vehicle Builders' Union and also holds a masters degree in Industrial Relations from the University of New South Wales and a bachelors in Economics from Cambridge University.

NEVER A WHITE FLAG

THE MEMOIRS OF
JOCK BARNES

EDITED BY TOM BRAMBLE

Victoria University Press

VICTORIA UNIVERSITY PRESS
Victoria University of Wellington
PO Box 600 Wellington
http://vup.vuw.ac.nz

Copyright © Jock Barnes 1998

Introduction and editorial matter © Tom Bramble 1998

ISBN 0 86473 344 5

First published 1998
Reprinted 1998

This book is copyright. Apart from
any fair dealing for the purpose of private study,
research, criticism or review, as permitted under the
Copyright Act, no part may be reproduced by any
process without the permission of
the publishers

Printed by South Wind Production (Singapore) Pte Ltd

CONTENTS

Introduction	9
Acknowledgements	29
A Chronology of Key Events	30
A Chronology of Key Events of the 1951 Lockout	32
A Who's Who	37

NEVER A WHITE FLAG: THE MEMOIRS OF JOCK BARNES

1   Life Before the Waterfront, 1907–33   41

   Home life; starting work; coming into politics and trouble in the Great Depression; persecution.

2   Onto the Waterfront, 1933–41   50

   Starting work as a wharfie; the Bureau system is introduced; no pig-iron to Japan!; the birth of the Waterfront Control Commission; the Kelly–Murray case; election as branch president.

3   War on the Waterfront, 1941–45   56

   Conscription is introduced; the yanks are coming!; battles with the Commission; action against jailing of freezing workers; election as national president; the Kaikorai gangway dispute; challenge to the preference clause; a living culture; end-of-war blow-ups.

4   The Short Life of Labour's New Order, 1946–47   74

   More battles with the Commission; the food for Britain fraud; emergency regulations abolished; our campaign for a guaranteed wage; FOL special conference; food for Britain, again; Cook Islands campaign.

5   The *Mountpark* Incident, 1948   90

Mountpark, round two.

6   The Cold War Hots Up, 1948–49   104

The carpenters caught in the cold war; conscription referendum; campaign for a wage increase; the Northumberland*; solidarity with the Canadians; toxic cargo on the* Barnhill*; sacked from the Waterfront Authority; taking action over safety, again; back on the attack over wages; electoral defeat for Fraser government.*

7   The Run-up to the '51 Lockout, 1950   130

Back on the waterfront; the break from the FOL; business as usual; lampblack again; the Authority hears our wage claim; the Rangitoto *dispute; yet another lampblack dispute; dispute over order of reference for Royal Commission.*

8   The Lockout Begins   156

The Royal Commission begins; negotiations for a pay rise continue; the anti-wharfie offensive; Waterfront Strike Emergency Regulations, 1951; taking a stand.

9   Support Floods In   171

WWU deregistered; rank and file on the move; the government's 'seven points'; friends and enemies.

10   Both Sides Dig In   189

Peaceful protestors bashed by police; FOL conference resolves on 'no action'; increased police repression; daylight robbery by the shipowners; Nash 'neither for nor against'; further police bashings; Bloody Friday, 1 June; public resistance grows; Labour's failure; my wife prosecuted.

Contents

11 To the Bitter End, and a New Beginning   218
    *Voting to return to work; early election called; two months' hard
    labour; fresh fields for sowing; life after the waterfront; reviving
    old memories.*

Appendices

1 History of the Waterfront Commission   241
2 Key Information on the Waterside Workers' Union
   (Auckland Branch), 1935–51   242
3 *Our Union is Attacked*, 1949   243
4 Messages of Support from Australian and Other
   Overseas Unions During 1951   251
5 Other Works on the Waterfront, 1935–51   254

Index   255

INTRODUCTION
Tom Bramble

From the 1930s until the 1950s the Waterside Workers' Union was at the centre of industrial life in New Zealand. The union was repeatedly in conflict with government and employers over wages and conditions and had made solidarity its byword, both at home and overseas. The wharfies were at the forefront in the battle against the Cold War anti-communist drive set in train by the Fraser government and taken up with gusto by the National government under Sid Holland. The final battle in 1951 ranks as one of the defining moments of New Zealand's history in the 20th century, as the forces of labour and capital were pitched against each other in a fight to the finish.

In this book, Harold 'Jock' Barnes tells the story of these events as they happened, from the day of his arrival on the waterfront in 1935 to the 1951 lockout and the destruction of the old union. Jock's account of life on the waterfront can be ignored by no-one. The man was at the centre of it all, from internal tussles for leadership of the union to moments of great national crisis. Jock Barnes's name was heard everywhere from Cabinet room to children's nursery—mothers used to warn their fractious children that 'Jock Barnes will come and get you if you don't settle down and go to sleep!'

The wharfies' union was once one of New Zealand's largest and most powerful unions. In the following description of the conditions of working life on the waterfront, I am indebted to the research of Dr Anna Green. Holding a central role in the export of agricultural and pastoral products and the import of manufactures and fertilisers, the nation's 8000 waterfront workers were in a critical position to affect economic activity throughout the country (Green, 1992: 102). From hesitant and uncertain beginnings in the 1880s, the wharfies built up their unions, saw them beaten back down again, only to rebuild them again stronger than ever (Roth, 1993). The waterfront drew in workers from all backgrounds: there were communists and Catholics, skilled and unskilled, native-born and immigrant, Pakeha and Maori.

But one characteristic the wharfies shared that took them through the tumultuous times was a unity forged around continuous battles with the bosses. In the early decades this meant the shipowners, but from 1940 onwards the wharfies also had to contend with the Waterfront Commission and government. The main shipowners operating to and from New Zealand were a mercenary, profit-driven cabal, comprising a British owners' conference line, Benmacow (consisting of Shaw Savill and Albion, the New Zealand Shipping Company, Port Line and the Blue Star Line), and the major local company, the Union Steam Ship Company (USSCo), owned by the British P&O Company (Green, 1992: 102–3). Profits were always protected at the expense of waterside safety and even the most basic canteen or washing amenities for wharfies.

The shipping companies invariably sought out tough ex-military men to manage their New Zealand waterfront operations (Green, 1996: 24), and this factor is commented on by Barnes, who notes the public-school 'born to rule' mentality of those whom he encountered (see Lowenstein and Hills, 1982, and Sheridan, 1995; 1996 for very similar accounts in Australia). The word of the boss was law, and although the union was able to gain control of overall recruitment to the workforce, under the 'auction-block' system, foremen were free to pick who was actually engaged on any given day. The shipowners had no compunction in requiring men to front up for work at six in the morning, sit on their haunches for three hours over the engagement period and, if still not hired, to wait around until lunchtime when the same process could be repeated. The men then had to return home with the entire day wasted and not a penny earned. In these circumstances favouritism was rife, and until 1937, when the auction block was replaced by the Bureau system of engagement, union activism sometimes meant missing out on the best jobs or the chances for overtime.

The cost of having a ship lying idle on the wharves was prohibitive, and the prime concern for the shipowner was to turn the ship around and get it back to sea. Work was dirty, hard, and frequently unsafe. The worst jobs were slag, lime and guano, but many others were regarded as obnoxious to handle. Bulk cargoes were stacked together in paper bags that often rotted. Jock describes the campaign for bonuses to handle lampblack (used for blackening tyres), but the union was also concerned for its men working in freezer hatches and elsewhere. Hernias and injuries of all kinds were common, and cuts and bruises just part of the daily work. In Auckland alone in 1938, more than 1300 injuries were reported to the Shipowners' Federation, arising mostly from problems in handling cargo and being struck by falling or swinging loads. At one stage roughly one third of all watersiders could be expected to be on accident compensation at some point during the year (Green, 1994: 147–54; 1996: 87).

The one constant in all statements from the shipowners throughout the entire period is their complaint that work standards were slipping, that pilferage was rampant, and that discipline needed to be restored to the waterfront. This refrain was maintained in times when the owners had complete control, as they did in 1915, and also when their 'rights' were under siege, as they were in the 1940s. None of the Auckland waterfront problems, of course, was due to abysmal facilities for the handling of cargo and the primitive levels of mechanisation. It was only with the arrival of American troops in 1942 that the Auckland waterfront was completely shaken up in this respect, and this 'can-do' mentality lies behind the respect evinced by Barnes towards the American top brass (Green, 1992: 106, 112; 1994, 147; 1996, 219).

Despite the shipowners' complaints, the city's wharves radically increased the amount of cargo handled from the time of Jock's arrival on the Auckland waterfront in 1935 to the 1951 lockout. Partly this was due to the war, partly it was due to a decision by the shipowners to reduce the number of ports called in at by ocean-going ships. Employment increased by two-thirds, with the result that Auckland went from having just over half the number of wharfies as in Wellington during World War One (967 as against 1735), to 10 per cent more (2000 as against 1840) 35 years later (Green, 1996: 34). The pressure of work explains the importance attached by shipowners and government to industrial discipline on the wharves. This placed a tremendous burden on the men, and long working hours became the norm after the mid-1930s, most especially during the war. Twelve-hour shifts were worked and work continued right through until 10pm. Men worked 60, 70 or even 80 hours for weeks at a time (Green, 1994: 155).

In the face of hostility from the entire industrial establishment and even from other unions, the Auckland wharfies developed a tremendous *esprit de corps* (see Sheridan 1994 for similar accounts of Australian wharfies). This was evident in the solidarity displayed in 1951, with barely two dozen scabs being recruited from their number. But it was obvious well before '51 and made their opponents reckon them up as tough adversaries. The group cohesion, manifest in the nicknames (Green, 1994: 158), their close working-class communities, the drinking in the same pubs, the following of sons into their father's trade, helped make the wharfies something of a 'race apart', in the words of academics Kerr and Siegel (1954: 191).

The worst sin on the waterfront was to be a scab. Once tainted, a man was marked for life. Jock notes that with the union in charge of hiring labour for the waterfront, good 'industrial character' was the number one requirement for engagement, and this ensured that workers who had been blacked from other industries for union activity were eligible for jobs on the waterfront. Like attracted like, and by the 1930s the wharfies included many old Waihi men, seamen and other survivors of past industrial battles.

It was this camaraderie that enabled the wharfies over time to win a series of improvements to their working conditions: the right to decide who should be employed on the waterfront, the right to decide whether to work in the rain, a limitation on the amount of overtime, regulation of the pace of work and the weight of slings, and payment for handling obnoxious cargo (Green, 1992; 1994). Particularly under Barnes's leadership, the union preferred direct bargaining and strike action to arbitration and conciliation. Through pressure of this kind in the 1940s, the union won an increased guaranteed wage and annual holidays, the right to refuse work deemed to be unsafe by wharfies themselves, and improved canteen and waiting-room facilities on the Auckland waterfront.

Conditions of work were very similar across the industry, with every worker on the award rate and not a penny more. Wage increases therefore had to be fought for nationally, so wharfies understood the importance of their national union. The wharfies resisted piecework and productivity bonus schemes proposed by employers in the 1930s and 1940s that would only have split up their collective identity. More controversially, rank and file members also rejected 'co-operative stevedoring', which would have seen some of their number effectively become managers of others (Green, 1992: 114).

The union won these gains primarily by exercising its industrial muscle. In the postwar years the loss of man-hours due to industrial conflict increased nearly tenfold. Auckland, of course, was at the centre of the agitation. Nearly three-quarters of all waterfront disputes in the postwar years were in this port. Nearly one-quarter of all hours of stoppage concerned disputes about dirt rates (e.g. the lampblack disputes), 18 per cent concerned danger rates (for example the dispute over tetra-ethyl of lead on the *Barnhill*), 12 per cent concerned spelling, and 11 per cent were over safety issues such as the *Mountpark* case. The continuous battle of wills between the wharfies' union and the Waterfront Commission accounted for a further 21 per cent of hours lost. In this book Jock covers all of these episodes and more (Green, 1996: 185–7).

The union packed a powerful punch because it was not only democratic in structure and participatory in nature, but also actively *controlled* by its members. Monthly stopwork meetings, which all members were required to attend, were held in the port buildings and, when the numbers attending grew close to 2000, were then moved to the town hall. Meetings could last up to four or five hours. Branch officials were elected by secret ballot and members of the Auckland branch executive were regularly overturned, with the balance swinging both left and right in the 1940s. It was not just an Auckland affair, of course. In 1949 a stopwork meeting was held at Lyttelton at which Barnes spoke for two hours and national secretary Toby Hill for one, followed by three hours of question and debate (Lane, 1981: 8).

The union's paper, *Transport Worker*, played a key role in informing members of union affairs and was edited by Dick Scott, who went on to become a professional writer of some repute. The paper was not just educational: it also served to mobilise the membership. It was a paper that *campaigned*, with full coverage of every issue of the day, whether it was the conscription referendum, shipowners' profits, battles over lampblack, a general election, Fintan Patrick Walsh's postwar anti-socialist 'stabilisation policy', or the split from the Federation of Labour (FOL) (Lane, 1981: 8). The paper did not shy away from history and included articles on the Red Federation of Labour and the early days of the labour movement. Contemporary Labour leaders were embarrassed by the regular reprints of their earlier statements on the restrictive nature of the arbitration system, to which they had now become enthusiastic converts.

In addition to the newspaper, the union also had an active publicity machine and, when under attack from either the Labour or National government or the Waterfront Commission, issued tens of thousands of pamphlets putting its case to the wider labour movement. The union also ran massive public meetings of a kind that any New Zealand union today would find impossible.

All of this took place in the face of consistent abuse from the Fraser Labour government, which regarded Barnes and the Auckland wharfies as 'deliberate enemies prepared to wreck the government to enforce their own will' (Green, 1996: 192). Perhaps ironically, at the same time as mercilessly criticising the Labour Party, the union was affiliated to the party and contributed more money to it than any other union (Lane, 1981: 7). The *Transport Worker* campaigned for Labour in all elections and gave over its front page in 1949 to an election message from Fraser.

The union was not just concerned with the immediate interests of its members but took a broader perspective as well. Jock talks about the campaign to ban the shipment of iron ore to Japan during its invasion of China. He also discusses the campaigns to expose the Food for Britain fraud and to stop the shipment of butter to the United States, which so embarrassed the government that it was forced to step in. The *Transport Worker* featured many articles attacking the Cold War politics of Fraser's government and its Tory successor, and in 1949 campaigned with Frank Langstone and others to oppose conscription. At a time when rugby was the religion of the country, the union argued that it was better that the tour to South Africa be scrapped than that Maori be excluded from the team. Like their brothers across the Tasman, New Zealand wharfies blacked Dutch shipping to Indonesia during the anti-colonial struggle of the postwar years. They also refused to load wool for Franco's Spain (Green, 1992: 105; Roth, 1993: 97). At home they were solid friends of workers in the freezing works and on the Mangakino hydro project, and also of Auckland carpenters and railway workers.

The wharfies' political platform was wide-ranging. They wanted the building of luxury dwellings banned. They wanted a programme of cheap housing introduced, paid for with the money saved by scrapping royal tours and Defence Force armaments. They wanted pensioners to be paid the same as MPs, prices to be frozen pending progressive reduction, abolition of wage discrimination based on sex, the nationalisation of key national resources and industries, and a minimum wage for all (Lane, 1981: 7).

Although this is the story of an all-male workforce, all records of the 1951 lockout bring out the role of the wharfies' wives and girlfriends. Although the hardships of the lockout broke up many families, for the most part the women supported their men to the bitter end. This support did not just materialise out of thin air, but had been consciously built by the union in preceding years. Families were involved in the life of the waterfront, not just because many lived close to the wharves but also because the union organised a Ladies' Committee, which looked after many social and welfare matters. There was also a hospital comforts fund, regular bucket collections to help out members in distress and, from 1942, a sickness fund (Green, 1996: 50). The union also involved families through its massively popular annual picnic days, which drew crowds of up to 10,000 and featured sports contests of all types, and even glamour contests for both men and women! All of these activities paid dividends in the course of the lockout, as the Ladies' Committee was transformed into the Women's Auxiliary, which helped the men by taking part in demonstrations and by harassing scabs and the wives of scabs, as well as more traditional activities such as preparation of food in relief depots.

As Dean Parker has said, the wharfies' union didn't just have militancy, 'it had a culture' (personal communication). The union had members actively involved in sports competitions. Jock notes his own interests in sports at school and he was certainly not alone. The kind of physique capable of withstanding tough work on the waterfront was the same demanded for inter-port rugby competitions. There were also soccer, cricket, swimming, boxing and wrestling teams, which took part in competitions across the country. Not just the body but the mind was attended to by the union. Jock comments on the success of the union's pipe bands, but the union also had a highly successful debating team, a drama group and a chess club.

Finally, of course, it is important to recognise that the battle between the wharfies and the industrial establishment was not simply the result of a personal vendetta between Jock Barnes and the world, as is sometimes implied in accounts of the time. Indeed, in Auckland the struggle involved all of the 2000 men on the Auckland waterfront, the vast majority of whom stayed loyal to the union for five long months in 1951. The national stature of Barnes was the result not just of his character and abilities, impressive though they were, but most importantly of the industrial muscle of the wharfies themselves. It was the wharfies who proved that a union leader is only as powerful as the members he or she represents. That was why the *New Zealand Herald*'s campaign against the union sought to demonise wharfies as a whole, while not stinting in its continuous character assassination of Barnes himself. The close connection between members and leadership was regularly reaffirmed at the monthly stopwork meetings.

Jock Barnes's career also proves the rule (by exception) that established labour movement leaders tend to react violently to any from within their own ranks or from outside who threaten the stability of the industrial status quo. His major labour movement opponents in the 1940s and 1950s were all former radicals who had now made their peace with the system. F.P. Walsh, Paddy Webb, Bob Semple, Angus McLagan, Peter Fraser, Ken Baxter and Jim Roberts all fall into this category. And some had done very well out of their accommodation to the system. Although the true story will perhaps always be shrouded in mystery, Walsh held numerous official union and government posts, died a rich man, and was a figure for whom De Leon's phrase 'labour lieutenant of capital' might well have been coined (De Leon, 1904). It was no accident that rank and file seamen ignored Walsh as their union secretary throughout 1951 and struck in support of the wharfies (Scott, 1952: 73–76; Bollinger, 1968: 226–32).

By contrast, Barnes was a working official for his entire time as president of the Auckland branch (1944–49). When the national presidency of the union finally became a full-time position, Barnes was paid less than many union members. In 1949, when the salary was first introduced, his weekly wage of £7.10 was 10 shillings less than 'his' members got for a 40-hour week at 4/- per hour. Working on the job made him intimately aware of the needs of members. How this contrasts with many of today's union officials, who are not only full-time office workers but may never have worked in the industry in which they are industrially active and, indeed, may never have held a full-time job outside the union movement since leaving university!

And while Walsh and FOL president Alexander Croskery's power base lay in the voting bloc represented by the industrial conscript clerical and shop assistant unions, Barnes's leadership was always contestable. To win the branch presidency, Barnes had to defeat the Jim Roberts machine. Roberts, 'the uncrowned king of New Zealand', had been the dominant figure in the union since the 1910s. Like so many other union leaders, however, on the election of the 1935 Savage government, Roberts forsook his union loyalties in favour of his allegiances to the Labour Party, of which he was now president. It was no mean feat defeating such a man and, once in office, Barnes was still not without opposition. The national union was not a monolith, and the various branches jealously guarded their autonomy.

Rows with the Wellington branch over the issue of commission control versus direct action were common, as indeed they were within the Auckland branch. At times Barnes crossed swords with Toby Hill and Alec Drennan within the militant wing of the branch, and also Noel Donaldson and others among the Labour loyalists (Roth, 1993: 91, 106). Despite these differences, Barnes maintained the loyalty of the Auckland branch in the face of continuous efforts by the Labour Party and FOL to unseat him.

Whatever one's interpretation of Jock Barnes, there is no doubt that the times made the man. What his opponents regarded as his bloody-mindedness was held by his supporters to be intransigent defence of the needs of the average wharfie in the face of united opposition from all corners. From the daily barbs of *Herald* cartoonist Minhinnick to the continuous attacks from F.P. Walsh and Minister of Labour Angus McLagan, Barnes was attacked not so much for the man he was as for what he represented: a body of 2000 men on the Auckland waterfront who were a permanent obstacle to wartime regulations, postwar 'stabilisation' and US military designs in Asia.

The 1951 defeat was a tragedy not just for the many wharfies who were blacklisted or cast to the four winds but for the New Zealand labour movement and, indeed, New Zealand society more generally. The defeat of the wharfies ushered in more than 20 years of nearly uninterrupted conservative rule, which secured for New Zealand an image as an intellectual and political backwater, locked into the British monarchy, rigid social and sexual mores, and fierce hostility to anything that might upset this idyll. Only in the late 1960s, when the labour movement finally shook off the shackles that Barnes's adversaries had so keenly locked upon it, did New Zealand society start to come alive again, not just industrially, but socially and politically as well. This wave too has passed and the country now suffers from a culture that knows the price of everything but the value of nothing. Only when the labour movement recovers the spirit that animated the militant unions of the 1940s and again in the late 1960s and 1970s will New Zealand's workers once again stand tall. Barnes's account in this book tells the story of how this happened in times past and gives us hope that such times may come once again.

Other Accounts of 'The Barnes Era'

There are two levels at which the great struggles on the waterfront can be understood (Green, 1996). The dominant and more traditional is the political–institutional, which sees 1951 as a Cold War battle between militant unionists, who renounced arbitration in favour of direct action on the job, and government and mainstream union leaders who were determined to gain the upper hand in the battle for 'industrial order' and postwar stability.

Within this paradigm can be found work both critical of and sympathetic towards Barnes and the wharfies' union. The critics include Gordon (1951), a serving officer of the National Party. The main supportive account is that by Dick Scott (1952), editor of *Transport Worker*. Both of these accounts were written by individuals closely involved in events and immediately after the dispute. The accounts by W.B. Sutch (1966), Michael Bassett (1972) and Bert Roth (1974; 1986; 1993), written many years later, are somewhat more distant from the events but are again written from the basic political–institutional perspective.

The second approach to 1951 takes the focus away from the Holland government and Federation of Labour and puts the spotlight onto the shipowners and the struggle for control over the labour process on the waterfront. Anna Green in particular portrays 1951 as the culmination of a 30-year battle of this nature (Green, 1996). From a situation of near total dominance of waterfront affairs in 1915, the shipowners were forced by union pressure to retreat in a range of areas, including the allocation of labour, safety issues, manning arrangements, discipline, forms of payment, and weekend work. The election of the Holland government in November 1949 and the gathering pace of the Cold War gave the shipowners the environment to confront the union and make up all the ground lost in previous decades. In Green's account, the Cold War factors are only background context for the main battle between employers and union.

This editor regards both these approaches as valid. The history of capitalism is the history of struggle at the point of production between capital and labour. As already mentioned, the key issue faced by the shipowners was rapid turnaround time, and this impressed upon them the need for close surveillance, particularly as regards spelling. To the extent that accounts of 1951 ignore this factor (e.g. Woods, 1963), they are clearly weakened. However, sidelining the political–institutional level is also problematic. The postwar years witnessed attempts by shipowners and governments to smash militant unionism on the waterfront and on the ships, not just in Auckland, but also on the West Coast of the United States, in London and Liverpool, and in Melbourne, Brisbane and Sydney. This was not merely coincidence but reflected the times: the postwar years were ones of titanic struggles between organised labour and Western governments as part of the Cold War drive. Politics was entirely polarised: Reds were not only under the bed but most probably in it as well. Labour governments in New Zealand, Britain and Australia all signed up as loyal partners in the United States attempt to snuff out all labour agitation on their side of the Cold War fence. Dockers on the waterfront in East London, metalworkers in Melbourne and carpenters in Auckland all felt the effects. They were not alone: workers in Nissan factories in Japan, farm labourers in southern Italy and railway workers in France also felt the lash. And in every case government politicians, social democratic, liberal or conservative, found allies in the union bureaucracy. F.P. Walsh, Angus McLagan and Ken Baxter had their brothers in Lord Citrine and Arthur Deakin in Britain, Walter Reuther and Phillip Murray in the United States, and Albert Monk in Australia. Similarly in the Eastern Bloc, where genuinely socialist, syndicalist or otherwise non-Stalinist currents in the labour movement were either crushed or driven underground in this period (Harman, 1983).

The strength of Jock's account of his time on the waterfront is that he deals with both the broader political context of the time, including his tussles with the Federation of Labour and the Fraser Labour and Holland National governments, but also details the on-the-job struggles waged by wharfies in their bid to wrest job control away from the shipowners. Jock describes how the union won the right to work in safe conditions, to have some control over manning rates and to work unmolested by American troops on the wharves. The ability to combine differing levels of analysis is one of the key strengths of *Never a White Flag*.

The Debates Over Barnes's Tactics
Key Criticisms

The story of the New Zealand waterfront in the middle part of this century is as controversial in its telling as it was in its living. Roth (1993: 143) has outlined some of the key issues at stake:

> Much has been written about the 1951 dispute, much has been argued. Could the defeat have been avoided by more flexible tactics, by making greater efforts to win friends in the forthcoming confrontation, by more willingness to compromise when retreat was the only alternative to total destruction?

Let us deal with each of these questions in turn. The mainstream interpretation of 1951 is that it represents proof that simple industrial muscle cannot prevail over the forces of state and employers combined. This was a lesson learned from the failed waterfront dispute of 1890–91, and the defeat of the Waihi coalminers and the Red Federation of Labour in 1912–13. As Olssen (1986: 25) has argued:

> Defeat was inevitable . . . Most unionists already knew that no union, or combination of unions, could defeat an elected government which chose to fight back. After 1951, all grasped the point.

The only way out for the wharfies by 1951 was some form of compromise with the government, FOL executive and shipowners.

Defeat was inevitable for the wharfies and compromise essential, the critics claim, because the union was isolated, even within the Trade Union

Congress. Roth points out that neither carpenters nor Auckland labourers helped the wharfies' cause in 1951, and only in Wellington did freezing workers and drivers take action. Railway workers only refused to handle scab goods rather than strike, while in Christchurch, a city with a strong TUC profile, not a single union struck in support.

Such isolation was avoidable. Roth is a keen exponent of the view that Barnes deliberately isolated the wharfies from the mainstream, cared not for the consequences, and thereby ensured the destruction of the union. According to Roth (1986: 138):

> Barnes and Hill . . . had no qualms about causing a split in the New Zealand movement. They had a blind faith in the power of their union and believed that the watersiders alone, without any allies, could fight and defeat the shipowners and the government.

By refusing to apologise for the damning letter sent to the FOL executive over the carpenters' deregistration, Barnes 'was intent upon a break' and 'walked into this trap without any prodding' (Roth, 1986: 130–31). In splitting from the FOL 'Barnes chose glorious self-destruction' (Roth, 1986: 138) and, 'By his super-militant tactics, Barnes effectively isolated his union and forfeited what public sympathy remained for the watersiders, but there is no evidence that he was either aware of or concerned about this' (Roth, 1974: 74). Unlike many union leaders of the time, Barnes had the full support of union members, but 'he repaid their magnificent loyalty by leading them to defeat and destruction' (Roth, 1974: 78). Similarly, Sinclair in his biography of Nash argues that by forming the TUC, the wharfies' union 'isolated themselves from the general union movement and sat out on a limb, waiting to be cut off. But of this they seemed entirely unaware' (Sinclair, 1976: 282).

This strategic failure is apparently rooted in Barnes's personality. His 'consuming personal hatred of Walsh, McLagan and other Labour politicians made it difficult for him to judge issues dispassionately, and Walsh by cleverly exploiting Barnes's weakness was able to manoeuvre him and his union into a position of increasing isolation' (Roth, 1974: 71). Roth is not alone in this assessment. Bassett (1972) argues that the wharfies' union selfishly put its interests above those of the broader labour movement (represented by the FOL executive) and that it was being driven by Barnes's desire for revenge. Barnes was motivated by deep political beliefs but was also 'a man seeking retribution' against his enemies who had deserted him in his fight for reinstatement to his public-service job in the 1930s. Barnes was, moreover, a man hungry for the spotlight (Bassett, 1972: 20; 41; 47). Similarly, Kevin Ireland, promoting his novel based on the 1951 lockout, describes Barnes as 'a mass of grudges . . . capable of carrying the wharfies to their doom' (*Auckland Sunday Star*, 7 April 1996).

Such views have been expressed not just by Barnes's strongest critics but also those who were his allies in 1951. Jim Healy from the Australian waterside union and the New Zealand Communist Party both argued at the time or soon afterwards that the union should have taken steps to ensure that it was not expelled from the FOL in 1950 (Roth, 1986: 133; NZCP, 1952). The split needlessly isolated the militants from the 'moderates', and prepared the way for the ruin of the union.

Some Responses

There are several arguments that can be made in Barnes's defence regarding strategy and tactics in the period leading up to the lockout and during the lockout itself. First, what would a compromise with the Holland government (and FOL) have entailed? The government's seven conditions for a peace plan in 1951 which are set out in Jock's memoirs involved serious concessions by the union. Some were accepted immediately, but some involved giving up key industrial gains that had been made in the previous decade or two at the cost of immense sacrifice in wages and hardship. One such condition was the government's insistence that the watersiders submit all their industrial claims to binding arbitration chaired by a government appointee. Since the early 1940s the wharfies had waged a series of industrial campaigns that were eventually successful in removing this very requirement, in the form of intervention by the Waterfront Commission. But this commission, Jock argues in his memoirs, consistently worked against the wharfies' interests. The second major sticking point was the government's demand that waterfront employment be 'opened up', i.e. to end union control over the selection of waterfront labour. The outcome of such a move would have been the reinstitution of the favouritism and patronage associated with the worst aspects of the 'auction-block' system.

These demands appeared quite unacceptable to the wharfies in the early days of the lockout and were rejected in meetings in every major port. Nonetheless, after the lockout had dragged on for two months the wharfies' national executive was compelled to accept them. Nash, who had prevailed upon them to do so, was exuberant. The following day, however, Holland added an eighth condition, demonstrating the government's real intentions for those who had not read the earlier signs. The government now insisted that the deregistered national union be broken up and replaced by the newly registered scab port unions. This, of course, had been the government's (and the FOL's) real agenda right from the start. In his memoirs, Sir Jack Marshall, New Zealand Prime Minister in the early 1970s and a member of the Holland government in 1951, noted of the lockout:

> The specific issues ... could have been settled in a few weeks if we had been willing to allow the old leaders to return to run the old union ... [but] we were determined to get rid of the militant troublemakers and to break up the national union (Roth, 1993: 143).

And so, just three weeks into the dispute, the Minister of Labour, Bill Sullivan, had refused to recognise Barnes and Hill as WWU negotiators, and two days later F.P. Walsh had called for wharfies to join the scab unions when they were established and to dump Barnes and Hill. Holland's announcement of the eighth condition was merely confirmation of this underlying goal.

The destruction of the national union and the removal of Barnes and Hill would not just have been a misfortune for these two personalities. It would also have meant widespread victimisation of all those loyal to the old leadership and the promotion of those, such as Noel Donaldson, who went on to play a leading role in the scab union in '51. This is clear from the situation at New Plymouth, where the leading militants of the old union were refused work by the shipowners in the 'screening' process after the branch independently voted to return to work early after a scab union was established. As Roth notes (1993: 143): 'Obviously this would have happened in Auckland too.'

Objecting to the government's escalating conditions was not selfishness on the part of the national leadership, but represented strong defence of the gains made through extensive sacrifices over the preceding 30 years. Had Barnes and Hill conceded in the obliteration of the national union, their names would have been dirt in the New Zealand labour movement ever after. Their refusal to compromise, furthermore, was backed repeatedly by the 2000 Auckland wharfies who voted support to the national leadership throughout the 151 days, even in the most difficult circumstances.

Neither the shipowners, nor the FOL executive, nor the government wanted a compromise. All were out to smash the wharfies' union, and whether the showdown came over the 1950 wage case or over the handling of obnoxious cargoes or over spelling was immaterial to them. On 30 November 1950, shipowners' representative Belford (Union Steam Ship Company) had admitted at the waterfront Royal Commission that a showdown with the union was likely (Scott, 1952: 15). The FOL executive was equally adamant. It had already destroyed the Carpenters' Union and in 1951 it took on the wharfies. Even the destruction of these two unions did not satisfy the appetite of F.P. Walsh and friends, whose red-baiting did not let up for another seven years until he was outflanked even further to the right by Peter Butler of the Labourers' Union in the late 1950s.

As for the political parties, Labour's Prime Minister Peter Fraser had referred to the wharfies as 'political blacklegs' at a special conference of the FOL early in 1947 (Bassett, 1972: 218), while Labour's Minister of Works, Bob Semple, was even more direct, accusing 'Mr Barnes and his ratbags' of being 'a real threat to the industrial peace and general welfare of the people of this country' (Bassett, 1972: 26). Labour's successors were no less forthcoming. Minister of Labour Bill Sullivan argued that 'Their wings have to be clipped or the system as we know it will fade and die', while Sid Holland declared that the country was 'actually at war' and was facing 'a very determined effort to overthrow orderly government by force' (Sinclair, 1976: 283). In this effort to maintain 'order' National was backed up in large measure by most leading Labour Party figures, with even the avowedly conciliatory Nash admitting that a Labour government, too, would have used the emergency regulations. Indeed, Nash's attempt to bring about a compromise deal with the government during the lockout and his 'neither for nor against' approach only gave the government greater confidence that the wharfies would be left to fight without any support from Labour (see Scott, 1952, Chapter 9 for more on the role of the Labour Party).

The level of determination of labour leaders, businessmen and Cabinet to crush the wharfies can also be demonstrated by the money that they were prepared to spend in this endeavour: up to £100 million, an enormous sum in those days. Given all these facts, the argument that some clever manoeuvre could have avoided the final confrontation is untenable.

What of the 'isolation' of the wharfies in 1951? Was this deliberate, was it welcomed, and in what way was the union actually isolated? That Barnes and his allies welcomed isolation is a bizarre claim. In his memoirs Jock repeatedly pays tribute to all those who took action alongside the watersiders in 1951. At the peak of the campaign up to 22,000 workers were taking action of some kind. This included, in addition to the 8000 wharfies, 7000 freezing workers, 4000 miners, 1000 hydro workers and 500 drivers (Roth, 1974: 76). Across the Tasman port workers throughout Australia refused to handle New Zealand shipping. For his union's pains, Jim Healy of the Australian wharfies' union was charged under the Crimes Act with obstructing trade and was later jailed with hard labour for six weeks. Thousands of Australian wharfies stopped work in protest and only lifted their bans at the request of their New Zealand counterparts, who said that they found material aid more useful at that point in their struggle. By the end of the lockout, Australian wharfies had donated approximately £40,000 through weekly levies. Within New Zealand tons of food were donated by supporters despite the best efforts of the police and Holland government. Canadian and American unions also refused to handle scab shipping.

Such solidarity was anathema to the FOL executive, which was intent on making the union a pariah long before the start of the lockout. Rather than the 1950 conference walkout by the wharfies representing a desire for industrial martyrdom, the split was forced upon the union. While arguing, as we have seen, that Barnes 'had no qualms about causing a split', Roth admits that:

> The prime responsibility for the FOL–TUC split lies at the door of the Federation leaders who were determined to crush the left wing opposition within the movement, and who did not hesitate, in the 1951 dispute, to help the National Party government destroy the watersiders (Roth, 1986: 137).

During the course of 1951 the FOL missed no opportunity to further isolate the wharfies. The executive actively opposed any aid to the watersiders and demanded that solidarity strikes be ended. As it had done two years earlier in the case of the carpenters, it then endorsed the formation of scab unions and urged locked-out wharfies to desert their union and join the scabs. By its constant pressure, the FOL succeeded in stampeding the railway workers back to work and forced them to handle scab cargoes, while striking freezing workers were whittled down to the Wellington and Taranaki branches. Harbour board employees also collapsed under pressure, Auckland freezing workers voted to load out meat for servicemen, and drivers resumed work. Mangakino hydro workers voted narrowly to return to work, and a national ballot by railwaymen voted to return also. FOL pressure also led to Waikato open-cut miners voting to return to work. The FOL executive mobilised across borders as well, linking arms with Albert Monk and Arthur Deakin, the leaders of the ACTU and TUC in Australia and Britain respectively, in recognition of the threat that all three faced from unions that were prepared to challenge the Cold War offensive against labour. The result was that dockers in both countries were instructed by their peak union councils to handle black cargo. Little wonder then, that P. Harrison, then president of the Auckland Rotary Club, could comment:

> I sincerely hope that we, as employers, will never forget that the last strike was not broken by the Government, although it did everything it could and provided the necessary framework. *It was broken by the responsible labour unions* (cited New Zealand Communist Party, 1952: 4) [emphasis added].

To describe this situation as in any way Barnes choosing 'glorious self-destruction' represents a complete inversion of the true situation.

Barnes certainly used rhetorical bravado at times but his actions refute the notion that the man deliberately sought to alienate support. Even the timing of the walkout from the FOL itself reflects Barnes's desire for his union to avoid isolation. To the extent that he had any room to manoeuvre at the 1950 FOL conference, the purpose of the walkout was to take as many supporters as possible, rather than risk being left truly isolated two months after the conference when the executive struck its blow, as was undoubtedly its intention. Barnes understood that there is a great deal of difference between formal organisational unity of the industrial conscript unions under the banner of the FOL and the potential for real concrete unity that could be achieved by workers in action, whether affiliated to the FOL or TUC. While Roth is correct in pointing to the failure of many TUC affiliates to support the wharfies in 1951, it is also true that miners, seamen and Mangakino hydro workers all pitched in, despite being affiliated to the FOL and despite the bitter opposition of their national leaders, Prendiville, Crook and Walsh.

Furthermore, the wharfies achieved unity not just across organisational boundaries within the labour movement but also with other oppressed groups. The privileged students of Auckland University may have voted nine to one to endorse the emergency regulations, but the wharfies found true friends among Maori organisations and in the Combined Women's Committee.

It is also worth reasserting that the wharfies could have won in 1951. Olssen's argument that 'no union, or combination of unions, could defeat an elected government which chose to fight back' flies in the face of union victories against even the most repressive of governments. If all unions adopted such a defeatist attitude, it is unlikely that they would ever have been formed in the first place, since unions across the world are frequently born in circumstances of the most bitter repression. The South African unionists who helped bring down apartheid by their mass strikes of the 1980s would never have attempted such rash action had they been so advised. The South Korean strikers would never have risked life and limb against vicious police and military action in 1987 and again 10 years later. In countries much more akin to New Zealand, workers have made similar gains, Australian unions breaking penal clauses by general strike action in 1969 and British unions actually bringing down Edward Heath's Tory government in 1974. Even in New Zealand itself, the success of the Public Service Association in twice forcing the Muldoon government to withdraw deregistration bills in the early 1980s proves Olssen's argument wrong.

We have seen the level of solidarity that was mobilised at the high point of the lockout. Wisdom after the event that 'defeat was inevitable' reeks of smug disdain for the struggles that were waged by wharfies and others in that notable year. It also acts as a cover for the criminal action by the FOL executive and Labour Party, who did their best to make sure that Olssen's prediction came to pass. As Keith Holyoake told Parliament in August 1960, the National government had been

> . . . fortunate in that the FOL, the responsible workers leaders, stood firmly

with the Government. The task would have been impossible without the Federation's aid (cited in Roth, 1974: 78).

Finally, even if we were to concede Olssen's argument that defeat was inevitable, would it have been better for the wharfies to have conceded defeat right from the start, rather than to have fought on to the bitter end? No union willingly goes into action anticipating defeat, and in most cases it is better for a union to seek some form of compromise rather than continue with action knowing that the odds are stacked heavily against it. However, 1951 was not just another minor struggle in which the wharfies could have conceded temporarily, replenished their resources, and come back and won revenge at the next round. As we have seen, 1951 was a year in which no compromise was possible. It was a year when the veil of class consensus was ripped from New Zealand politics, revealing the harsh reality of a bitter class conflict. Conceding in these circumstances would have meant utter demoralisation of the entire militant wing of the labour movement. Barnes and Hill would have been regarded as the worst form of cowards; as braggarts who turned and ran.

This appears to be the preferred course of action for Bassett, whose description of the government's responses to Walter Nash's attempts to broker a compromise indicate that the government was happy with nothing less than the total destruction of the union. That the wharfies still decided to resist the dismemberment of their union is put down to the belligerence of Barnes and 'a strong sense of impending martyrdom' of its members (Bassett, 1972: 27). Given that their fight was doomed from the outset, the fact that the wharfies chose to engage in an unwinnable battle served only to consolidate the National Party in power and to lower the reputation of trade unions and the Labour Party in the eyes of the general public for years afterwards. In order to avoid 'untold damage to the cause which working men still hold dear' (Bassett, 1972: 212), the union should evidently have agreed to its own break-up at the beginning of the year so as to avoid the awful conflict that befell all concerned.

Now it is true that the outcome of the wharfies' defeat was significant demoralisation within the labour movement, evident in the electoral gains for the Holland government later in 1951 and the years of industrial passivity that followed. F.P. Walsh and the arbitrationist unions had clearly beaten back the challenge from the threat from militant unionism and were to remain in this comfortable position until the revival of industrial action in the late 1960s. In this sense, Barnes's assessment at the time that the lockout was merely 'round one' of the battle was incorrect. But the question remains: was it better that battle was entered into and lost rather than conceded without a single blow being landed on the enemy? Clearly for Bassett, the latter was preferable: it would have avoided the Labour Party being put on the spot at the very least. However, as Barnes was to write in reviewing Bassett's book 20 years after the event: 'We had no option as unionists and men but to fight back and make our attackers pay as dearly as possible. In this we succeeded' (*Sunday Herald*, 27 February 1972). If the union had simply given in, there is no guarantee that the Holland government would not have gone amok, overrunning all the welfare measures from the Savage years.

While one camp in the labour movement could draw the conclusion that the wharfies were wrong to fight, others could draw much more radical conclusions concerning the true friends and enemies of New Zealand's working class. That knowledge was essential training in the education of future generations of union militants and even now is instructive for those who wish to learn. As Scott (1952: 204) wrote:

> Thousands learned fast while the mask was down and tens of thousands stored impressions which will mature at the first stimulus of activity. The worth of secret ballots, the purpose of law-making, the genuineness of arbitration, the value of solemn undertakings, the role of the state forces—the full face of the ruling class was bared, the naked class basis of society exposed.

We might contrast the situation with the 1990s. Forty years after the '51 lockout, the Council of Trade Unions, the successor of the FOL, refused to mobilise for an industrial confrontation with the Bolger government over the Employment Contracts Act. Since enactment, the CTU has also been at pains to avoid industrial action that might constitute breaches of the act. Can it seriously be proposed that the New Zealand union movement has benefited from this cautious strategy? Union membership continues to fall, workplace union organisation is in disarray if not collapsed in many former strongholds, and cynicism about unionism is widespread. Over the long term, passivity is far more damaging to the union movement than defeated upsurges, for it saps the very life from the unions and lends no lessons to union activists other than frustration and resignation.

References

Barnes, J. 'Only part of '51 strike story told', *Sunday Herald*, 27 February 1972.
Bassett, M. (1972): *Confrontation 51: The Waterfront Dispute*, A.H. & A.W. Reed, Wellington.
Bollinger, C. (1968): *Against the Wind: A History of the Seamen's Union*.
Gordon, J. (1951): *Crisis on the Waterfront*, Wellington.
Green, A. (1992): 'Spelling, go-slows, gliding away and theft: informal control over

work on the New Zealand waterfront 1915-1951', *Labour History* No. 63, 100–14.
_____ (1994): 'The unimportance of arbitration? The New Zealand waterfront 1915–1951', *The New Zealand Journal of History*, 28 (2), 145–59.
_____ (1996): 'British Capital, Antipodean Labour: The New Zealand Waterfront, 1915–1951', unpub. manuscript.
Harman, C. (1983): *Class Struggle in Eastern Europe 1945–83*, Pluto Press, London.
Kerr, C. and Siegel, A. (1954): 'The Inter-Industry Propensity to Strike—An International Comparison', in A. Kornhauser et. al. (eds.): *Industrial Conflict*, McGraw Hill, New York.
Lane, T. (1981): 'Watersiders: the Conscience of the Working Class', in *Socialist Action Review* (Auckland), 7–8.
Lowenstein, W. and Hills, T. (1982): *Under the Hook: Melbourne Waterside Workers Remember, 1900–1980*, Australian Society for the Study of Labour History, Melbourne.
New Zealand Communist Party (1952): *The Waterfront Situation: A Statement by the Political Committee, New Zealand Communist Party*, Auckland.
Olssen, E. (1986): 'The New Zealand Labour Movement, 1920–40', in E. Fry (ed.): *Common Cause: Essays in Australian and New Zealand Labour History*, Allen and Unwin, Sydney.
Roth, H. (1974): *Trade Unions in New Zealand: Past and Present*, Reed Education, Wellington.
_____ (1986): 'The New Zealand Trade Union Congress, 1950–51', in E. Fry (ed.): *Common Cause: Essays in Australian and New Zealand Labour History*, Allen and Unwin, Sydney.
_____ (1993): *Wharfie: From Handbarrows to Straddles. Unionism on the Auckland Waterfront*, Waterside Workers' Union, Auckland.
Sheridan, T. (1994): 'Australian wharfies 1943–1967: Casual attitudes, militant leadership and workplace change', *Journal of Industrial Relations*, 36 (2), 258–84.
_____ (1995): 'Baggage taken ashore: The outlook of senior waterfront management in the 1950s', *Journal of Industrial Relations*, 37 (4), 562–86.
_____ (1996): 'Shipowners, stevedores and foremen: Divergent management attitudes to waterfront labour in the 1950s', *Journal of Industrial Relations*, 38 (3), 412–40.
Sinclair, K. (1976): *Walter Nash*, Auckland University Press, Auckland.
Scott, D. (1952): *151 Days: Official History of the Great Waterfront Lockout and Supporting Strike, February 15–July 15, 1951*, reprinted in 1977 by Labour Reprint Society, Christchurch.
Sutch, W.B. (1966): *The Quest for Security in New Zealand, 1840–1966*, OUP, Wellington.
Woods, N. (1963): *Industrial Conciliation and Arbitration in New Zealand*, Government Printer, Wellington.

A Note on the Editorial Process

I first became aware of Jock Barnes's memoirs while conducting research in Auckland in December 1995. I had gone to interview Jock in order to further my understanding of New Zealand trade unionism in the postwar years and for help in writing a chapter that appeared in Chris Rudd and Brian Roper's book, *The Political Economy of New Zealand* (OUP, Auckland, 1997). At the end of the meeting Jock pulled out an enormous package comprising the first draft of his memoirs entitled *Never a White Flag*. This had been written in 1987 and was at that stage 382 pages long, without illustrations, chapters or sub-headings. The text had been typed at this time by his granddaughter.

In the nine years since it had been written, *Never a White Flag* had been distributed within limited academic and union circles, but no-one had made a commitment to publish it. So it was that Jock asked if I would try to find a publisher. I took on this job on my return to Australia in new year 1996.

In order to get the text into the form that you now have before you, I edited it heavily, cutting out about one-third of the text, mainly material that was extraneous to the narrative. On my next visit to Auckland in December 1996 I then went through the revised version with Jock for his approval of the changes and to clarify some points of uncertainty. Further changes were made on my return to Australia on the basis of more information from secondary sources and primary sources provided by Jock.

In editing the text I sought to remain faithful to the spirit of the original draft. This is especially relevant when it deals with Jock's forceful opinions on individuals with whom he crossed swords. The argument, which was made to me from several quarters, that sections of the original text were defamatory was certainly a factor in some of the editing process. I sought to eliminate material that suggested unproven criminal or illegal activity on the part of key individuals whilst keeping Jock's *political* assessments of such figures, distasteful though they may be to some. There are other parts of the original manuscript that remain in this book which I believe may not be entirely correct or where at least credible alternative interpretations of events are possible. But these are Jock's memoirs and in these circumstances I chose as editor to maintain a light hand.

During the follow-up visit to Auckland in December 1996 I selected the photographs and cartoons that are included in this book. Jock also gave me his entire collection of archival material for referencing. This included complete sets of the union's journal, *Transport Worker*, from 1943 to 1951, minutes of national council meetings for the same period, and copies of correspondence within the union and between the union and outside individuals and bodies, including the government, Federation of Labour and Waterfront Commission. Jock's collection also included reports to the annual conferences of the Federation of Labour. These are now lodged, on Jock's instructions, at the library of the University of Auckland and were all consulted in final editing of the manuscript.

ACKNOWLEDGEMENTS

Many people lent assistance in the production of this book. Tom Bramble would like to express his thanks to Dean Parker, Keith Locke of One World Books, and the editors at Victoria University Press for their encouragement and advice, to Professor John Deeks and his colleagues at the Department of Management and Employment Relations at the University of Auckland, who made me welcome during a three-week stay in Auckland in December 1996, to Dr Anna Green for the loan of her manuscript, to Christine and Jim Devine for hospitality during my visits to Auckland, and to Georgina Murray for support throughout the project from start to finish. The book would also not have been published without generous support from Terry Ryan of the Waterfront Workers' Union, David Morgan of the Seafarers' Union, Bill Andersen of the National Distribution Union, and Maxine Gay of the Trade Union Federation.

A CHRONOLOGY OF KEY EVENTS

1935
Jock Barnes arrives on the Auckland waterfront.
Election of first Labour government under Michael Savage.

1937
Bureau system of engaging labour established in main ports.
Union boycotts Japanese shipping in protest at Japanese invasion of China.

1939
Labour government amends Industrial Concilation and Arbitration Act to enable the Minister of Labour to deregister a striking union and to cancel relevant awards.
Labour government enacts Strike and Lockout Emergency Regulations.

1940
Waterfront Control Commission takes control of the wharves.
Kelly–Murray case.
Ted Girven replaces Bill Cuthbert as WWU Auckland branch secretary.
Conscription introduced.

1941
Jim Roberts steps down as national secretary and is replaced by Toby Hill.
Barnes defeats Tom Solomon for position as branch president.

1942
American troops arrive at Auckland and Wellington.
Cuthbert and Solomon appointed to Waterfront Control Commission.
Disputes over *Chios* and *Kartigi*.
Labour government enacts Economic Stabilisation Emergency Regulations.

1943
Dispute over *Waiana*.
Westfield freezing workers released from jail.

1944
Jock Barnes defeats Jack Flood for national presidency.
Appointment of Jim O'Brien as Minister of Labour.
Kaikorai dispute over gangway.
Strike wave through New Zealand industry.

A Chronology of Key Events

1946
Dispute over Waterfront Commission decision on guaranteed wage.
Union imposes ban on Dutch shipping to Indonesia.
Retirement from office of O'Brien and appointment of Angus McLagan as Minister of Labour.
Boycott of wool for Barcelona in protest against Franco.
Walsh economic stabilisation report.

1947
Campaign against repression in Cook Islands.

1948
Mountpark dispute.
Labour government enacts Economic Stabilisation Act.

1949
Labour destroys communist-led Carpenters' Union.
Solidarity with Canadian seamen's strike.
Labour's conscription referendum.
Dispute over *Barnhill*.
Nationwide waterfront lockout.
Formation of New Zealand Port Employers' Association.
National wins the general election.

1950
Royal Commission of Enquiry into the New Zealand Waterfront established.
Formation of Trade Union Congress after split from FOL.
Lampblack disputes.

1951
Waterfront lockout.
State of emergency declared and emergency regulations promulgated.
WWU broken up and replaced by 26 port unions.
National wins re-election.
National makes substantial amendments to Industrial Conciliation and Arbitration Act and the Police Offences Act and introduces the Union Funds Distribution Act, all of which severely penalise militant unionism.
Barnes sentenced to two months' hard labour for criminal libel.

1952
Report of the Royal Commission.

Source: Adapted from Green (1996)

A CHRONOLOGY OF KEY EVENTS OF THE 1951 LOCKOUT

JANUARY

31 Arbitration Court hands down general wage rise of 15 per cent.

FEBRUARY

8   Negotiations between wharfies and shipowners over pay rise on waterfront fail to reach agreement.

13 WWU national executive meets with shipowners: 'final offer' of 4/7½ per day (9 per cent) in response to WWU claim of 6/-.

14 Overtime ban imposed in response to employer offer. Employers threaten to dismiss all wharfies refusing overtime.

16 WWU negotiating committee meets with Cabinet (Holyoake, Sullivan and Webb) and shipowners (Blakely, Marchington, Belford, Robertson, Congdon and Dobbie).

17 Holland returns from Washington.

19 Branches all confirm readiness to resist employer ultimatum. Employers lock out men refusing to work overtime. The '151 days' begins.

20 John Foster Dulles (US State Department) arrives in Auckland from Japan.

21 Holland declares state of emergency. Troops begin to work the wharves soon after.

25 Meeting held in Christchurch attracts 1500 to hear the watersiders' case.

26 Meeting of Trade Union Congress votes support for WWU.

26 First Auckland WWU illegal bulletin issued, the first of several dozen over the following five months.

27 Waikato and King Country miners, freezing workers, hydro-electric workers, Portland and Golden Bay cement workers, coolstore workers strike against regulations and in defence of WWU, followed by blacking of scab cargo by railway workers and gasworkers.

28 Deregistration of the WWU and seizure of union funds by Public Trustee. Ken Baxter (FOL president) denounces WWU actions.

A Chronology of Key Events

MARCH

1-2   F.P. Walsh calls a meeting of affected unions at Trades Hall and insists that WWU accepts binding arbitration on its claim.

6   WWU negotiating committee, plus representatives from miners and freezing workers, meet Sullivan and Bert Bockett, secretary of the Department of Labour. Sullivan refuses to acknowledge Barnes and Hill as legitimate representatives of the wharfies, the WWU having been deregistered.

7   Further meeting held between WWU and miners and freezing worker reps. WWU accepts binding arbitration in principle and nominates the other two unions to negotiate on its behalf.

9   FOL special conference at Wellington Town Hall calls for the WWU to reject direct action in favour of conciliation and arbitration and votes for the convening of a conference involving all affected parties. F.P. Walsh subsequently attacks WWU leadership as communist stooges and calls for the removal of Barnes and Hill as the WWU's national leaders.

12   First Wellington underground bulletin produced.

13-15   Discussions between FOL executive, government and representatives of freezing workers and miners over the lockout. FOL attempts unsuccessfully to have the WWU hand over carriage of the dispute to it. Minister of Labour finally nominates the conditions for a return to work—the 'Seven Points', including 'open' employment.

14   Government succeeds in establishing scab union at Whakatane.

16   FOL executive and seven other affected unions endorse the government's Seven Points.

17   WWU rejects government's insistence on open employment and demands union maintain control over recruitment (while accepting several of the other government conditions). Government responds by demanding permanent dismantling of the WWU.

21   Extension of state of emergency for a further month.

21   FOL executive calls upon workers to return to work and to handle blacked goods. Several key unions respond, including Auckland drivers, Mangakino hydro workers and railway workers.

29   Walter Nash calls for a compulsory conference and agrees at a public meeting in Hamilton, also attended by Ken Baxter, that Labour government would also have used the emergency regulations.

APRIL

3   WWU national council meets and reaffirms basic union demands; all rejected by the government.

5   Emergency strike committee established by rank and file mine-

	workers. Reaffirms blacking of coal production and distribution. Effective in Waikato, Buller and West Coast.
7	Sullivan sends letters to the home of every registered wharfie in New Zealand inviting him to return to work or be assumed to have abandoned employment on the waterfront.
9	Auckland police unsuccessfully attempt to prevent meeting of WWU at Trades Hall.
10	Seamen and Wellington drivers reaffirm decision to strike.
12	Walter Nash meets with WWU negotiating committee and then makes representations to the Holland government on behalf of the WWU. Barnes eventually accepts all Seven Points, including compulsory arbitration.
20	Holland announces an 'eighth point' as a condition of settlement of the dispute: that separate port unions be established and the national union be broken up.
23	Public Trustee seizes funds of Wellington Freezing Workers' and Drivers' Unions and of Golden Bay cement workers.
24	FOL conference decides to take no action against emergency regulations.
30	Dynamiting of Huntly railway line in Waikato: no culprit ever found.
30	Scab union formed in Auckland with 191 members. R.S. Belsham, 'new union' president, attacked in his home.

MAY

1	*Auckland Star* editorial calls on government to ban any gatherings by wharfies in the vicinity of the wharves, and for police to shoot at groups of workers who defy such a ban. Government extends emergency regulations to forbid 'loitering' of strikers and sympathisers, and establishes a civil emergency organisation, consisting of volunteers, to provide 'essential duties'.
2	March by Wellington wharfies broken up by police in Cuba Street. Early scab union formed at Bluff following decision by Timaru WWU branch to return to work on employer conditions.
3	Scab union members start work in Auckland: 5000 wharfies and supporters demonstrate outside the town hall. Shipowners announce a 50 per cent increase in freight charges.
4	Walter Nash issues a press statement complaining about suppression of free speech by the government and police force.
11	Wellington branch leadership meets Minister of Labour to discuss government's conditions. Government further extends its Seven Points, now insisting on separate port unions, open employment,

A Chronology of Key Events

screening by employers, prohibition of 'spelling', and government regulation of waterfront employment conditions through a series of nominees. Wellington rejects conditions.

13   TUC convenes a public rally of 9000 in Auckland Domain: Nash declares that he is 'neither for nor against' the wharfies.

18   Bashings of wharfies in Queen Street and nine arrests.

18   Scab union formed in Dunedin.

20   Government temporarily lifts ban on members of the WWU addressing public meetings. Mass public meetings follow in Auckland and Wellington town halls to hear WWU speakers present their case.

21   Scab union formed in Lyttelton.

24   Mass public meeting at Dunedin Town Hall.

28   Members of new scab union start work in Wellington.

30   Joint meeting held between national executives of FOL and Labour Party in fruitless attempt to work out a common policy on the lockout.

JUNE

1   'Bloody Friday': police attack Queen Street demonstration of wharfies and their supporters in Auckland.

3   17,000 gather in Auckland Domain to hear the WWU present its case. Some 3000 attend public meeting in Wellington Town Hall.

6   Mass public meeting in Christchurch Town Hall. Government re-imposes ban on WWU public meetings.

6   Australian police raid offices of Waterside Workers' Federation (WWF) in Sydney and Melbourne in an attempt to destroy the leadership. Mass walkout by Sydney wharfies in protest.

7   Port Chalmers votes to return to work.

13   Australian WWF lifts ban on handling ships sailing with black cargo following condemnation of its stand by the ACTU and the threat of mass fines.

13   Combined meeting of representatives from seamen, miners, freezing workers, drivers and labourers confirms resolution to fight until 'honourable settlement' is reached.

11-13   Labour Party holds annual conference in Christchurch. Delegates endorse stance of Labour Party and FOL executive.

13   W.F. McMullen, ex-Grenadier Guards, elected president of the scab Auckland 'Maritime Cargo Workers' Union'.

14   Freda Barnes appears on a charge of 'inciting disorder'. Found guilty and fined on 22 June.

14   Full complement of scabs now at work in the port of Auckland.

	Minister of Labour rejects any possibility of former wharfies returning to their old jobs in Auckland on cessation of the dispute.
21-22	Meetings by drivers and Waikato miners vows to continue the fight, but evidence of weakening among other mineworkers, railway workers and others.
25	Wellington branch leadership engages in independent negotiations with Minister of Labour. Deadlock.
26	Strike committee meets. Seamen advise WWU to return to work on government's terms.
26	Parliament reconvened.

JULY

4	Mineworkers return to work. Lyttelton branch of WWU votes to return to work but then reverses its decision awaiting a national outcome.
9	National Strike Committee (seamen, watersiders, freezing workers, miners and drivers) votes to call off combined action.
11	Seamen return to work.
11	WWU national executive votes to recommend a return to work.
12	Holland announces early dissolution of Parliament to contest a general election.
16	Watersiders return to work where they are able. Widespread victimisation in Auckland and Lyttelton.
25	Emergency regulations lifted.

AUGUST

2-3	Justice Jenner Wiley hears a case of criminal libel brought against Jock Barnes by Constable Robert Edwards. Barnes sentenced to two months' hard labour in Mount Eden Prison.

SEPTEMBER

1	Holland government takes four seats from Labour to win re-election.
12	Barnes's appeal against sentence dismissed.

OCTOBER

3	WWU national executive votes to wind up national union with Barnes in jail.

NOVEMBER

10	Barnes released from Mount Eden.

A WHO'S WHO

Allum, Sir John Andrew: Mayor of Auckland 1941–53; member of council of Auckland Chamber of Commerce 1923–63; KCMG 1950.
Anderson, Captain James Alfred: manager of Roose shipping company.
Baxter, Ken McLean: secretary of Federation of Labour 1944–69; secretary of New Zealand Printing Union 1932–44.
Berendsen, Sir Carl: New Zealand ambassador to US, 1944-48; KCMG 1946.
Bockett, Arthur Ernest: secretary of Waterfront Control Commission 1940; general manager of Waterfront Control Commission 1946; Chairman of Waterfront Control Commission 1948–51; KCMG 1974.
Bockett, Herbert Leslie: secretary of Department of Labour 1947–64; KCMG 1968. Like his twin brother Arthur, an accountant by training.
Coates, Joseph Gordon: Reform member for Kaipara; Prime Minister 1925–28; Minister of Public Works, Transport and Unemployment (Coalition government) 1931–35.
Croskery, Alexander: vice-president of FOL 1945–46; president of FOL 1946–52; secretary of Amalgamated Society of Shop Assistants for 25 years; vice-president of Wellington Trades Council.
Dalglish, Judge Douglas James: chairman of Waterfront Industry Commission 1947–48; chairman of Waterfront Authority 1948–51; deputy judge, Court of Arbitration 1947–52; judge of Compensation Court from 1952.
Forbes, George William: Liberal then United member for Hurunui; Prime Minister 1930–35 (coalition government from September 1931).
Fraser, Peter: Labour member for Brooklyn; Prime Minister 1940–49; secretary of Parliamentary Labour Party 1919–35.
Holland, Sidney George: National member for Fendalton; Prime Minister and Minister of Finance 1949–57; Opposition Leader 1940–49.
Luxford, Judge John Hector: principal stipendiary magistrate in Auckland 1941–51; Mayor of Auckland 1953–56.
McLagan, Angus: president of FOL 1937–46; secretary of United Mine Workers' Federation 1927–46. Appointed to Legislative Council and position as Minister of National Service and Industrial Manpower 1942. Resigned 1946 to successfully contest seat of Riccarton for Labour; Minister of Employment, Labour, Mines and Immigration 1946–49; member of Economic Stabilisation Commission 1940–45.

Minhinnick, George Edward: cartoonist *New Zealand Herald* 1930–75; OBE 1950; KCMG 1976.

Moohan, Michael: secretary of Labour Party 1940–47; Labour MP for Petone 1946–67.

Nash, Walter: Labour MP for Hutt 1929–64; secretary of Labour Party 1922–32; president of Labour Party 1935–36; Minister of Finance 1935–49; Deputy Prime Minister 1940–49; Opposition Leader 1950–57, 1960–63; Prime Minister 1957–60.

O'Brien, James, Labour MP 1928–46; Minister of Labour 1945–46.

Ongley, Frederick William: chairman of Waterfront Industry Commission 1946–47; judge of Compensation Court from 1945.

Price, Captain R.E.: president of Harbour Boards Association and Waterside Employers' Association; member of Wellington Harbour Board for 23 years (13 as chairman).

Roberts, Jim: secretary of Waterside Workers' Union 1915–41; secretary of Alliance of Labour 1920–35; vice-president of Labour Party 1934–37; national president of Labour Party 1937–50; member of Waterfront Control Commission 1940–46.

Semple, Robert: Labour member for Wellington East 1928–46 and then for Miramar; member of Savage and Fraser ministries as Minister of Works 1935–49; published *Why I Fight Communism* 1948.

Sullivan, William: National MP for Bay of Plenty 1941–57; Minister of Labour, Employment, Mines and Immigration 1949–57; KCMG 1957.

Walsh, Fintan Patrick: vice-president Federation of Labour 1946–47; 1948–53, then president 1953–63; president of Seamen's Union 1927–63; president of Wellington Trades Council 1937–63; president of Wellington Clerical Workers' Union 1936–63; member of Industrial Emergency Council during World War Two; member of Economic Stabilisation Commission from inception until closure in 1950; member of War Assets Realisation Disposal Commission.

Webb, Patrick Charles: Labour MP for Buller 1913–18; 1933–46; Minister of Mines, Labour and Telegraphs 1935–45.

Source: *Who's Who in New Zealand* 1932, 1941, 1951, 1961

NEVER A WHITE FLAG

THE MEMOIRS OF
JOCK BARNES

To my grand-daughters
Adrienne Susan and Jennifer Jane
for their invaluable assistance
and to all who fought fascism
in New Zealand in 1951.

1 LIFE BEFORE THE WATERFRONT, 1907-33

Home Life

I was born in Auckland on 17 July 1907, the son of a father and mother who had been raised in the Scottish border area of Cumberland in England. My father, Robert William Barnes, was apprenticed as a painter, paperhanger and decorator, for which privilege his parents had to pay. The conditions of his apprenticeship were appalling—hours of work 6am to 6pm, winter and summer alike, and six days a week. Slave labour if you like. The only good feature was that, after five years of that, anyone who survived was an expert in all branches of the trade. After working for some time in England, Scotland and Ireland, my parents decided to seek a better life for themselves and their children and emigrated to New Zealand.

In 1904 my father left first to establish a home in Grey Lynn. My mother, Catherine, followed with my older brothers and sisters: Roy, five years, Marjorie, three, and Arthur, one. There were no assisted passages in those days and the voyage took six weeks. Such a venture took real courage. Although a big improvement on the conditions left behind, life in New Zealand for working people was no bed of roses. Family allowances, unemployment pay, paid holidays and a host of other 'benefits' accepted today were unheard of.

As a tradesman, my father would bow his head to no-one. Despite the fact that he was recognised as a first-class man at his job, many a day he was out of work. And my mother, a very great and courageous lady, suffered too from the harsh conditions. Some of my earliest memories are of standing by my mother at night while she did the day's washing by candlelight. This after a day spent in feeding, working and caring for five young children. She made sure we never went to bed hungry but, looking back, I am afraid many a time she did.

At a very early age I used to think that all of this was wrong. Why should good, honest working people have to suffer while others who did no work lived in luxury? I guess a little iron entered my soul at a very tender age.

When I was four we moved from Grey Lynn to Mount Albert, at that time right out in the country. My father kept a good garden and from then on there was no shortage of vegetables and fruit, although never much money. We went picking mushrooms from the paddocks and gathered firewood. At home we had fresh eggs from our hens, even honey from a couple of beehives. Arthur and I only had to walk down the road to catch eels. Beautiful fresh watercress was in abundance. We would walk over to Point Chevalier and, fishing off the rocks with our homemade bamboo rod, get a bag full of piper. It was a longer walk to Blockhouse Bay where schnapper were caught off the rocks and the mud flats were alive with flounder. The Manukau Harbour in those days was fresh and clear.

And so to school at Point Chevalier with its memories: some good, some bad. In those days the guiding rule was spare the rod and spoil the child. There were quite a few teachers who, I am satisfied, achieved pleasure out of thrashing helpless children. On the other hand, there were many kind, dedicated teachers of whom I still have pleasant memories. I was seven and in Standard One when I struck one of the former type—a prize bitch if there ever was one! I was the only redhead in the class and she made my life a misery. She had a good ally in the headmaster of this school. Any time she thought I should have a good thrashing she would call on his services. He used to have his strap and cane always on display and thrashed you in front of the class. No questions ever asked—referral from that bitch was enough. This at seven years of age. I have always regretted that in later years I never caught up with the sadistic bastard.

My father and mother got to hear of this and paid a visit to this legalised child basher. My father left him in no doubt about who would be getting the bashing if this continued. They took me to another school at Edendale, of which I have nothing but pleasant memories.

I often wonder how many rebels are created by sadistic teachers, together with some of our magistrates and judges of a like type. Anarchist and communist movements do not create rebels. At a later stage they only recruit them.

At my second school I never saw a strap or cane displayed. My memories of one woman teacher are fond indeed.

When I was nine and Arthur 11, we got *Auckland Star* rounds. Houses were few and far between and streetlights just about non-existent. We each had a run of three or four miles every night. I got 2/6 a week and was proud to hand that over to my mother.

In 1921 I transferred to Auckland Grammar School, and in the following year at the age of 15 was a foundation pupil at Mount Albert Grammar School, which had just opened. The headmaster, Fred Gamble, was a man of outstanding qualities and humanitarian ideals. With two exceptions, the form masters were of the same type. No doubt Fred Gamble had had a big say in their appointments. For the three years I was at Mount Albert I was active in the school's cricket, rugby football and athletics teams, winning prizes and the occasional record along the way. I also became a keen boxer. These experiences all stood me in good stead for my later selection playing serious rugby for the city club and later in a match for Auckland against Hawke's Bay. On the scholastic side, I still have two books given as prizes and won a bursary to attend university. It was at Mount Albert that I picked up the nickname 'Jock' (on account of my assumed Scottish parentage), one that has stuck with me ever since.

Starting Work

On leaving school in 1925 I joined the Lands and Survey Department as a draughting cadet. The department conducted two exams—one for draughting and one for computing. In those days computing was done in your head and not by a machine, and to pass the exams it was necessary to have a good knowledge of advanced mathematics, and so I used my university bursary to attend classes in advanced mathematics. I passed both exams and was then admitted as a public-service draughtsman and 'computer'.

In those days you worked on Saturday mornings and there were no such things as tea breaks. Hot water was not even provided and you had to have your lunch at your draughting table. That is, unless you had it at some restaurant, and on a salary of £80 per year few could afford that. The annual increase was £15. Hardly an environment to turn one into a budding capitalist!

While I was working at the department I was courting Freda Jacobs, who I had met in 1924 at a church social. Like me, Freda was born in New Zealand to English parents who had emigrated to this country. Unlike mine, however, Freda's parents were quite well off, her father eventually becoming chief engineer for the Auckland Hospital Board. Freda had gone to a good grammar school, then undertook legal training and steady work in a solicitor's office. Four years after we met, at the age of 21, we were married at St Luke's Church in Mount Albert. Our daughter Dorothy was our first child, followed later by our son Eric William (Bill).

Coming into Politics and Trouble in the Great Depression

No sooner had I started work than New Zealand began its long slide into what became the Great Depression of the 1930s. Depression? I prefer the word oppression. This was a land filled to overflowing with the necessities of life—food, clothing and the means of shelter. A country still in the early stages of its development degenerated into, for the vast majority, a land of poverty, misery and starvation. Financial manipulation by the criminals who controlled the world's monetary systems was the cause of this disaster. Sir

Otto Niemeyer, the chairman of the Bank of England, was the evil genius who preached to New Zealand and other countries the philosophy of poverty in a world of plenty. Starvation and misery for the many but a further accumulation of wealth for the interests he served.

Freda and I had not long been married and conditions for working people continued to get progressively worse. By 1930 there were 51,000 unemployed in New Zealand. Unemployed street marches seemed to be a daily occurrence and soup kitchens were the only thing that stopped many people from starving to death. Slave camps were established in country areas, the main purpose being to get the unemployed out of the towns in an endeavour to stop them organising. So-called wages of about 14/- to 15/- per week were the norm, with thousands of men separated from their wives and families. The seizure of household goods and evictions continued to grow. Our next-door neighbour, Mrs Marcus Jones, who was in her seventies and lived with her daughter, fell behind with her hire purchase payments. She only owed a few pounds but it was enough—the vultures arrived and stripped their home. Mrs Jones wasn't the only one to fall victim of course, and soon working-class districts began to establish anti-eviction groups, which fought pitched battles against the bailiffs and their goons. Direct action was the only language these Shylocks understood. In 1935 the new Labour government passed legislation protecting the rights of tenants against these ghouls, but in the Depression it was up to ordinary folk to do what they could. All the time you had the fat cats and the politicians bleating their slogan of 'everyone is suffering but it is equality of sacrifice'.

My horror at the circumstances that I could see everywhere drew me into socialist politics. I began to write articles for unemployed workers' papers and also sent the odd article to the *Labour Daily* in Sydney, which was run by New South Wales' rebel Labor Party state leader Jack Lang. I joined the Labour Party and in coming years was to become secretary-treasurer of the Morningside branch, a councillor for the Mount Albert Borough and an approved parliamentary candidate.

In 1930 an imperial conference was held in Ottawa. On his return, Liberal Prime Minister George Forbes announced that wages of public servants would be cut by 10 per cent and that relief work wages would be cut from 14/- to 12/6 per week for married men, and to only 9/- for single men. This was too much for the Labour members who had backed the Liberals until this point, but was carried with the support of Gordon Coates and his Reform Party. Another of the Forbes government's measures was the scandalous scheme known as 'No. 5', which allowed local authorities to employ men at relief rates of pay. Of course this resulted in permanent employees being sacked and employed again at unemployed rates.

Forbes was driven by only one idea—to slash anything pertaining to

Gordon Coates, Reform Party
Prime Minister 1925–28
(News Media: *Auckland Star*
collection)

workers' rights and conditions, and at this stage he formed a coalition government with the Reform Party. The unholy alliance went from bad to worse. The protection of award wages was removed and even highly profitable employers, such as the Chelsea Sugar Refinery, responded by slashing wages to the bone. Forbes went to the country on his austerity budget, promising that all were sacrificing equally and that austerity would soon be rewarded by recovery and prosperity for all. The Labour Party, then led by Harry Holland, was unprepared and Forbes and his United government was returned to office, albeit with a reduced majority.

By the end of 1931 there were 100,000 registered unemployed out of a population of just over a million and a half, and that figure did not include unemployed women. The ranks of the unemployed were made up not only of tradesmen and labourers but also of many of the professional classes. Sickness and malnutrition were endemic. One of the worst features was the effect on a generation of undernourished children, which became so apparent in later years. Cases of death from starvation were not unknown. Old people simply faded away.

Of course we had the usual platitudes. Anyone in real need could get help from charitable aid sources, generally administered by hospital boards. And what an inquisition applicants had to face for any meagre assistance that might be given! Ruthlessly cross-examined and stripped of their last shreds of human dignity, to be eligible for anything it was essential to prove you no longer had any household effects, and this included even a bed.

By now many thousands of workers and unemployed were asking themselves: 'How much longer are we going to take this?' An explosion was inevitable. The first was in Dunedin on 8 April 1932 when men and women, driven desperate by starving children, stoned and stormed a relief depot. The police, who were kept well fed throughout the Depression, faithfully fulfilled their usual role.

This was the precursor of the big Auckland riot six days later.

When 10 per cent cuts on public servants' salaries were announced, once again a protest gathering of public servants was called by the Post and Telegraph Association in Auckland. It was to march up Queen Street for a meeting in the town hall and, as an employee of the Lands and Survey Department, I was in the thick of things. As we lined up we were joined by unemployed workers with their respective banners: Auckland Central Unemployed, Mount Albert, Onehunga, Grey Lynn etc. The march itself was peaceful.

I was in charge of keeping order at the main town hall door in Queen Street and was therefore in a better position than anybody to see what actually happened on the day.

About 30–40 police were lined up by the door and on the footpath. Public servants were inside and unemployed workers had started to enter. Unemployed seamen had just gone in. Contrary to what has been freely stated, the hall was not full. At this point the police decided to move in to bar the entry of a contingent of Auckland Central unemployed led by Jim Edwards, then the most prominent figure in the Auckland unemployed movement.

Two police told me to close the doors. I refused, telling them it was a lawful meeting and the hall was not full. They tried to close the doors and I resisted. The unemployed seamen were just inside. Needless to say, the men outside started to get restive. Jim Edwards turned to speak to them and, with his back to the police, he was batoned down. Desperate men did the rest. It was all on.

The doors had not been closed and out poured as tough a bunch of men as you would find anywhere—the seamen. They were followed by the rest from inside and with those still outside it was all over in about a minute. Then came a charge of mounted police, who had been held in reserve at the Rutland Street drill hall. They were dead out of luck. Construction work was going on alongside the Civic Theatre, bricks and what-have-you were lying everywhere and down went this lot, horses and all. It was Bastille Day all over again. Pickets were ripped off a nearby fence and the police fled the scene. Bricks were thrown through the windows of a pawn shop opposite the town hall and then it was the rest of Queen Street. Men driven beyond human endurance wrecked and looted Queen Street. They had total control of Auckland city until about 1am next day, when armed naval forces arrived.

Colin Scrimgeour's Friendly Road radio station was then located near the foot of Queen Street. 'Scrim' broadcast details of the riot as it took place. The government tried to block the news leaking out of the country but to no avail. News travelled fast and early next day I got a cable from the Sydney *Labour Daily* to send a full account. I did this right away and it was headline news not only in Australia but further afield as well.

The following night there was rioting in Karangahape Road, as well as riots in Wellington.

This was the nearest thing to revolution that New Zealand had ever seen, but in no sense was it such. The majority had no wish to turn their country into a socialist republic, although that idea was becoming fairly prevalent amongst a minority of workers and young people. Faced by riots and political polarisation, the government realised that unless misery was lessened, it faced more disturbances. Conditions were somewhat eased— not to any great extent, but enough to prevent what might otherwise have been open revolution. In practice, misery, starvation and distress continued to be the lot of tens of thousands until 1935.

Persecution

My activities had not gone unnoticed in Wellington and my public-service dossier must have been bulging at the seams. The breezes blowing through the corridors of government buildings got very chilly. My union, the Public Service Association, was no help at all. It had done nothing to defend the interests of public servants and now did nothing to defend one of its most active members. On two occasions in the summer of 1932 the union secretary, F. Millar, paid me a visit and warned me against continuing my political activities. On the second occasion he informed me that the Public Service Commissioner, Paul Verschaffelt, wished to see me in Wellington to discuss my political activities. I refused to go to Wellington.

One week later, on 30 July 1932, the commissioner made his move against me. In an urgent telegram to the chief surveyor of the Lands and Survey Department at Auckland, the commissioner instructed the department to transfer me to the New Plymouth office. I refused this transfer because at this time I had an application for exemption from pay cuts still lodged with the public service's Adjustments Committee. This committee was established to hear claims of special hardship and such was my case, trying to live on a weekly wage of £3.15/8 and supporting a wife and two children. Furthermore, the commissioner's request was ludicrous: the New Plymouth office was already amply staffed.

The real reason was clear: to remove a political irritant from the country's major city and to shunt me into a country town where, they believed, I could cause no mischief. The United government had only recently passed the notorious clause 59 of the Finance Act, which imposed serious restrictions on the activities of state employees. The commissioner had been informed of my activities in the 1931 general election in Roskill, where I had exposed the financial interests of the conservative candidate at a public meeting and had been instrumental in causing his defeat. I had been implicated in the Queen Street riot and had defied government instructions in cabling news of the riot overseas.

On refusing the transfer, I was summarily dismissed. Or, in the commissioner's view, I had dismissed myself by refusing to accept the transfer. There then followed a six-year campaign in which I endeavoured to get reinstated to the Lands and Survey Department. Many good men came to my aid. Four months after my dismissal John A. Lee, Labour member for Auckland, promised me that I would be reinstated with backpay on Labour winning the next election. Mr McVeagh, a well-known Auckland solicitor, took up my case on a no-win, no-fee basis. I had never met McVeagh before but he said he was very disturbed by aspects of my case. Nevertheless, it was nearly a year before my appeal was heard by Justice Reed in the Supreme Court, in June 1933. The court case was a farce, the commissioner refusing to answer any pertinent questions, claiming privilege. The secretary of my union, Millar, did nothing to help, even taking his lunch with the commissioner while my legal counsel and I ate our sandwiches in Albert Park! Little wonder that I lost the case. My only option now was to petition Parliament and in September 1933 my petition appeared on the Order Paper, along with 30 others. Labour was still in opposition and my petition therefore failed. I petitioned again in 1934 and 1935. My local Labour member, Arthur Richards, held out the hope that when Labour won I would be reinstated, and when Michael Savage won the 1935 election things began to look up for me. On the very evening before the election I had been on the stage with Savage at Auckland Town Hall and when we repaired for coffee afterwards Savage leaned over and said, 'My boy, one of the first things we will do is reinstate you and see that you get adequate compensation for the wrong that you and your family have suffered.'

However, I was to face the first of many betrayals by the Labour Party as, no sooner were they in office than they dropped me like a half-sucked acid drop. In February 1936 the new Labour Minister for Lands, Mr Langstone, sent me a letter that read:

> It is not competent for me to bring about your reinstatement in the Public Service. I am informed by the Public Service Commissioner that he had good grounds for ordering your transfer to New Plymouth and that such reasons were not political. I am sorry that it is necessary to send such an unfavourable reply, but I must support the fundamental principle of discipline and obedience to authority on which all organisation must be based.

I was astonished by this discouraging reply but didn't give up hope. John A. Lee appealed the matter, putting my case before Prime Minister Savage. However, Savage supported his minister's decision. Lee also tried to find me work in the Housing Department, which at that time was advertising in Australia for staff. No go here, however. I was then offered temporary work in the Railway Department for a maximum of 12 months at £275 p.a., £60 less than I would have received had I remained at Lands. I refused both, insisting on reinstatement, and petitioned Parliament again in 1938 and was again unsuccessful. At this point I gave up all hope and ceased my campaign.

While all of this was going on, I had had to find work to feed my family. However, the authorities, for whatever reason, appeared to be trying to make life difficult. After my dismissal I did not receive any unemployment allowance for nearly six months, nor did I have my superannuation payments refunded. I had to get by earning a few shillings hawking toilet articles, soaps and scents door to door. No longer in the Public Service Association, I joined the unemployed workers' movement and was soon vice-president of the Mount Albert Unemployed Association.

2 ONTO THE WATERFRONT, 1933-41

Starting Work as a Wharfie

In late 1933 the Chelsea Sugar Refinery offered me a job on the waterfront discharging sugar from the company's lighters. It was non-stop labour for 44 hours and all hard work. Pay was a miserable £3.8/9 per week. I joined the Sugar Workers' Union. Soon after starting work I was nominated to a position as delegate to the Auckland Trades Council. From then on I was a marked man in the eyes of the company. Within 12 months I was sacked after refusing to load sugar on two Matson line ships, *Mariposa* and *Monterey*, which were regular visitors to Auckland from San Francisco en route to Sydney. American longshoremen had blacked these ships as they were being run as scab operations during one of the bitterest disputes that the United States labour movement has ever had to face: an 11-week strike by American wharfies the length and breadth of the Pacific Coast, from Seattle to San Diego. True to the best traditions of the New Zealand waterfronts, Auckland watersiders refused to work them. We were ordered by CSR to load sugar onto the *Mariposa*. Two of us, myself and Jack Roberts, an ex-seaman, refused. The sack followed.

It was a bad time to be out of work but word had got around amongst the wharfies and Jack and I did not have to wait too long before we were accepted as members of the Auckland branch of the Waterside Workers' Union. The year was 1935. Jack and I were proud members of the WWU. One didn't just join the WWU—you had to be accepted by them first. They only took strong union men. With their history of long years of suffering and struggle in an endeavour to obtain a reasonable living from some of the world's most vicious employers, this was perfectly understandable. In the union ranks were many veterans of the 1913 strike and many who had been jailed after Waihi. They knew what it was all about. If the world has ever known a better-organised, stronger, more disciplined or knowledgeable body of men I have yet to hear of it. As such, they constituted a threat and a menace to the privileged position of the master class.

The union ranks constituted a veritable league of nations. Race, colour, religion meant nothing; background and outlook were the dominant factors. Here we had men who had sailed windjammers around the Horn, who had fought in strikes, lockouts and struggles in Britain, the US, European and Scandinavian countries, as well as Australia and New Zealand. These were men who had been forged in fire.

The Bureau System is Introduced

When I started work the auction block system of engaging labour was still in force. Early each morning men would line up before the shipowners' representative, who would then pick and choose from amongst them. Needless to say, those who were prominent in union affairs or job action, or had a record of working-class activity, were not called. They only worked when no other labour was available. Hours of call were 7.45–10.30am six days a week.

Ordinary hours of work were 8am to 5pm Monday to Friday and 8am to noon Saturday, with overtime until 10pm Monday to Friday and 6pm Saturday. However, if a ship was due to sail it would be worked until midnight, with meal breaks also being worked. Overtime was optional, but because the men had no guarantees of their next job they always took it. There was no such thing as attendance money and many were those who, after a week of fronting up at the wharf each morning, had to return to their wives and families with nothing. Efforts to achieve a fairer system by representations to the shipowners were met with steadfast refusal. Only by direct action did the union win a new system that promised some fairness: this was the 30-hour system, which was established late in 1933.

The 30-hour scheme was a big improvement. Under this, any member who had finished a job or who had worked 30 hours or more for the week had to stand down, allowing one of his workmates the chance of work. The bosses could do nothing about this, as we operated and policed it ourselves.

While a vast improvement on what previously applied, it still did not provide for an equal division of work. This only came about with the introduction of the Bureau system. This system was first trialled at Lyttelton in June 1936 and there was widespread interest in the scheme up and down the country. The men deputised me and Victor Nugent, another wharfie, to investigate how it worked in practice. The Bureau system, which was operated by and paid for by the shipowners, required each worker to be allocated a job on the basis of strict rotation. This was clearly an improvement on the 30-hour scheme and did bring about an equal distribution of work. However Victor, an older man than me, of wide experience and considerable intelligence, could also see the dangers inherent in such a system in that it put all power in the hands of the owners. Men could no longer take days off for a break and nor could they refuse to take a job to which they had been allocated on pain of fines or suspension from the scheme. While we recognised this problem, it was also clear that the owners had given up on the old auction block system. It was on this basis that the men accepted it in Auckland and in all major New Zealand ports in September 1937. As a condition, we insisted in Auckland on having our own full-time Bureau officer elected and paid for by the union. We also warned the owners against any attempt to use the Bureau as a further means of attacking the union.

No Pig-iron to Japan!

However, the owners were not getting to let a chance slip by and we did not have to wait long. In September 1937 the Japanese invaded China, a prelude to the Pacific war. Although all military attacks are ruthless and merciless, the atrocities committed by the Japanese in China shocked the world. That is, all except those who profited from the war, and that included sections of business in New Zealand and Australia. Exporting scrap iron to Japan was a lucrative business and the government had no intention of intervening to stop it. The money that business was making from the industry was enough to encourage them to turn a blind eye to the atrocities, the tragedies, and the inhuman suffering that they were aiding and abetting.

The Auckland wharfies, however, followed by our Australian fellow workers, took a stand against this obscene trade and at a stopwork meeting in October refused to load scrap iron for Japan. In came the Labour government in full support of the dealers in death. We had a stopwork meeting addressed by Paddy Webb, Minister of Labour. Paddy, like his fellow ministers Peter Fraser and Bob Semple, had once been a red-hot militant and had done time in jail for agitating against the Great War. They now accused us of wanting to dictate New Zealand foreign policy, and this was something that the government could simply not tolerate. Mind you, had New Zealand wharfies actually run foreign policy, a lot of subsequent tragedy might well have been avoided! We sent Webb running back to Wellington.

No more scrap iron for Japan left the port of Auckland. Having seen off Webb, we were now faced by the shipowners, who were keen to get this dirty trade moving again so that they could get their cut of the money. It was at this point that the owners took advantage of the Bureau system to teach us a lesson. Men who refused to lift their discs from the engagement board were penalised and denied other work. Under the old auction block system this would have been impossible as men simply would not have lined up for such a job and there was nothing the employers could have done about it. We could now see out in the open their motivation in agreeing to the new system. They wanted absolute control over the

Patrick Webb, Labour Party Minister for Mines, Labour, and Telegraphs, 1935–45 (*NZ Herald*)

Peter Fraser, Labour Party Prime Minister 1940–49
(News Media: *Auckland Star* collection)

workforce. While it looked as if they held the trump card, we were helped by a wave of public opinion in favour of our stand. Many New Zealanders were becoming increasingly concerned by Japan's increasingly expansionist military and particularly by the atrocities in China. Committees to aid China were being formed and we raised almost £100 to assist in the adoption of Chinese children orphaned by the war by organising a charity concert by our union band. Politicians did nothing to help, but with an election coming up, the government, the shipowners and the industrialists were forced to back down. The wharfies had done their bit to reduce the Japanese military build-up.

The Birth of the Waterfront Control Commission

However, this was a temporary victory. Before long we were faced with all-out world war, with the Labour government, now under Peter Fraser, New Zealand's No.1 war party. Early in 1940 the Labour government took unto itself unlimited powers and all civil rights were suspended for the duration. One of the first targets of the government was the waterside and a Waterfront Control Commission was soon in place, which took over management issues from the shipowners and pay determination from the Arbitration Court. In many of the unlimited powers the government took unto itself that year, it was as fascist in character as the fascism we were fighting overseas. The commission's powers were specified in the Waterfront Control Commission Emergency Regulations 1940 and it comprised three members, all appointed by the government: one from the union, one from the shipowners and one so-called independent chairman (see Appendix 1 for full details). To ensure that a union representative on such a body acts in the true interests of the men he represents, one thing is essential. He should be elected by the union membership and subject to recall by the union. However, this did not occur in this instance as Jim Roberts, at that time our national secretary, but also national secretary of the Labour Party and confidant and close ally of the government, was appointed by the government to the position, with Captain R.E. Price as commission chairman. Many of us thought that Roberts could not serve two masters: he had to make a choice between the union and the commission.

Many of our members were veterans of World War One and had past experience of so-called wartime emergency regulations. They knew that they had a habit of becoming permanent and aimed only at the workers. They knew that waterfront control meant wharfie control and that if the waterfronts of New Zealand were not to become concentration camps, abuse of the commission's authoritative powers would have to be resisted in the traditional way. Opposition to the commission was particularly strong in Auckland, the largest and most militant port, and wharfies in Auckland waited patiently for some response from their president (Tom Solomon) and secretary (Bill Cuthbert). None came, however—for them, soft and lucrative jobs with the commission were already beckoning, with Cuthbert appointed Auckland wharf superintendent in June 1940 (see Appendix 2 for full listing of WWU office-holders).

The Kelly-Murray Case

Matters came to a head within the union with the unilateral decision by the commission to stretch wharfies' working hours to 11 at night, to overcome the growing labour shortage caused by the military call-up. Men would not get home until after midnight and yet they were expected to be fit for heavy work again at 8am. Rebellion in the ranks surfaced.

Most of us exercised our legal right to refuse overtime and ceased work at 5pm. There was nothing the commission could do about this. But five elected to work until 10pm and then knock off as a direct challenge to the new hours and the commission. They were immediately sacked and debarred from any work on the waterfront. Two of the five were well-known militants—Joe Murray and Jack Kelly.

Despite being sacked the five reported for work every day and fellow members made sure that the five and their dependants did not suffer. Things drifted along for a while, but rank and file demands for action got nowhere. I had had enough and at one stopwork meeting went to work on Solomon and Cuthbert, who had refused to even lodge a protest. I moved that if the five were not reinstated we would take industrial action until they were. The motion was carried by an overwhelming majority by workers determined to defend their working conditions in war as well as in peace.

Wartime conditions and an acute shortage of labour rendered the usual appeal for scabs a useless exercise. Similarly, the armed forces could not be ordered to scab. The government was in a no-win situation and was forced to step in, ordering that the matter be the subject of an inquiry before Mr Gilmour, industrial magistrate. The five nominated me to represent them in court. The case, which became famous as the Kelly–Murray case, resulted in a total win for the union. Mr Gilmour rejected all the commission submissions and ordered the immediate reinstatement of the five. Captain Price's attempt to break the power of our union had backfired!

Election as Branch President

This successful outcome resulted in increased feeling against Solomon, who had refused to take any action. A motion of no-confidence in him was passed and within weeks Solomon bailed out to join his old mate Cuthbert on the commission. This created a vacancy and at the next branch elections I was asked by many of my workmates to stand for the presidency of the Auckland branch. This presented me with something of a problem. While I was a delegate to the Auckland Trades Council I had stood for no other position. I was studying accountancy by correspondence in the limited free time I had, and in my first exam passed in three subjects—Mercantile Law, Joint Stock Companies, and Secretarial Law and Practice. However, with the union under ever-growing pressure, it was obvious that if I won I would have to drop my accounting studies.

The choice was obvious. I had become too prominent in the union and the fight against the commission and the shipowners to back down. Came the election and I won the position of president of the Auckland branch, New Zealand Waterside Workers' Union, beating the old vice-president. These elections saw the militants in our branch sweep out all the old Roberts and Cuthbert supporters and we were now in a solid position.

3 WAR ON THE WATERFRONT, 1941-45

Conscription is Introduced

I had no illusions about the fight that lay ahead of us. As in all wars, there would be two fronts—the foreign and the home. Already we had experienced many attacks on the home front and it was axiomatic that, as the war progressed, these would be intensified and workers would have to fight back. We had many in our number with experiences of 1914–18, many veterans of bitter struggles for elementary rights, many who knew that police batons under a Labour government were as hard as police batons under a Tory government and many who since 1935 had seen the Labour Party abandon all talk of socialism until it had become a dirty word in the ranks of its leadership. And many who knew the background of the two greatest jingoes in New Zealand, Fraser and Semple. We did not have long to wait.

The Labour Party and Federation of Labour (FOL) were totally committed to the war effort. On 21 February 1940 a joint statement on war policy had been issued by the executives of the Labour Party and the federation. It was signed by Jim Roberts, president, and Michael Moohan, acting secretary, on behalf of the Labour Party and by Angus McLagan, president, and Fred Cornwell, secretary, on behalf of the FOL. Among other things, it said:

> We are opposed to conscription for military service either inside of New Zealand or overseas. We are satisfied that there is no need for conscription; our young men will rally to the cause of the defence of their freedom against any aggressor.

Three months later another joint statement was signed by the same individuals introducing conscription and pledging full support to the Labour government! It was the first of a series of anti-worker dictates that, in many cases, lasted until well after 1945. The betrayal of labour principles by Fraser and Semple was particularly galling. In 1916 the pair of them had been sentenced to 12 months' jail for sedition. Semple had argued at the time:

Conscription was not intended in this country to fight the Kaiser but to fight trade unionism and the working class. They are more afraid of the trade unionists, the capitalists are, than the Kaiser. Why? The Kaiser belonged to the same school that they belonged to. The Kaiser stands for despotism, robbery, plunder, oligarchy. The worker stands for liberty. They fear the rising of the working class a sight more than the Kaiser, because the Kaiser belongs to the same school as the robbers in the rest of the world.

Now in government, these same people turned against all that they had stood for in past years. Nice people we had to deal with—renegades of the worst type!

By the beginning of 1941 all forms of democracy had disappeared in New Zealand and for all practical purposes it was a dictatorship. Press

Bob Semple, Labour Party Minister of Works 1935–49 (*NZ Herald*)

censorship was drastic and the treatment of conscientious objectors a disgrace to any civilised country. Pacifists were brutally treated and many jailed. Appeal boards were set up to hear appeals from conscientious objectors. However, as with the vast majority of such boards, they were a farce. That there was a good deal of corruption in the appeal process is also beyond doubt. In the face of rising trade union protests, the super-patriotic Labour government advised the Auckland Trades Council that it could elect a representative to act on the Auckland Appeals Board. I was elected but was never allowed to sit.

The year saw a spate of emergency regulations directed against workers. All existing awards were abolished and all work stoppages made illegal. Direction of labour was introduced. Despite these measures, however, workers struck to maintain their wages as prices and profits soared. Workers fought to prevent the war overseas against fascism being used as a means of destroying the trade union movement in New Zealand. An uneasy truce prevailed.

The Yanks are Coming!

In December 1941 Pearl Harbour was bombed, and in June 1942 the first American troops landed in Auckland, which served as their main South Pacific base for some considerable time. No attempt had been made by either the government or the Waterfront Control Commission to negotiate an industrial agreement on work for American forces on the waterfront. As far as Fraser was concerned, the Americans had an open go and could do what they liked. The Commission, likewise, stood well clear: its role was to control watersiders, not Americans! As it turned out, the American top brass were reasonable men. I never experienced any untoward difficulty when negotiating with them, and we made a most satisfactory working agreement. They were astounded at our extremely low wage rate and we agreed on an increase of 2/- per hour. Better conditions were also obtained. This provoked Fraser into immediate action and, using the emergency regulations, he reduced the rise to a shilling.

Dealing with some of the lower ranks was a different story, however. These men had been dragooned from American jails in some cases, or were good ol' boys from the Deep South. They became regular bullies, and were racist towards our Maori comrades to boot. Things blew up when these men were stationed as armed guards in the ships' holds and on Princes Wharf, Victoria Park and other areas on which storage sheds were erected. The place was by now crawling with US soldiers. Returned men who had been fighting overseas long before Pearl Harbour but who were now back on civilian duties as a result of sickness or injury were not going to stand for this. Similarly our Maori members quickly got sick of the racist attitude that they experienced. The watersiders walked off as one in protest at the standover tactics.

On going to the scene I was told bluntly and in no uncertain terms that they had shot longshoremen overseas and they would do the same here. I told them that the first one shot would be their last, and that they would get more fight than they ever wanted right there on Princes Wharf without leaving New Zealand! We declared their ships black. Very soon, however, after discussions with their officer in charge of Princes Wharf, Colonel Chianese, the guards were lifted and there was never another attempt to have armed guards stand over New Zealand watersiders. Work resumed, but that was not the end of problems between the American military and New Zealanders. A few months later a riot erupted in Wellington. American troops objected to Maoris drinking in the same services club as them. It ended in a four-hour battle through the streets of Wellington in which some Americans were killed, news of which was successfully hushed up. They had to learn the hard way that they were not back in the southern States.

Many of the American stevedores, both civilian and military, were inexperienced or just plain incompetent. In their rush and bash tactics, elementary safety precautions were ignored. Left to themselves, they might well have blown up Auckland. Matters came to a head when one of our members, Jim Hamilton, was killed because of criminal negligence and incompetence on their part. Jim left a widow and two young children and so we approached the US military HQ in Shortland Street for compensation. We were told that the military and therefore the waterfront was operating under US law and that Jim's family would get paid out a maximum of $500 allowable by Washington. They were adamant that, because of Washington's directive, this was the maximum that would be paid. I was equally adamant that they were going to be subject to the laws of New Zealand—not Washington. I called a stopwork meeting and it was unanimously agreed by the men that, until we were covered by New Zealand law, their ships would not be worked.

The government went berserk and I was off to Wellington again. I took with me the union's Auckland lawyer, Bob Fawcett, and we met the full Cabinet. Fraser said he could have me shot for interrupting the war effort. But we knew this was just bluster: I told him that if I had been harmed in any way, wharfies around New Zealand would have been drawing lots for the honour of knocking him off! I had great pleasure in letting that collection of renegades, hypocrites and numbskulls know what I thought of them. The result of our almighty showdown was that the government had to back off. All workers in New Zealand working for the US military were now to be covered by New Zealand law. So much for Washington's $500! We obtained a substantial settlement for Jim's widow and children.

The next battle occurred over an attempt by some of the Americans to stitch up our men for stealing cargo. With such a huge quantity of supplies moving through Auckland, it was not surprising that racketeers operated. Fortunes were being made on the black market. The main force behind this were two Yanks who operated a real Mafia outfit and when they left New Zealand they owned plenty, including farms and racehorses. It was big business. However, it was our boys who were the target of some Pinkerton detectives who were brought in to clean up the racketeering. On returning from dinner one day on the wharves, our members found a gang of American military police standing over their kitbags containing their food and other personal belongings. The police moved in and arrested six of our men. The Yanks planned to hold them under armed guard at Victoria Park and to charge them before a military court with stealing US equipment—to wit officers' gloves. Others had been shot for this, so they said. However, if they thought that our boys were gullible, they got a big shock. It so happened that working on the Princes Wharf were, among others, about 300 of the first-echelon boys, who knew all about American military police, who had made their lives hell on overseas service. They knew that the contents in the bag were a plant and that this was a set-up to

George Minhinnick, *New Zealand Herald* cartoonist 1930–75
(News Media: *Auckland Star* collection)

teach the wharfies a lesson. Uproar ensued and it was on for young and old. The nearest the MPs got to Victoria Park was an upstairs office on the quay to which they fled and locked themselves in, besieged by hundreds of wharfies baying for their blood.

I was called in and on my way I could hear the row from about two miles away. When I arrived I told the men that I was going in to see the Yanks and if I was not out in 10 minutes, to do the rest. What a frightened bunch. Maybe they had visions of past occasions when they had lynched blacks. This time, they got plain talk. Many outside were veterans of three years of fighting and many of our men would have welcomed the chance of squaring accounts. If this wasn't settled very smartly they were likely to be found floating in the Waitemata. I was out in five minutes.

The Pinkerton bunch were sent back next day. Our six members were released and the US military gave an unconditional guarantee that if they ever had occasion to make complaints about such things as alleged theft, they would be made through the New Zealand police.

I rang Inspector Jack Southworth, who was in charge of the waterfront police. Naturally they had heard the row. He said they had kept out of it, being quite happy to have our boys settle it. There would be no action from them.

Considering the vast quantity of cargo handled, however, disputes with the Americans were few. After we had made it clear to them that they were not an army of occupation and that at all times their actions would be subject to New Zealand law, industrial unrest was conspicuous by its absence.

This was more than could be said for the Waterfront Control Commission.

Battles with the Commission

Bill Cuthbert and Tom Solomon, who had now been promoted to chief controller and assistant controller for the port of Auckland, now set about doing the dirty on their old union and their sights were firmly set on Auckland. Both of them had a simple formula—the watersiders were always wrong and shipowners always right. With Cuthbert in charge, constant trouble was inevitable.

Unlike the Americans, the Waterfront Control Commission was completely intransigent. In fact, Cuthbert simply ran the commission in Auckland as an extension of the government and shipowners, with one goal only in mind—to destroy the power of the WWU, starting with Auckland. The unholy alliance of government, commission and shipowners was aided and abetted by the press, which maintained a continual barrage of hatred and abuse against the Auckland wharfies. This was particularly true of the

New Zealand Herald and its cartoonist, Minhinnick. As a creator of class hatred, this man was in a class of his own. It would seem that if it were not for his despicable caricatures of watersiders, he would have been bereft of ideas. While our men were useful, productive and hardworking members of society, Minhinnick and his type sought to crucify them. Press coverage throughout this period was completely one-sided, and when we proved their lies and calumnies wrong or libellous they never used headlines to set the record straight in our favour.

The year 1942 saw growing unrest throughout the country. The Fraser government continued to push our war effort to ridiculous lengths. Rationing was at an absurd level and, with soaring wartime profits, signs of rebellion were surfacing in the workforce. Strikes were increasing, with that of the Huntly miners perhaps the most notable. Due principally to Fraser and Semple's policy of conscription, industry was near to total collapse, and in the following year 17,000 men were even withdrawn from the armed forces and drafted to work in essential industries to keep production going.

On the waterfront we continued to work longer hours than any other industry and, generally speaking, disputes were few. But, war effort or not, the commission's main objective was to smash the Auckland branch. The appointments of Cuthbert and Solomon made that abundantly clear. This obsession overrode any intelligence they may have possessed.

Commission chairman R.E. Price was domiciled in Auckland and we had to suffer him most of the time, rarely seeing the other two national officers, T.H. Bowling and Jim Roberts. Price never forgot the hiding he took in the Kelly–Murray case and pursued a non-stop vendetta against the Auckland branch in general, and myself in particular.

One example was the dispute over the ship *Chios*, which was being managed while in the port of Auckland by Captain J.A. Anderson of the Union Steam Ship Co (USSCo). Beyond all doubt, Anderson was the most provocative shipowner's agent on the waterfronts of New Zealand. Anderson had taken on men to work on the *Chios* for Saturday afternoon only and under the terms of the Commission's Order he was obliged to give notice to the men on Saturday morning if he wanted them to work through Sundays, the only day that the men ever got to see much of their families. At 3.30pm one Saturday Captain Anderson ordered the men to attend work on the following day to help unload the *Chios*. This was an illegal instruction and a clear breach of the Commission's Order under which we worked. Naturally the men refused.

The dispute drew in Cuthbert, who upheld Captain Anderson and said that he would withdraw all appeals for exemption from military service currently lodged by Auckland watersiders if we didn't agree to work on Sunday. This was blackmail to which no union could submit. At this time

War on the Waterfront

SONG AND DANCE

THE SOLUTION

"PIPING ON THE SHIFT" BY THE NEW WATERSIDERS' PIPE BAND

there were few single men working on the waterfront and all the appeals were for married men with at least a couple of children. For reasons best known to itself, the government had never declared New Zealand's waterfronts to be an essential industry, although they had done so to many others of little or no importance.

Realising that we would get no satisfaction from the commission we took the matter up with Paddy Webb, Minister of Labour. Captain Price had issued a summons against me for holding up the *Chios*. At the meeting with Webb he made no mention of it and, until I raised the matter, neither Webb nor Price's colleagues knew about it. Price got his coffee in no uncertain manner and the commission was told to rescind the order to work on the Sunday. That Price and Cuthbert were not sacked over this matter could only be explained by the fact that despite this flagrant and barefaced attack, they had the support of the government. Any doubts about this were made abundantly clear by their continued attacks.

Undeterred by their *Chios* defeat, the commission and shipowners continued their unholy alliance. The war effort ran a bad second to their attempts to smash the union. At times it was not even in the race: minor disputes of no real significance and inseparable from the nature of the industry frequently occurred. However, serious breaches of our award by shipowners and the unrestrained offensives went unheeded. One would be naive indeed to think this possible without government connivance.

One such barefaced attack was in January 1942. Men on the *Matthew Flinders*, in accordance with clause 5 of the Commission's Order, took a ballot on whether or not to continue working in the rain. The procedure for stopping work in the rain was clearly laid down and was correctly carried out. Shipowners called in Auckland gauleiter Cuthbert who, once again, in complete violation of the Commission's Order, sacked the men. However, of greater significance was the statement of his boss, Captain Price, who said that a verbal order of any member of the commission, irrespective of whether it conflicted with the written provisions of the Commission's Order, was valid and must be unquestionably obeyed. And we were at war with Hitler and Mussolini!

To accept such a situation meant that our union no longer existed and workers' rights were a thing of the past. They got the only possible answer. I called a stopwork meeting and it was decided the port would strike unless the men were immediately reinstated. Further, our legal working conditions were to be recognised and observed at all times and not subject to the whims of any jumped-up dictators. Realising that they had created another situation they could neither defend nor substantiate, they capitulated.

After licking their wounds for a while, the commission and shipowners had another go at us, involving the very same principles. In August 1942

Captain Anderson ordered that non-union labour be used on the *Kartigi*, with the clear intention of creating a non-union reserve of scab labour. This clearly flouted the commission's own transfer clause as laid down in section 22 of the order and occurred at the same time as all our endeavours to admit more men into the union were being denied by both shipowners and commission. However, they didn't count on the excellent relations we had with the non-union men who received the full protection of the union and worked under the same conditions. The non-union gang concerned refused to accept this illegal order and were sacked. Cuthbert lined up with his old pal Captain Anderson and endorsed this gross breach. For good measure, he imposed a penalty of two days pay on the gang concerned, stating that a serious breach had been committed by the men and that he would report the matter to his head office in order that further disciplinary action could be taken against them.

When shown section 22 of the Commission's Order, which prevented summary transfer, Cuthbert assumed full responsibility for Captain Anderson's actions and declared that he could arbitrarily waive the terms of the order any time he thought fit. After his previous effort, incredible but true. We took this up in Wellington, and again he got a rap over the knuckles, albeit with a feather duster.

About this time a few of our members and their families were subjected to dawn raids by police. The excuse was that they were searching for pillaged goods. We believed it was further harassment of waterside workers and was policy dictated from Wellington. The outcome was a stormy meeting with Fraser, Justice Minister Mason and the Commissioner of Police, and believe me it was stormy! I told them if they had good reason to make any house searches, they could be made in the accepted and appropriate manner. Our members were incensed, would not tolerate it and if there was another, there would be a strike. The Police Commissioner found I could shout just as loud as he could. That was the end of the dawn raids.

The next big row with the shipowners and the commission occurred in April 1943. It was over the *Waiana*—Captain Anderson and the USSCo again.

This started as a minor dispute, once again involving the wet-weather clause. It is significant that, despite the vast amount of cargo handled for the Americans, there was not one single dispute over wet weather. This, of course, was in marked contrast to any ships involving the commission, a fact that should speak for itself.

As usual, the men acted lawfully and in accordance with the provisions of the Commission's Order, but this was of no concern to Solomon. Without any discussion, this little Caesar sacked them.

It being a Sunday, the men rang the union walking delegate, Walter

McLean, at his home. It was his job to handle these matters and, if possible, to settle them there and then. On his arrival he was met by Solomon and police who, on Solomon's instructions, escorted him to the wharf and refused him the right to speak to the men.

From being a minor dispute it thus became a major one that well might have precipitated a national stoppage. For good measure Cuthbert endorsed his junior's actions.

Police action in denying the right of a union official to speak to his members was an issue affecting the entire New Zealand trade union movement. It would be accepted by none—least of all by watersiders. And, as another issue, who gave this petty upstart and rejected union official the authority to instruct police to act in any manner at all, let alone an illegal one? Members had had a gutful of Cuthbert and Solomon. A no-confidence motion in the two of them was carried and a resolution passed that this issue would be fought to the finish.

The issue was immediately taken up nationally with the commission and the Minister of Labour. Realising that they would not be dealing with watersiders alone but with the trade union movement as a whole, they speedily washed their hands of the matter, leaving Cuthbert and Solomon to clean up the mess. But, believe it or not, these two were left alone to hatch more villainy.

In boxing parlance, Cuthbert by now would have been barred from the ring, but his Wellington trainers had different ideas. After every time he was counted out, they threw him in for another one. By now, however, there was widespread concern within our union about the antics of Cuthbert and Solomon in Auckland. While all ports had had their problems, none had experienced anything comparable with Auckland's. In 1941 our conference had asked for an inquiry to be held into the conduct of these two men, but two years later nothing had been done. At our next biennial conference, held in Wellington in November 1943, we again demanded that the minister carry out an inquiry into the Auckland commission. Again we were rebuffed, as the government was hell-bent on sacrificing workers to the war effort.

Action Against Jailing of Freezing Workers

With rationing at absurd lengths, wages pegged while profits soared, and men and women directed to industry whose sole motive was wartime profiteering, the seeds of discontent were being freely scattered. We suffered for this approach, but so too did other New Zealand workers. Industrial unrest was rising everywhere and strikes well away from the waterfront were on the horizon. In the freezing industry, appalling working conditions were constantly being worsened by profiteering employers using the pretext of the war effort to squeeze out still more production. Finally, workers at the Westfield freezing plant struck in protest. Summonses were instantly issued by the government. Despite assurances from Paddy Webb that there would be no jailing, after a trial in the Auckland Town Hall 213 of them were imprisoned in Mount Eden. The effect of a couple of hundred more admissions into that disgraceful institution can be imagined. It was disgusting, filthy and unfit for animals, let alone human beings.

At a meeting of the Auckland Trades Council, on behalf of our Auckland branch, I moved that if they were not released the Trades Council call a general strike in Auckland. It was carried. Up came the usual summons from Fraser and Co and another trip to Wellington. We had another ding-dong battle, but the government caved in and the workers were released to general jubilation in the ranks of the union movement.

Election as National President

Dissatisfaction with the government increasingly led to dissatisfaction with leaders of our union who placed allegiance to the Labour government, whatever the issue, above loyalty to their union. Members knew that I was prepared to fight, no matter what the colour of the government, and late in 1943 I was asked to stand for national president. A national ballot was held in February 1944 and I was elected, beating Jack Flood by a narrow margin, to the great consternation of the government and assorted Labour Party apologists.

The Kaikorai Gangway Dispute

We did not have to wait long for the next offensive. It was almost a dead heat with our election result and concerned Captain Anderson and the USSCo again. The ship was the *Kaikorai* and the issue was safety. We wharfies took the question of safety extremely seriously. There had been all too many fatalities and serious injuries, with the employers tossing a two-headed penny. When it came to a compensation case for a fatal or serious injury the employers would plead, often successfully, a case of contributory negligence. They claimed that the man or men had known it was not safe and should not have worked until conditions were made safe. However, when we did just that, we were accused of being irresponsible saboteurs!

Labour was engaged for a 1pm start after it had been raining all morning. On arriving at the job, one look was enough to see that the gangway was unsafe and a request was made that it be made safe before men boarded the ship. This was refused and the USSCo called in its commission friends. They adopted their customary role, declared it safe, ordered the men to board the ship and, on their refusal, sacked them.

That this was a politically inspired move to create a major confrontation was made quite clear by their next action in declaring the ship a preference ship. This was a tactic designed to starve men back to work by locking them out. It simply meant that this ship had to be worked before any labour was engaged for any other vessel. In short, it was a port lockout.

Failing to get any union men to scab on their mates, they then tried to get non-union labour. They got none.

This continued for eight days, with work in the port coming to a standstill.

Further evidence of the organised nature of this attack was the blitzkrieg by muckraking press throughout the country. One would have thought the only war was on the Auckland waterfront. Editors, cartoonists and others who could not tell a gangway from a pushchair had a field day.

The issue was simple. Did the gangway comply with the provisions of the General Harbour Regulations? It did not. It did not even meet the first requirement, which was security from ship to shore. Was it safe? That answer was given after seven days when the wire strop supporting the gangway broke and it collapsed. This was with nobody on it. The result, had it been full of workers, is obvious—a disaster.

But then the double-headed penny of contributory negligence would have been produced. Workers were to blame. They knew it was not safe and should not have used it.

They ducked this one by shifting the ship to another berth where a gangway was correctly fitted and work in the port resumed.

Even for the press and politicians this was a particularly vicious campaign. The collapse of the unoccupied gangway and the shifting of the ship to another berth merited just the odd line. The cartoonist of the *Herald* had to look for another subject.

The port had been locked out for eight days and men had wrongfully lost wages, all due to illegal and unjustifiable actions by the commission and USSCo. These super-patriots had knowingly hindered the war effort, but never was there the slightest suggestion of any action against them. From the viewpoint of politicians and shipowners it was just another lost round in the battle to smash the union. On the credit side, they had created more public feeling against watersiders. They would try again: the events of 1951 did not erupt overnight.

Challenge to the Preference Clause

The next blow-up must rank as one of the worst attempts to frame a union official in the history of New Zealand. On 19 May 1944, in clear contravention of the long-established clause that stipulated that union men must be given preference in employment, the Labour Bureau, acting under instructions from Cuthbert, insisted that the three ships—the MV *City of*

Lille, SS *Waipara* and MV *Catrine*—be unloaded using non-union labour. At this time there were between 400 and 500 members of the Auckland branch standing by awaiting engagement. On the morning of 20 May I advised all parties that unless union men were in these jobs by 10am, the jobs would be stopped. This was not done and at 10am approximately 400 men went home until Monday morning.

By the Monday the Bureau had given in and union men were soon hard at work on all three ships. Nothing more was heard until 2 June when three summonses were served on me, to be heard on 22 June. I was charged under sections 3 and 4 of the Strike and Lockout Emergency Regulations 1939, that on or about 20 May I did incite certain persons, to wit, waterside workers employed on MV *City of Lille*, to be, or continue to be, parties to a strike. Similar summonses were issued in conjunction with the *Waipara* and *Catrine*. On 6 June a meeting was called of the Auckland branch executive. The executive unanimously agreed on the following resolution, which was submitted to a mass meeting of the branch on the same day and also carried unanimously:

> 1. Direct union representation on the Control Commission as resolved by the last biennial conference.
> 2. No summonses to be issued against any member of the union for union activities without first a conference of the parties concerned being called, the Minister of Labour to preside.
> 3. That in the event of any member of the union being imprisoned or excluded from the waterfronts of New Zealand for union activity, no work be done on the waterfronts during the course of imprisonment or exclusion.
> 4. That an inquiry be conducted by the Minister of Labour into the activities of Messrs Cuthbert and Solomon as officers of the Waterfront Control Commission.

On Monday 12 June Labour Minister Paddy Webb met the officers and executive of the Auckland branch and gave a typical politician's performance. If I would plead guilty he would see that only a small fine was imposed. However, his assurances to the Westfield freezing workers were too recent for anyone but a fool to accept.

The cases came before Mr J.H. Luxford at the Magistrate's Court, Auckland, on 9 July. V.R. Meredith, Crown Prosecutor, led the charge in a case lasting two days. At the conclusion, without hesitation or delay, Mr Luxford dismissed all charges.

The three summonses were sworn by Smith of the Labour Department and, despite all his assurances, the instructions to the Crown Prosecutor had never been varied. He was to endeavour to get the maximum of three months on each charge. In an endeavour to conceal this political frame-up, Smith was never called. Not that this was to any avail, as it was clear from start to finish that the Labour government was 100 per cent responsible for the attempted frame-up.

Of particular interest was that Mr Luxford held that the actions of the commission and shipowners in fact constituted a lockout under the provisions of the Strike and Lockout Emergency Regulations. However, we waited in vain for the minister to prosecute either the commission or shipowners.

This case had seen the usual spate of anti-waterside workers propaganda in the press but one had to search diligently to find the verdict published. Nor did we see a *Herald* cartoon showing the minister and his mate with egg on their faces.

While the verdict was the subject of congratulations, not only from my own members but from a wide section of other unionists, it was a disappointment to the handful within our own ranks who put loyalty to the Labour Party ahead of their own union.

A Living Culture

While the press made us out to be no more than a pack of thugs and wastrels, the activities of our union at this time told a different story. Our union was not just interested in the industrial welfare of our members; we also attended to cultural and sporting interests. We staged a boxing carnival

Wellington and Auckland watersiders rugby league teams, 1950 (Jock Barnes)

at the town hall, where one of our members put away an American Golden Gloves winner with his first punch. We ran highly successful inter-port cricket and rugby competitions. We sponsored bands involving members and their families. Our junior band, with boys of between 11 and 13 years of age, was top class, winning the New Zealand C-grade championship in 1946 and a year later the B-grade championship of Australia and New Zealand, which was staged in Newcastle, NSW. The proceeds of the carnival went to the Red Cross. Our senior band was the national champion and we also maintained a pipe band. Members of all of these bands were later in the first national band that won the world championship in Holland after the war. The union's bands played for no charge at hospitals of all kinds, for St John's Ambulance, at RSA events, for schools and even at the naval base.

The union also took collections for many worthy causes. Since early in the century the Auckland branch maintained a Hospital Comforts Fund, which distributed gifts worth thousands of pounds to patients in public and mental hospitals. In just five years theamount totalled £4357.15/7. The union also made annual donations to the Makagai Leper Fund and St John's Ambulance and frequent donations to charitable and public organisations ranging from educational concerns to surf clubs. None of these achievements was worthy of consideration by press or politicians.

Auckland Watersiders' Junior Silver Band (Jock Barnes)

End-of-War Blow-ups

With the war drawing to a close, industrial unrest became the rule rather than the exception. Workers were making it known that they had had more than enough of ever-rising prices and profits while wages remained pegged.

A strike by dairy workers provoked the usual hysterical charges from Fraser, with his customary blackmail threats to immediately draft them into the army. This brought a quick reaction from the trade union movement so, in the best traditions of Hitler and Mussolini, he settled for directing troops to scab on their mates. Within days, there followed a major strike of railway workers. Workers everywhere were demanding a sample of the long-promised 'New Order'. Fraser was running out of armed forces personnel he could order to scab.

The railway dispute was settled by the Auckland Trades Council, which assured the government that if railway workers' demands were not fairly met, they would have the support of the whole trade union movement. I, with others, spoke at a mass meeting held in Carlaw Park and assured them of the full support of our union. We were united with them in a common fight against a government that had betrayed every principle of the labour movement.

Fraser kept his nose out of it this time and the workers received a fair settlement. Even those stooges in our own union who blindly supported every action of the Labour government could no longer defend its scab-herding activities, open hostility to the trade union movement and servile toadying to the forces of reaction.

Strikes became so prevalent that the government was forced to grant workers annual holidays and minimum wages. These they had resisted for years and were finally obtained not because of a change of heart among politicians, but because of widespread industrial action forcing them to concede.

After the failure of their summonses against me in the *City of Lille* case, we had for a while a reasonably quiet period in the latter half of 1944. With the minister, shipowners and commission still licking their wounds, their fascist friends from other circles took over the hate campaign. The *Herald* and *Star* carried articles by assorted military blimps and reactionaries accusing our union of everything from slow and poor-quality work to an alleged failure to contribute to a charity carnival organised by the RSA. Needless to say, our attempts to set the record straight were either not published or were cut to ribbons.

Commissioner Cuthbert, however, was getting impatient and decided to have another go at us. This involved a safety dispute on the USSCo

Karepo. On 28 February 1945 the commissioner sent the following letter to the Auckland branch:

> Following on the arbitrary action of Union members in ceasing work on several occasions recently to enforce settlement of disputes instead of resorting to the procedure laid down for the settlement of same, the Commission is compelled to take steps to enforce its authority in order to maintain existing conditions of employment for those Union members who are prepared to fulfil the obligations resting upon them under the Orders of the Commission.
>
> It has been decided therefore, that notwithstanding anything previously existing to the contrary that all such workers who ceased work on the *Karepo* shall not be permitted as from the day of the date hereon to share in the benefits derived from the contracting system, and it is hereby directed that failing a resumption of work their rights under such Order shall cease to exist and they will no longer be considered available for work on the Auckland Waterfront.

Even for Cuthbert, this action was incredible. Without any inquiry or any approach to the union for the facts of the case, he proposed to deny union members the right to work. A statement from Captain Anderson of the USSCo was enough for him.

He got a response at once. We called a meeting of the Auckland men and won solid support for the men concerned. I then wrote to Commissioner Cuthbert, telling him that, until his threatening letter was unconditionally withdrawn, all work in the port would cease and that, in accordance with Mr Luxford's decision, we would issue a summons against him for creating a lockout under the provisions of the Strike and Lockout Emergency Regulations.

Cuthbert wasted no time in withdrawing his letter and, for good measure, said the commission would do all in its power to hold an inquiry at an early date for the purpose of hearing the union's grievances against Captain Anderson and the USSCo

And even after this barefaced attempt to create another major dispute, Cuthbert remained in office. We looked in vain for any mention of this gaffe in the press, and the customary cartoon was absent from the *Herald*.

And so the war ended with the unholy alliance having suffered several setbacks but, urged on by the press and government, still determined to settle scores with the nefarious Auckland wharfies.

4 THE SHORT LIFE OF LABOUR'S NEW ORDER, 1946-47

More Battles with the Commission

The shipowners, Waterfront Control Commission and government often claimed that I was stubborn, a troublemaker and had led the men astray. They received a response from the men themselves in the biennial election for national president in January 1946. The rank and file gave their verdict on my leadership in no uncertain manner and soundly endorsed my policy of putting the union's interests above those of any political party, irrespective of label.

It was soon made clear that any spirit of peace and goodwill that the recent victory in the war and the Christmas break may have engendered in the hearts of shipowners or commission had disappeared early in the New Year. On 14 January the Blue Funnel Line freighter *Reavely* arrived for loading. A member who had been engaged to work a winch was ordered to work on the wharf. This was in direct conflict, not only with the Commission's Order, but also with Bureau rules. On refusing this illegal order, he was sacked. Cuthbert endorsed his sacking. Perhaps this was an opening shot to see if the festive season had softened us but, whatever the reason, it had to be resisted. The port was put on a go-slow and the matter taken up with the Minister of Labour. Neither shipowners nor commission had a snowball's chance in hell and they soon capitulated.

We were helped in the *Reavely* case by the new Minister of Labour, Jim O'Brien. Jim had never lost his West Coast roots and stood in marked contrast to the openly hostile Prime Minister Fraser, FOL president McLagan and Co. Jim was prepared to listen. His usual style was 'come and have a beer and tell me what it's all about'. It was a tragedy when, after only a short time as Minister of Labour, he fell seriously ill and was forced to retire, dying soon afterwards in September 1947. Had he lived longer, the whole course of events that unfolded after the war might have turned out quite differently. About all that Jim left was his old West Coast cottage. That is about the biggest tribute one could pay him. There are exceptions to every rule and such a one was Jim O'Brien. He entered Parliament as a

Arthur Bockett (Waterfront Control Commission) and Bert Bockett
(Department of Labour), 1975
(News Media: *Auckland Star* collection)

workers' representative and died that way.

Early in March we had a major dispute in Lyttelton. The port controller, Captain H. Brockett, was determined to make his mark. The ship in question was the *Korowai*, another USSCo vessel, and its cargo was lampblack (a pigment used for blacking car tyres), which was filthy, obnoxious and in a shocking state.

A penalty rate of 1/6 per hour was claimed on behalf of the men. This was refused by both shipowners and commission but the more serious aspect was a letter from the general manager of the Waterfront Commission, A.E. (Arthur) Bockett, who repeated Cuthbert's threat to permanently sack from the waterfront all men who refused to accept his decision. We decided to put an end to this abuse of powers once and for all. The dispute was taken over by the national union and I proceeded to Lyttelton. Jim Roberts attended for the commission. No longer having a Minister of Labour who supported all their actions, however, the commission was forced to back down. The men got their claim in full and Bockett not only had to withdraw his ultimatum but also apologise.

Of particular significance was the reporting by the Christchurch daily papers. It was fair and did not have the usual lying attacks and scurrilous cartoons.

We did not have to wait long for more from Cuthbert, however. Spurred into action by Captain Brockett's attempt to usurp his position as chief provocateur, he chose the *Herekino* as his weapon. A most unfortunate choice for him. This was a small coastal ship carrying cement. With a port full of shipping and an acute shortage of labour, Cuthbert decided to provoke another dispute by declaring this small coaster to be a priority ship. In 1944 we had entered into an agreement that certain ships could be declared priority ships. This was to ensure that munitions ships could be dispatched to combat zones with the utmost expedition in consultation with the union. Now, with the war long over, we felt that it was time that the commission was disbanded and all the wartime regulations lifted. Most of the shipping in port was loading for Britain, where food was badly needed. This shipping was not fully manned, yet here we had a decision, and an illegal one, that left the ships short of labour while preference was given to a small coaster.

Cuthbert was followed onto the scene by Captain Price, who spouted off about his powers under the wartime regulations and threatened all sorts of dire measures if we did not unload the *Herekino*. We told him that eight months after VJ day it was time for him and his commission to be sent off to pasture. Instead of using his powers, Price referred the matter on to the minister. Another mistake! With Jim O'Brien as minister we were on safe ground. Jim castigated the commission in no uncertain terms, directed that the *Herekino* engagement board be cancelled and that in future the government, not the commission, would be the body to declare any ship a priority one.

This was complete vindication of the union's stand, with the blame placed fairly and squarely where it belonged. The press, however, in their usual performance, launched a particularly vicious campaign. All references to the truth of the matter were completely ignored as the *Star* and *Herald* took advantage of another opportunity to malign and vilify watersiders. The *Star* was bad, the *Herald*, with its usual apology for a cartoon, worse. Here we had a watersider portrayed as a monster standing over a grovelling Fraser who allegedly had once again given in to the wreckers. If truth is the first casualty in war, then we were at war.

The Chamber of Commerce, too, joined in the hymn of hate. The heaviest thing most of them had lifted as war effort would have been a knife and fork, but then the war was over and so was all talk of a new order. As a union in the forefront of the fight for social justice, we were a menace. Case-hardened though we were to lying propaganda, the campaign of lies was almost incredible. More of the seeds of '51 were being scattered.

The Food for Britain Fraud

The fact that we had been completely vindicated and the commission exposed for what it was received not one line of press coverage. This was the norm, but the orchestrated campaign was not allowed to fade away. The next barrage came from a self-styled Food for Britain Committee, consisting of the usual worthy and concerned citizens.

This bunch of imposters proposed to organise volunteers to load ships when watersiders' hours of work had ceased. They would do it for no pay. The *Herald* kept the momentum going, seeing an opportunity to further attack watersiders.

The fact that a host of auxiliary services would also be required either had never occurred to them or was deliberately ignored. Arrangements would have to be made for workers to cover the freezing works, coolstores, railways, wool and other stores, as well as drivers, crane and winch drivers, seamen, dairy workers, harbour board employees and tally clerks. Nobody but a moron would advance such a proposition, but moronic though it was, it was more fuel for the great conspiracy and its propaganda machine.

A similar attack had recently been made on miners, but no invitations to take up a pick and go down a mine had been accepted. Golf clubs were easier on the hands and the 19th hole a more pleasant environment!

Five-eighths of nothing was the total knowledge of real problems possessed by this collection of spivs, yet columns of the press were readily available for such drivel. That food and other supplies were already being used for political purposes was common knowledge among seamen and watersiders. Questions could well have been asked as to why some ships ostensibly loading for Britain were being discharged elsewhere. But that could have resulted in the exposure of vested interests who benefited so handsomely from profiteering, of which these public-spirited citizens were typical.

Within a matter of a few weeks Prime Minister Fraser dropped a bomb that for a while silenced our critics. The Auckland branch was instructed to load 10 million pounds of butter for the US where food was plentiful and there was no rationing. The first consignment was to be carried by the *Mariposa*. Following the hysterical campaign conducted against us over Food for Britain, this one rocked the country. For once we had mass public support that was beyond the powers of the press to change. Not only watersiders but the vast majority of New Zealand people were angry. Complete silence was the response from the Food for Britain Committee.

Utmost secrecy surrounded this deal and even the opposition under Sid Holland was ignorant of it. For the only time in his career, Holland was compelled to support our stand in refusing to load the butter bound for the US. We received not only a flood of supporting letters but also cables of congratulations from overseas.

All conjecture about the real reasons and facts behind this scandalous deal were soon satisfied. Sir Carl Berendsen, New Zealand minister in Washington, let the cat out of the bag when he complained about huge quantities of food being exported from the US to Japan. With the guns of war hardly silenced, the US was already building up Japan as a bulwark against the Soviet Union. As an excuse for further vilification of waterside workers, the issue was dropped like a hot scone by most, but not so the *Star* and the *Herald*. A scandal that in many countries would have been sufficient to bring down a government was sidetracked and ignored. Those hackneyed and grossly abused phrases of 'law and order' and 'the government must govern' were dragged out and dusted off by the press. An abusive editorial in the *Star* and further calumnies in the *Herald* followed. The theme song from the scrap iron for Japan campaign was again top of their hit parade.

F.P. Walsh, vice-president, Federation of Labour, 1946–53 (News Media: *Auckland Star* collection)

Emergency Regulations Abolished

Two matters of considerable significance now occurred. First, Jim O'Brien, as Minister of Labour, announced the abolition of the Waterfront Control Commission and its draconian wartime emergency regulations, and its replacement by a new five-man committee, the Waterfront Industry Commission. The new commission consisted of two representatives from the union, two from shipowners and the usual 'independent' chairman. After a national union ballot I was elected with a big majority, with Jack Flood as my colleague.

The chairman, F.W. Ongley from the Compensation Court, was a judge with no experience of waterfront work and little knowledge of any industrial problems. On the shipowners' side we had G.L. Almond representing overseas interests and K.A. Belford of the USSCo. Almond was a typical product of his class, with the necessary old school tie and plum in the mouth. Belford was an Australian and a shifty character. It was a part-time and largely judicial body and, as with most of its kind, it meant a 3:2 vote for the boss class. We were not too optimistic.

The second major event was the publication by F.P. Walsh, president of the FOL, of a new report on the waterfront. This recommended the continuation of wartime policy against workers and an open go for the employers. The Walsh report was hailed by employers, chambers of commerce, press and reactionary forces everywhere and equally condemned by the whole trade union movement. As an instance, the Otago Trades Council, not noted for its militancy, condemned it lock, stock and barrel as disastrous to the labour movement. While workers' wages had been the subject of strict control during the war years, company profits had increased by 80 per cent.

Not that we expected anything better from Walsh. In Walsh and his confreres, Ken Baxter and Angus McLagan, we had three more penitent sinners in the mould of Fraser and Semple. Baxter was secretary of the Federation of Labour and worked hand in hand with Walsh. Formerly active and prominent members of the Communist Party, they were now dedicated disciples of Senator Joe McCarthy and anxious at all times to prove they had truly recanted.

Our Campaign for a Guaranteed Wage

Workers across New Zealand were looking for some reward for years of sacrifice during the war and industrial unrest was now rampant throughout the country. Our major claim at the time was for a guaranteed minimum weekly or monthly wage, or 'appearance money' as the press called it. The nature of the industry was such that work came in fits and starts. One moment our men would be working their guts out, the next they would be forcibly idled as work dried up. Because the shipowners couldn't guarantee when labour would be required for loading and unloading, they insisted that men be available on the dockside from 8am to 10am, even if there was no work for them. If not working they were not paid, and nor did they receive payment for travel expenses if they showed up but were not given work. Some of those who did not find work in these hours would then be called back for the afternoon shift at 1pm; others were simply sent back home. If those who were called back at 1pm lived a way out of town they simply stood around the wharves wasting another three hours of their day. This represented a massive abuse of employer authority and was a source of great discontent among the men. Our minimum demand was for each man to be guaranteed work each day, Monday to Saturday inclusive, to the value of not less than 14/- or, failing the provision of such work, payment of equivalent to that sum. Our preferred option was for each man to be paid the equivalent of a 40-hour week whether taken on or forcibly idled.

In the circumstances of significant labour unrest, the new commission handed down a couple of modest improvements to our conditions. For the first time we secured payment for statutory holidays and meal money for men ordered to work overtime. Even this was no great gain, however, seeing that they had been for years the right of almost all other workers. Our major claim, for a guaranteed wage, was deferred by the commission, with employers freely quoting the Walsh report and the benefits to all of continued stabilisation of wages.

These modest changes have to be set against the free-for-all going on at the top of society. While the government and Arbitration Court continually preached the benefits of stabilisation, in September 1946 the government granted substantial salary increases to the Governor-General, Sir Bernard Freyburg, and members of the judiciary. Sir Bernard, who was already in receipt of a very substantial army pension, was given another £2500 a year, and all judges (including Judge Ongley) an additional stipend of £250. This increase amounted to the total annual income of many workers and, in some cases, a good deal more. For good measure, our politicians had recently awarded themselves substantial pay increases, plus an expense allowance of £250. In accordance with the best traditions of the House, the usual farcical sham fighting that would have shamed professional wrestlers was conspicuous by its absence and the vote was unanimous.

We were not alone in our protests against these exorbitant pay rises, and requests from other unions demanding action poured into the Federation of Labour. With that body dominated by Walsh, however, it was foolish to expect any action from that quarter.

Once again we experienced the immutable laws of capitalism: largesse

Ken Baxter, secretary,
Federation of Labour, 1944–69
(News Media: *Auckland Star*
collection)

for those who only sponged off the system and nothing for the creators and builders of the country's needs and assets.

The forced resignation due to ill-health of Jim O'Brien, Minister of Labour, in November 1946 was a great loss to the labour movement and to New Zealand, and the appointment of Angus McLagan as his successor was a tragedy. McLagan was an ex-communist, ex-president of the FOL and ex-miners' leader, whose sour face had never been creased with a smile. His chief purpose in life seemed to be proving to his former enemies the sincerity and depth of his recantation, and an integral part of that formula was to dispute the legitimate claims of workers. Trouble was inevitable.

Our claim for a guaranteed wage, adjourned in October, was heard early the next month. As usual, Belford of the USSCo and his frosty-faced mate, G.L. Almond, were united in their opposition to any legitimate claims. If it were not for saying 'no', they could have been dumb. It was therefore the chairman's responsibility to bring down a decision. Judge Ongley waited until after the parliamentary elections held later that month, in which the Fraser government was returned with a very slender majority. Six hundred votes the other way in the Auckland area would have seen it defeated. This was indicative of the fact that workers had had a gutful of one-way stabilisation.

Why Ongley had waited was soon obvious as he handed down a monthly guarantee of £25. In effect, it was a nil decision. Due to the excessive overtime we had to work on some days, that amount would be exceeded by all over the course of a month, but there was still no guarantee that men would be paid for appearing for work at the daily labour engagement between 8am and 10am. And if a man should miss appearing on just one morning, even if sick, he would be paid nothing for the day and would lose any guarantee of a monthly minimum wage—the shipowners had our men both ways!

Bad as all of this was, it paled into insignificance when compared with the rest of Judge Ongley's decision concerning manning arrangements. For 30 years we had had clauses in our award governing the number of men in gangs and the conditions under which they could be transferred to other work. These were vital to our existence as a union. These clauses had never been mentioned at any meeting of the commission, had never been on any of its agendas, and in no way were they a matter for the chairman's adjudication. Yet this judge, not satisfied with a nil order on our guaranteed wage claim, amended these clauses so that they would operate at the whim of the employers. He was handing us over, gagged and bound hand and foot, to that gang of international pirates known as shipowners. A more brazen misuse of power would be hard to imagine.

One would have thought that in any country purporting to have a free press, this completely illegal and provocative action by a judge would have been headline news. We had the editorials and headlines, but without the slightest mention of Ongley's repudiation of every legal concept he was supposed, as a judge, to uphold. As far as the press were concerned, the war had finished on the Western Front and shifted to the waterfront. Unable to present a case for Ongley's illegal and indefensible decision, they completely ignored it, while day after day saw a continuation of their diatribes against us.

Obviously we were in for a big fight and a meeting of the national executive was called early in December 1946. Opinion was unanimous. There was no way Ongley's gift to shipowners would be accepted and an overtime ban and 40-hour week would be observed at all ports until a satisfactory agreement was obtained.

Many requests were received from other unions anxious to hear the truth of the case. Like us, they had had a gutful of waiting for the much-vaunted new order. Meetings were held at most ports and were addressed by rank and file members, as well as officials. From the Auckland branch we sent out members to talk to workers and officials from the Auckland Trades Council and Auckland branches of the Freezing Workers' Union, the Transport Workers' Federation, the New Zealand Workers' Union, the New Zealand Engineers' Union, the Glassworkers' Union, the Gas Workers' Union, the General Labourers' Union, the Brick, Tile and Pottery Workers' Union, the Plasterers' Union, as well as the Otahuhu branch of the Railway Workers', and at meetings of workers at R. & W. Hellaby, Korma Mills, and at the Karapiro Hydro Works.

Everywhere except at R. & W. Hellaby, resolutions were passed endorsing our claims. Of particular significance was that passed by the Auckland Trades Council, representing the largest group of workers in New Zealand.

We called a meeting of our national council for 14 January 1947 and 34 delegates from all but the very small ports attended. Bill Richards and Percy Hanson, president and secretary of the New Zealand Transport Workers' Federation, representing railway workers, tramworkers, drivers and harbour board employees, were also there.

This was not a fight with our traditional opponents, the shipowners, but with the Labour government, and there were one or two on our council who were very suspect on such an issue. When moving the adoption of the national executive's report, vice-president and respected trade union fighter for many years Alec Drennan minced no words. He made it crystal clear that any delegate who placed the Labour government above the interests of his union should declare himself and report back to his rank and file in an endeavour to get approval. There were no takers. The report was adopted unanimously.

In the face of the storm of protest and our no confidence vote in him, Judge Ongley resigned as chairman of the commission. McLagan then formed a new one-man commission as a temporary step, appointing its former general manager, Arthur Bockett, as its chairman. We then had three meetings with Fraser and his Cabinet, with F.P. Walsh lurking in the background. Despite a sustained attempt to undermine our case by Fraser, McLagan and Walsh, our unity in the face of attack, the injustice of Ongley's decision and the solid support from other major unions forced the government to agree that there would be no worsening of our conditions and that we would get a daily guaranteed wage. Arthur Bockett was empowered to act as commissioner for the case.

FOL Special Conference

Meanwhile, a special conference of the FOL had been called for the following week (late in January 1947), the purpose of which was to put our head in the noose, with Fraser, McLagan and Nash on the platform as willing executioners. Guarantees we had just received from them were ignored, as was Ongley's infamous decision. Walsh and his friends diverted the whole issue from a debate on workers' rights to a motion of confidence in the government. They sought to bind the union movement to the fortunes of Fraser, with any opposition marked down as the work of communist and outside agents. They would have made Senator Joe McCarthy green with envy. Fraser's attacks on the watersiders and other militant unionists were exceeded only by those of Walsh, McLagan and Baxter.

However, Walsh and Co had misread the mood of the country's workers and unions, who by now had had quite enough of Labour's one-way stabilisation programme. Fraser attempted to bluff his way through, even threatening to resign, but many delegates agreed that that was the best thing he could do in the circumstances. The longer the conference went on, the greater was our support, as many delegates were hearing the truth for the first time, as against lying propaganda. Delegates representing labourers, carpenters, tramway workers, dairy workers, railwaymen and others formed an informal bloc with the wharfies at this conference and together we were able to push Walsh and Co back.

The platform moved a resolution that, in future, all disputes should be handed over to the FOL executive before any direct action was taken. Opposition to this was so strong that it was dropped. A resolution to endorse continued stabilisation was deferred for consideration by the FOL national council, which was due to meet in the following month. The executive had been well and truly trounced.

After this debacle we were left alone to settle our claims with Bockett, who had no option but to hand down a decision involving a daily guarantee of two hours' attendance pay and weekly £5 guarantee, to be payable at all ports, as well as an assurance of improved amenities and a promise that wages would be increased in the near future. Bert Roth in his book *Trade Unions in New Zealand* argues that this was a significant victory for the watersiders in the face of opposition from the shipowners, the commission, the government and the FOL. I'd prefer to say we finally obtained common justice.

In May our national executive had a meeting with McLagan to discuss claims for a long-overdue wage increase and the long-promised measure of worker control in the industry. A fundamental Labour Party policy in place since its formation was the socialisation of the means of production, distribution and exchange. After all, it was an avowed socialist party. However, with its return as the government in 1935, we saw a continuous reduction in socialist rhetoric, coupled with a complete failure to implement any socialist policies. With Fraser at the helm, backed up by hatchetmen such as Walsh and McLagan, all pretence at being a workers' government was abandoned. Eventually the party did the decent thing and struck the policy from its platform. This abandonment of even the rhetoric of socialism meant that even Savage's promises to eliminate middlemen on the waterfronts of New Zealand and to hand control of stevedoring over to newly formed co-operative union-run companies were abandoned by his successors. Fraser and McLagan dropped all camouflage and made it clear that they would never permit worker control of any industry.

In July 1947 we saw McLagan give his maiden speech in Parliament. Sheltered by the privilege and protection of his coward's castle, he delivered an outrageous and slanderous attack on the Watersiders' Union in general and myself in particular. We were witnessing an extreme case of paranoia. According to McLagan's twisted interpretation of industrial reality it was no longer reds under the bed, but wharfies.

McLagan also had his sights firmly set on the Carpenters' Union, whose waterside section was run by the exceedingly able Bill McAra, a member of the Communist Party. McLagan at first refused to allow a pay rise for carpenters employed in laying dunnage in ships' holds for fear that this would enhance the reputation of both McAra and myself. A settlement

Johnny Mitchell at the opening of the new canteen for Auckland waterside workers (Jock Barnes)

was only obtained after direct action by workers on the Auckland and Wellington waterfronts. This, of course, was another field-day for the press which published the usual vilification of watersiders but made no mention of McLagan.

Food for Britain, Again

August 1947 saw the return of Fraser from a jaunt to Britain. With the war over for more than two years, the chorus was still 'Food for Britain'. The choir consisted of the usual patriotic profiteers, parasites and union bashers generally. This humbug was still being mouthed, although it was no longer a secret that produce from New Zealand was being sold on the open market and to the highest bidder. For instance, butter in the US fetched 34 cents a pound more than in Britain. We were still suffering from wartime rationing, but of course that was good business. With a world shortage, the less consumed in New Zealand, the more there was available for export to the best markets.

In October 1947 Fraser and Walsh convened a Food for Britain conference at Parliament to discuss the economic situation. Some 250 attended, of whom only 20 represented the people most affected—the unions. The other 230 were hand-picked and beyond doubt would have represented the greatest collection of spivs and bludgers ever assembled in a room in New Zealand. Fraser spoke of his latest junket and put on an act worthy of an Oscar. The plight of the British people had never been so bad. No mention was made of the new order for New Zealand workers. He was almost sobbing, and his command performance was heartily applauded by 230 of the 250 present.

This gave the opening for Walsh, seconded by Baxter and supported by McLagan, to propose a National Industries Emergency Council with authoritarian powers that were almost unbelievable: powers to abolish awards and place the union movement under the jackboot. With Food for Britain the excuse, one did not need to be Sherlock Holmes to see that our union was again the target.

I could stomach no more. While in Britain, Fraser had been wined and dined in style by a variety of bigwigs. Some London dockers had sent me a menu from one of his banquets. It took about two minutes to read and was full of luxury items that most British workers had never even seen. I told those assembled that the war was long over and our attention should be on the interests of New Zealanders. The purpose of an emergency council could only be to hamstring the union movement, the watersiders in particular, all for extra profits for the 230 drones and the interests that they represented. These people did not give a damn for the British worker and never would. I was followed by two stalwarts of the Freezing Workers'

Sid Holland, Walter Nash and Peter Fraser (speaking), at the Food for Britain conference, 1947 (*NZ Herald*)

Union, Con Doyle and Sid Giles, who were equally blunt, and then by Fred Craig of the Timber Workers' Union. Fred was anything but a militant, but even he had had enough. That was the end. Uproar ensued and the conference, together with the plan for an emergency council, was over. In their efforts to smash our union, Fraser and Co would come at anything. The abject failure of this latest conspiracy rendered some other form of waterfront control essential.

McLagan finally found it expedient to appoint a new Waterfront Industry Commission to replace Arthur Bockett, who had been sole commissioner for nine months. Whereas it had been a 3:2 vote against us in the old commission, McLagan now proposed to make it 4:2—two from the government, two from shipowners and two from the union. Again he failed when we protested, and the former arrangement prevailed. His selection of Judge D.J. Dalglish as chairman was typical of McLagan's approach. Dalglish was from the Crown Law Office and had absolutely no knowledge of waterfront workings and would not have known a merchant ship from a submarine. However, he suited McLagan's purpose in being certain to follow the minister's instructions.

On the basis of Fraser's instruction that union representatives were 'not to be looked upon as delegates from the union', Toby Hill and I, who had been our union's representatives on the previous commission, decided not to stand. After a national ballot Jack Flood of Lyttelton and Reg O'Donnell of Wellington were elected in our place. Meanwhile, we were holding elections in our own ranks for the positions of national president and national secretary. I was elected unopposed but Toby Hill was opposed by Jim Napier of Wellington. At the subsequent national ballot, Toby was re-elected with a large majority. Thus did our 7000 members give their answer to Fraser, McLagan, Walsh and Co. For good measure, the 1947 conference re-elected Alec Drennan as national vice-president. Alec was a member of the Communist Party but this was not an issue for our members, who judged him on his ability as a trade union leader, not on his political affiliation. No longer could the press claim that we did not represent the views of our members.

Cook Islands Campaign

For some time we had been receiving disquieting reports about labour conditions in the Cook Islands—New Zealand territory. Our union was not alone in our concern and at the FOL conference in June 1946 deep concern was expressed by many delegates. Representations to Fraser in his capacity as Minister in Charge of Island Territories met with the usual whitewash. Auckland Trades Council adopted a firmer attitude and demanded a full and open public inquiry into the alarming conditions that were being revealed.

Matters came to a head when, early in December 1947, 14 Cook Island watersiders were arrested and chained to the courthouse at Manihiki Island following their refusal to accept a tribunal award of 6/- per day. On its arrival at Rarotonga, the government motor vessel *Maui Pomare* was not worked for 10 days. It did not call at Manihiki, and the action was taken by Cook Island wharfies in support of their fellow workers. When work resumed, it was by 'irregular' labour, or scabs, as we preferred to call them. When the *Maui Pomare* arrived at Aitutaki it was declared black and not worked. Waterside workers there too failed to differentiate between 'irregular' labour and scabs! The ship returned to Auckland with its cargo still in its holds.

The *Dominion* of 18 December carried the following headline: 'Islanders Were Not Chained, Mr Fraser tells Mr Barnes' and in the accompanying article: 'One of the arrested persons was handcuffed to a post, one member was tied to a post with twine and twelve were squatted in the courthouse veranda in the care of the police helper.' A variation, it must be conceded, of the 'shot while trying to escape' theme! However, Fraser's story was blown apart by A. Osborne, his undersecretary, who admitted that the 14 had indeed been chained. This was at a time when Fraser and Nash were preaching to the rest of the world on the rights of minorities. The dispute was resolved after Fraser was forced to increase their wages from 8/- to 9/- per day, and there was no more chaining of waterside workers in the Cook Islands.

So ended 1947, a year with never a dull or idle moment. A year in which eternal vigilance had been essential in the preservation of working and human rights. Contrary to the scurrilous and lying fulminations against us by the press, politicians and big business alike, the past year had shown that, in every dispute, the Waterside Workers' Union had been justified. To destroy our union, rightly regarded as the spearhead of the industrial movement, had become an obsession with the forces of reaction, and we did not have long to wait before the next offensive launched by the unholy twins: the Waterfront Industry Commission and the Union Steam Ship Company.

5 THE MOUNTPARK INCIDENT, 1948

SS *Mountpark*, (News Media: *Auckland Star* collection)

This latest attack by the commission and the Union Steam Ship Company involved two ships, the *Cape York* and the *Mountpark*, and the issue at stake was both fundamental and elementary. Were we human beings with human rights or were we, as cattle, completely at the disposal of the master class? This was to become one of the biggest and most significant disputes ever to surface on the waterfronts of New Zealand. The facts are incredible.

The safety of our members was one of our primary concerns and a medical record recently furnished by a Macquarie Street specialist on 150 Sydney waterside workers revealed some of the problems that the men faced. There were many cases of men who had suffered spinal injuries, multiple fractures and finger amputations through their work. Respiratory diseases were abundant and the high prevalence of abnormal thickening and hardening of the arteries was clear indication of premature old age. Many of the men had suffered from rheumatoid arthritis and severe duodenal ulcers.

The Mountpark Incident

Some had had their gall bladders removed. Many large and inoperable hernias—always prevalent in occupations involving heavy lifting—had been found. A similar survey in any major New Zealand port would have furnished the same results. Despite taking all possible precautions, accidents and fatalities in such a high-risk occupation would always happen, but men had the right to see they were given the maximum protection.

In its report to Parliament the commission had acknowledged that, on questions of safety, men had the right to strike. In practice, however, it was quite a different story, as the *Cape York* and *Mountpark* episodes illustrate well.

The *Cape York* was discharging bagged phosphate from Tunisia. An obnoxious cargo and dangerous to the men's health at any time, this cargo was the worst I had ever seen. Bags were rotten and it was not much better than a salvage job. It was classed as basic slag, for which an agreement existed including, among other things, the provision of milk and respirators for the men. A penalty payment of 3/- per hour had been directed by Bob Jones, who was assistant port controller to Cuthbert in Auckland. However, Cuthbert rejected this, reduced the payment to 2/6 and refused milk. He also refused to give a couple of the men respirators to replace their existing ones, which were worn out after 12 months' use.

On my instructions the *Cape York* gang knocked off until respirators were supplied. Before the port committee had even met, Cuthbert announced his decision, which inevitably went against the union. However, this action only backfired against him. The USSCo was dismayed by his haste in making the decision, and for once refused to back him. The company made a joint agreement with our union that the men would be provided with new respirators after 12 months. They also agreed that milk should be supplied. To complete discharge, the *Cape York* went to Whangarei, where a penalty payment of 3/- per hour was again paid willingly by the employers, despite a commission instruction to pay only 2/6. This demonstrates that Cuthbert's aim was to disrupt work at all times, the better to have us vilified by the press. In the case of Auckland, the *Herald* gladly obliged, seizing on our work stoppage as the opening of its 1948 union-bashing campaign. As usual, there was complete distortion of the facts and Cuthbert's actions were ignored. It was clear by now that the only explanation for Cuthbert remaining in office was that he was faithfully carrying out McLagan's instructions.

The *Mountpark* incident, however, topped the *Cape York* for sheer audacity on the part of the commission. On each of three previous visits of the USSCo's *Mountpark*, complaints had been made about the condition of its hatches but these had been ignored. The passage of time and further usage had caused still more deterioration in their condition by the time of the fourth visit in February 1948. Work on the ship began on 9 February and protests were immediately entered about the state of its hatches. They were again ignored. Men continued to work under protest until 13 February when, after several hatches had fallen below, any one of which could have caused a fatality, James Gatt, gear inspector for the Marine Department, was called in. Gatt ruled that the hatches were not safe to handle and did not comply with minimum regulations.

This report was never rescinded.

The union had long been concerned about unsafe hatches and in the previous two years several serious accidents had occurred at the port of Wellington—all attributable to faulty hatches. These included:

1. William George Winter: serious spinal and other injuries.
2. Leslie Archibald: killed.
3. W.F. Easton: serious head and other injuries, permanently incapacitated.
4. Stanley Bennett: killed.
5. Walter Pym: serious injuries sustained through hatches similar to those of the *Mountpark*.

On 19 February two gangs refused to work on the *Mountpark* unless hooks were supplied for the purposes of lifting the hatches by mechanical means. This was met with the sacking of all men concerned. There followed an on-again, off-again campaign on the issue. We claimed that the *Mountpark*'s hatches were badly warped and the hand-grips were unsafe: they were liable to fall in on the men working below. All it would have taken was for the company to provide hooks for each of the hatches and the dispute would have been resolved. But the company was pig-headed and refused even to allow the union solicitor, Bob Fawcett, onto the ship to take photographs of the offending hatches. At a meeting involving Judge Dalglish, Captain Anderson from the USSCo and our union representative on the commission, Jack Flood, the union demanded that gangs should be reinstated without loss of pay, that hooks should be supplied for all hatches, that action should be taken against three ship captains for flagrant violation of the regulations and that hatches not complying with regulations should be replaced. Only the fourth of these demands was agreed to. The commission also added fuel to the fire by declaring the *Mountpark* a preference ship (which meant that it had to be worked on before any other ship), which was equivalent to locking out the men across the port of Auckland, given our decision to ban work on this vessel.

On 2–3 March Toby Hill and I met the Waterfront Industry Commission in Wellington. Judge Dalglish, the chairman, was not present, and his place as chair of the committee was taken by J.O. Johnson, port controller at Wellington. Also present were G.L. Almond and Captain J.A. Anderson for the shipowners and Jack Flood and Reg O'Donnell for the union. I recounted the history of problems on the *Mountpark*, including our previous complaints that had not been attended to. This was a dispute that should have been settled on the first day and the question arose as to why that was not done. The answer lay in the fact that *before* Dalglish had declared the *Mountpark* to be a preference ship, he had sought permission from his minister, Angus McLagan. This was readily granted. So much for an independent chairman!

On the morning of Tuesday 4 March, at a special stopwork meeting, the Auckland branch unanimously decided to perform no work on any USSCo ship in Auckland after noon that day unless permission was granted to the union solicitor to visit the job and get the necessary evidence. Later in the day we were advised by the commission that it had reconsidered its attitude and that Bob Fawcett could now visit the *Mountpark*.

On the same day we were advised by Mr Fawcett that Captain Atkins, acting marine superintendent of the Marine Department in Auckland, had officially told him, as late as the morning of 28 February, that Mr McLeod of the Marine Department had looked at the hatches of the *Mountpark* and that they were unsafe. Further photos taken by Fawcett confirmed that fact beyond all doubt a week later.

That these further facts did not settle the dispute then and there is incredible but true.

The Auckland branch unanimously passed a vote of no confidence in the Waterfront Industry Commission, as did the Wellington branch at a stopwork meeting which I addressed. Ongley had been bad enough but he was looking like a union advocate when compared with Dalglish! Meanwhile, Auckland watersiders continued to be locked out and more ships became idle.

A meeting of our national executive was held in Wellington on 11 March. This meeting unanimously endorsed the stand of the Auckland branch and made every possible attempt to get a settlement. An offer was made to isolate the *Mountpark* until the matter was legally determined and, in the meantime, to work all other ships in the port of Auckland. This was rejected. The *real* chairman of the commission, Angus McLagan, had only one intention—to starve the wharfies into submission.

Our national executive then instructed Bob Fawcett to immediately institute legal proceedings against the Waterfront Commission and/or the Union Steam Ship Company, and a meeting of our national council was called for March 22. Our third-largest branch, Lyttelton, also unanimously passed a resolution of full support at a special stopwork meeting.

On 16 March Mr Fawcett had a meeting with Judge Dalglish and proposed that the matter be heard in the Auckland Magistrate's Court the following Monday. Judge Dalglish refused, saying: (1) that his legal advisers would not be ready; and (2) that he would not accept a magistrate's decision. This reply from an individual with the status of a Supreme Court judge! This was the individual who had caused the dispute, prolonged it, and still refused a settlement. That in practice he was only a dummy for his ventriloquist master did not alter that fact.

Two days later Judge Dalglish again somersaulted and agreed to our proposal. Maybe his legal advisers had had time to advise him of his stupidity.

It was agreed that:

1. Work will be resumed on all vessels including the *Mountpark*.
2. Work will be resumed on the *Mountpark* in a manner that will not expose the men to any of the danger alleged by the union.
3. Penalties against watersiders will be cancelled.
4. All ships in port will be manned as labour is available.

This agreement had been made by Bob Fawcett and Judge Dalglish and was accepted by the membership of the Auckland branch at a stopwork meeting.

As soon as the formula for settlement had been accepted, both the Waterfront Commission and the Labour Bureau were advised that men would be available for a 1pm start.

On reporting to the Bureau for the purpose of lifting their discs and proceeding to their allotted work, watersiders found that the only job available was again the *Mountpark*. Despite the agreement, Dalglish and Co had again made it a preference ship. Long accustomed though we were to double-dealing, this act was almost unbelievable.

It needs no imagination to know what would have happened if engagement boards for all ships had been deployed and we had refused to supply labour. It would have been a Roman holiday for press, politicians and big business. But McLagan and Fraser were dumb, both *Herald* and *Star* had no headlines as to why the port was still not working and, in small type, explained it as a 'misunderstanding' on the part of the commission.

That the intention was to provoke a strike is clear. If it were not for the fact that the strength of our union was its informed and disciplined rank and file, this contemptible act would have succeeded. The following morning, engagement boards for all ships were deployed and normal work was resumed. *Mountpark* hatches were lifted by hooks.

Anybody would have believed that, apart from legal argument, the dispute was over. But no, this incredible plot continued. A few days later we had another amazing somersault from Judge Dalglish. The commissioner had continually stated that he would facilitate a court hearing in every

Walter Nash, Deputy Prime Minister, 1940–49; Leader of the Opposition, 1950–57 (News Media: *Auckland Star* collection)

possible way and to this end Bob Fawcett arranged a special fixture before Mr J.H. Luxford. Judge Dalglish then said that he was not prepared to accept a magistrate's decision and wanted the case heard by a judge. On his assurance that he would facilitate this, the union agreed. Now he came up with another classic—he had had *another* change of heart and now did not believe that a Supreme Court judge had any jurisdiction in the matter. This, while Fraser and McLagan were insisting that there is never any justification for workers to take strike action in view of the ample legal remedies readily available!

In April 1948 at the annual conference of the FOL McLagan had the hypocrisy to dwell on this very argument. Needless to say, he got the works from our union delegates. I challenged him to come down to the wharves and argue this before the rank and file. There was no reply. Nash gave his usual heart-rending exhibition. Three years after the war he could still talk of little else but food for Britain. It did not go over well, being by now generally recognised for the racket it was. Fraser, McLagan and Nash could have gained little satisfaction from this conference. People had had enough of stabilisation of wages while profits soared.

Fraser clearly intimated at our conference that peacetime conscription was on the cards. He was firmly in the camp of his right-wing friends in Britain and the US. The Soviet Union, our recent ally in the fight against fascism, was now our bitter enemy. An army of conscripts would serve a double purpose. When not fighting Russians, it would scab on watersiders. Everyone knew they were Soviet agents. And he had used conscripts as scabs before.

Reporting on the FOL conference in the June issue of the *Transport Worker*, I wrote:

> Throughout the curse of the last war I constantly preached the doctrine that the only New Order workers anywhere could achieve would be solely by their own efforts. Today a survey shows us that this philosophy was 100 per cent correct. Reaction everywhere is in the saddle and workers are compelled to struggle not for any visualised New Order but for the maintenance of everyday working conditions with their standard of living continually falling. Such had been the aftermath of every war this system of society had known and, coupled with the offensive against workers, the seeds of the next war are being sown.

Mountpark, Round Two

Meanwhile, back on the waterfront, peace prevailed as hatches were removed by slings and all work in the port proceeded without a hitch. But not for long. The occasion was the return of the *Mountpark*. Legal action was still in limbo. In accordance with the agreement, men began to remove the hatches with slings. However, they were ordered to remove them by hand and, on refusing, were sacked.

Incredible but true. We were back to square one and Dalglish had done it again. What price the word of a judge?

On 26 May Toby and I had another meeting with Fraser, McLagan, the commission and employers. The government offered to appoint a tribunal presided over by a judge of the Supreme Court. We agreed, conditional on the agreement entered into by Bob Fawcett and Dalglish being observed. The USSCo refused. Even the *Star* and the *Herald* were starting to ask questions.

After a month, with men being called every day for the *Mountpark* and then being penalised, all pretence at desiring a legal settlement was dropped and on 24 June the *Mountpark* was again made a preference ship. Having failed to starve us into submission at the first try, McLagan was giving it another go.

Reg O'Donnell and Jack Flood, our representatives on the commission, had had more than enough. They resigned. Reg O'Donnell sent the following letter to McLagan:

> Dear Sir,
>
> In accordance with the Waterfront Industry Commission Regulations I am tendering, in writing, my resignation from the commission.
>
> When the Commission was established, it was clearly understood by all parties that the Commission would be the arbitrator and arbiter on all questions affecting the waterfront industry. On the grounds of logic and equity alone, only upon this basis of authority, could the Commission possibly perform its duties.
>
> However, since the *Mountpark* decision of the commission on March 17, which evidently met with your displeasure, I have been forced to conclude that the overriding authority on waterfront affairs is yourself, and that the Commission possesses administrative authority which is more apparent than real. With this conviction in mind it is impossible for me to remain as a member of a Commission divested of its fundamental powers.
>
> My feelings were confirmed last night, June 24, when Judge Dalglish advised the Commission that he had been in communication with the Government and that the Government had requested that the *Mountpark* be declared a preference ship in the Port of Auckland.
>
> As you must be aware, declaring the *Mountpark* a preference ship will, within a period of ten days, completely immobilise the Port of Auckland. This is a grave responsibility, and I am not prepared to share it, especially when the act is in the name of the Commission.
>
> In my capacity as a union nominee I protested against the acceptance by the chairman of this direction from the Government. It is proof that constitutional authority in this field of industrial administration had been subjected to political influence.
>
> I assert that the action which must lock out the Port of Auckland is not the decision of the Waterfront Industry Commission. It is the decision of the Government. If the decision is the responsibility of the Government, I consider that the Government should have honestly conveyed the decision to the Union, the employers and the public, so that all could see where the responsibility for this most serious affair truly rests.
>
> Yours faithfully
> R. O'Donnell

McLagan and Dalglish both denied the accusation.

With no union representative on the commission there was no quorum and it became inoperative, but this was no problem to McLagan, who by now had a pathological obsession to smash our union. Amending regulations were approved by the Executive Council, which permitted a quorum of three, including Dalglish himself. The two shipowners' representatives could now pass any resolution they thought fit and against which there was no appeal. This affected not only Auckland but also every other port in New Zealand.

Government by regulation, in which all pretence of justice and legal rights were abandoned, had begun. Sid Holland in 1951 was not the innovator in this respect. He only used the precedent established by the Fraser Labour government.

The first act of the junta was to suspend payment of the guaranteed daily and weekly wage in the port of Auckland. Starving workers into submission by the preference-ship method was taking too long. This was answered by every other member of the New Zealand Waterside Workers' Union paying a weekly levy for the relief of their Auckland comrades. They were 100 per cent behind their fellow workers and were equally determined that our hard-won rights were not going to be destroyed by famine tactics. The overture to '51 was being played under the batons of Angus McLagan and Peter Fraser.

The arrival of the *Broompark* saw still more autocratic and provocative action by the commission and the USSCo. Larger than the *Mountpark*, it had similar hatches, which were lifted safely and completely by slings. In doing this, the men were acting strictly within their rights, following a pattern that had been used many times previously. This suited neither the commission nor the USSCo. Showing complete disregard for any concern other than unquestioned obedience, the commission ordered the men to do this by hand. On refusing, they were sacked.

In the best tradition of dictators everywhere, Fraser and McLagan gave broadcasts on national radio and excelled themselves in their vilification and downright lies in the case of the *Broompark* and *Mountpark*. We offered to buy time to reply, but to no avail. Some more of the scenario for Holland in '51 was being written.

Our union decided that we should instead hire the Auckland Town Hall so that I could present our case to the public. Mr J. Allum, Mayor of Auckland, agreed to chair the meeting and also made representations to Fraser that it should be broadcast. The Prime Minister refused, but on 4 July the meeting went ahead regardless. The town hall was packed out and several hundred people braved rain to listen to proceedings on a loud speaker in Grey's Avenue. It was not plain sailing at the start. My argument that the waterside workers had been double-crossed by the Waterfront Industry Commission and the Minister of Labour was greeted with a mixed reception of cheers and boos. However, after a few minutes there were practically no interjections. The meeting then unanimously passed this resolution:

> This meeting of Auckland citizens is of the opinion that the watersiders have justifiable grievances in connection with the *Mountpark* dispute, and, in the

best interest of all concerned, calls upon the Government to hold a public inquiry into this dispute and the workings of the Waterfront Industry Commission. Pending such an inquiry, and in order that the work of the port may proceed, we ask the Government to put into immediate effect the agreement of March 18, relative to the *Mountpark*'s hatches.

At the conclusion of the meeting, together with the Auckland branch executive, I had further discussions with the mayor and, as another compromise, proposed the following:

1. That the facts of the dispute be determined by some well known and respected Auckland citizen, to be accepted by all parties concerned.
2. That, in the meantime, the agreement made on March 18 between the union and the Waterfront Commission should be honoured.
3. If no agreement on the independent mediator is reached, the union will accept a person nominated by the senior magistrate of Auckland, Mr J.H. Luxford.

True to form, our offer was rejected and Fraser, in the House of Representatives, made an attack on the Mayor of Auckland for 'patronising meetings of the communist-led watersiders'. However, Fraser made a major admission in the same speech when he confirmed that McLagan himself had made the *Mountpark* a preference ship.

Our national council met with delegates from the Transport Workers' Federation on 7 July. Any illusion that Toby Hill and I did not truly represent the entire national union were soon dispelled, as full and unconditional support for our stand on the *Mountpark* was forthcoming. A meeting with Cabinet was arranged for 9 July. After the lies they had been told by McLagan and Fraser and after hearing the union version, some Cabinet members were not very happy. The result was that pressure was brought to bear on Baxter and Fraser by their Cabinet colleagues. After months of sabotaging any attempt at a settlement, they now agreed to appoint a tribunal consisting of two from our union and two from the shipowners, to be presided over by a Supreme Court judge.

But McLagan had to have another go. He insisted on drafting the terms of reference. If we had agreed to this we would have been sunk before we fired a shot. The arrogance of this man was unbounded. It was not until 15 July that we reached an agreement with the commission and shipowners in which the minister was told to keep his nose out of the tribunal's affairs.

In the meantime, both Auckland dailies conducted an all-out campaign against us for not accepting McLagan's terms of reference. In its edition of 9 July the *Herald* ran a lengthy article headed: 'These Men Betray Their City'. It would have to rate as one of the most malicious ever printed, with its sole design being to incite the general public against watersiders. Our town hall meeting proved its value. Thousands of Auckland citizens had

> **The New Zealand Herald**
> AUCKLAND, FRIDAY, JULY 9, 1948
>
> **THESE MEN BETRAY THEIR CITY**
>
> THE waterfront troubles which to-day are Auckland's shame are slowly shaping themselves as a threat to Auckland's civic eminence. This city is the greatest in New Zealand simply because it is a great port—the doorway to a rich and fertile area containing more than a third of the Dominion's total population. Destroy or even reduce its sea-borne trade and the five countries' defence problems at once conjures up a picture of their forces standing at bay with backs to the Atlantic. The mind turns inevitably to the possibilities of aid from North America. Canada's participation in the talks as a North American Power conforms with what one of her statesmen, Mr St. Laurent, has said about the eventual constitution of a world-wide system of regional defence arrangements, as possibly the long-sought design for collective security.

unanimously endorsed the justice of our case. They had spread the word. Already very suspect to many, the only casualty was the credibility of the *Herald*.

On 14 July the *Herald* printed another lengthy leading article, headed: 'Mr Barnes Trails his Coat'. It was just as vicious and misleading, with its complete disregard for truth, as the article of 9 July. But the time was not far distant when, together with the commission, McLagan and the shipowners, the *Herald* was to get the public exposure so long overdue and so richly deserved.

On 15 July the tribunal personnel were announced. Presided over by the Chief Justice, Sir Humphrey O'Leary, our union representatives were Toby Hill and Alec Drennan, with Captains Anderson and Belford of the USSCo representing the New Zealand Waterside Employers' Association.

The *Mountpark* was not to be worked until the decision of the tribunal was announced.

The hearing began at the Auckland Supreme Court on 26 July and lasted 12 days.

I appeared for the New Zealand Waterside Workers' Union, C.A. Hamer for the New Zealand Waterside Employers' Association and G.G. Watson and T.P. Cleary for the Waterfront Industry Commission. Messrs Watson and Cleary were barristers and solicitors from Wellington. Mr Watson had been the Law Society nominee for Chief Justice and, not very long after the *Mountpark* case, Cleary was made a judge of the Supreme Court.

The stage was set for a hearing where there was no place for the scurrilous lies of press and politicians. It was being played in a vastly different theatre from that of the previous six months.

It took me five and a half days to complete my opening address, which involved the calling of 20 witnesses. Opposing counsel, particularly Cleary and Hamer, seemingly fully cognisant of the bankruptcy of their case, made an all-out attempt to discredit the witnesses. In this they completely failed, as was evidenced by these words of the Chief Justice:

I should say something of the credibility of the witnesses as the Committee was invited to hold that the witness was unreliable and exaggerated. The men gave their evidence in a manner and with such convincing detail and apparent truth as to make it impossible for me to disregard or disbelieve them. They were subject to lengthy cross examination but this had no apparent effect on the accuracy of their evidence.

But the most important section of the 26-page decision of the Chief Justice and complete vindication of the union's stand is as follows:

> A standard of reasonableness has to be established and if reasonable men think that a particular method of working or the use of a particular class of gear is dangerous to life or limb then they are justified in either refusing to undertake the work or to discontinue same when serious danger arises.
>
> I adopt the words of a former commission relative to the *Meerkirk*, cited by Mr Barnes, that even though gear is declared safe by an expert, a worker who genuinely fears that it will endanger his life and limb can refuse to work such gear.

In plain and unequivocal words, the Chief Justice of New Zealand accepted that the worker was the final and legal arbiter on matters of safety. Not commissions, not alleged experts, not shipping companies, but the workers.

On 9 August, after the day's proceedings had finished, Mr Watson approached me. He said, 'I want to congratulate you and shake hands, Mr Barnes, for you have won. The hearing will finish tomorrow. I am going back to Wellington tonight.'

The hearing did in fact finish the next day and the Chief Justice reserved his decision. This he delivered on 15 August.

The two most vital and important questions set by the order of reference were questions one and two (below). We contended that, not only legally, but also from the angle of safety to life and limb, our actions in every way were justifiable and correct. For six months we had been condemned in the most vicious possible manner by politicians, press and union bashers generally. Were we to be justified or were the actions of government, commission and shipowners to be upheld? Here are the questions and answers.

> *Question 1:* Were the *Mountpark* hatches safe to remove by hand on 20 February 1948 and on subsequent days, having regard to the letter of 13 February 1949 from the government inspectors of waterside gear, Auckland, and to the relevant provisions of the New Zealand General Harbour Regulations and to all other relevant considerations, and was the Union Steam Ship Company of New Zealand Limited justified in dismissing the men employed, and were the men properly placed on penalty on 20 February 1948 and on subsequent days? If the Union Steam Ship Company of New

Zealand Limited was not so justified, what payment if any should be made to the men dismissed on 20 February 1948, and if the men were not properly placed on penalty what payment if any should be made to the men so placed on penalty?

Answer: The *Mountpark* hatches were not safe to be removed by hand on 20 February 1948 and on subsequent days and the Union Steam Ship Company of New Zealand Limited was not justified in dismissing the men employed and the men were not properly placed on penalty on 20 February 1948 and on subsequent days. A payment of £935.12/10 should be made to the men in respect to Friday 20 February, Monday 23 February, Tuesday 24 February and Wednesday 25 February.

Question 2: Having regard to all relevant considerations, was the decision of the Waterfront Industry Commission on 25 February 1948 a proper decision, and were the men entitled to refuse resumption of work on the *Mountpark* in accordance with that decision either on 26 February or any subsequent days? Should any payment, and if so how much, be awarded to the men placed on penalty on 26 February and on subsequent days?

Answer: The decision of the Waterfront Industry Commission on 25 February 1948 was not a proper decision and the men were entitled to refuse resumption of work on the *Mountpark* on 26 February, 27 February and 28 February. A payment of £363.14/8 should be paid to the men placed on penalty in respect of Thursday 26 February and Friday 27 February; 28 February was a Saturday.

We had won a smashing victory! On 16 August work resumed on the *Mountpark* and hatches were removed with slings—not by hand.

The combined fee of Messrs Watson, Cleary and Hamer was 1800 guineas. I received £15, being two weeks' pay at £7.10 per week. In addition, I was voted two weeks' holiday on pay. After working at pressure for over two weeks on an average of 20 hours a day, I needed it. I mention this for one reason alone. So much is said of union bludgers and their rich rewards. The value of any official to the workers he represents can be measured by the volume of abuse heaped on him by press and politicians. His monetary rewards are in inverse proportion. Conversely, for those whose main purpose is to sell out and betray the people they represent, monetary rewards and sycophantic publicity are plenty.

So ended a six-month campaign of unmitigated lying and unscrupulous tactics from Fraser, McLagan, the commission, shipowners and the press. The verdict received no headlines. From the *Herald* there was no comment, no apology or retraction of any of its slanders and outright lies. It was satisfied with publishing in small print the order of reference and decision with no comment. On 24 August it did publish an address by Sir Michael

Myers, a former Chief Justice, on the *Mountpark* and the independence of the judiciary. He was extremely critical of McLagan and the government. In a lengthy address he said another objectionable feature was that of a judge (in other words Judge Dalglish, who although not a judge of the Supreme Court, had what was called the status of a Supreme Court judge), having to give evidence and submit to cross-examination to justify his actions. To say that he was giving evidence as chairman of the Waterfront Commission and not as a judge was not a valid answer to the objection that it was contrary to both public policy and constitution of principle that a person holding high judicial office with the status of a judge of the Supreme Court should be placed in a position involving such an indignity! Sir Michael Myers said he ventured to hope that the happenings in the *Mountpark* case would not be regarded as precedents to be followed.

On 26 August the *Christchurch Press* published a leading article along similar lines which commented, *inter alia*, 'At every step the government blundered more deeply into pitfalls which it had itself dug.'

Since then, there has rarely been mention of the *Mountpark*. It exposed too many in high places and had to be buried with the minimum of publicity.

Further endorsement of our action was provided by a conference held at the head office of the Marine Department on 7 October involving the secretary of Marine, the Chief Surveyor of Ships, representatives from the Harbour Boards' Association of New Zealand, the Overseas Shipowners' Committee, the New Zealand Shipowners' Federation (including Belford), the Waterfront Industry Commission, the Waterside Employers' Association, and Toby Hill and myself. The conference was convened on instructions from F. Hackett, Minister of Marine, to deal with safety on the waterfront. Truly a case of shutting the stable door after the horse had bolted, only called, of course, because of the *Mountpark* case, which had convincingly proved the need for radical amendments.

Among other recommendations made were:

(6) That a new Regulation (No 73A) be added to the General Harbour Regulations, 1935—
'That all hatch covers exceeding 112 lbs net weight must be handled by winch, crane or other mechanical means.'
(9) That it be a recommendation to all New Zealand shipowners that, where practicable, all single hatch covers be converted to slab hatch covers at the next annual survey.

The fact that, with the exception of Belford, these amendments were unanimously approved, casts serious doubt on the integrity of those who so recently had given evidence to the contrary. Belford's excuse was that he had to report back to his supervisors.

6 THE COLD WAR HOTS UP, 1948-49

With the *Mountpark* settled and the 1948 budget just announced, our union directed its attention to the economic and political problems facing not only watersiders but all New Zealand workers. We summarised these in lengthy statement that read:

> Promises of relief to workers are not enough, and just claims for wage increases must continue. Wage earners are heavily taxed and their wages are deplorably low. With rationing of goods and excessive control of imports the people are denied large quantities of goods just as effectively as by a naval blockade. Mr Nash could be viewed as a one-man navy.
>
> Some time ago we announced that we were going ahead with a claim for a wage rise of 1/- per hour. After considering the budget, that demand will be continued. We regard the budget as one of great expectation, but wage earners and their families cannot live on expectation. Immediate issues before the trade union movement are to seek substantial wage increases, to oppose military conscription in peacetime, to bring about effective control of prices and profits, and to ensure that workers have a sufficiency of real money and cheaper and better goods.
>
> The inclusion of the conscription question in this group of subjects may seem strange. The fact is, however, that the drafting of thousands of our young men into military camps would have a serious economic effect by lowering production. Our Union regards with concern the kite-flying which has been going on over peacetime conscription.
>
> History shows that in Britain, France and the US the primary purpose of peacetime conscription is strike-breaking. To talk of the necessity of parade ground drill in New Zealand in this age of atomic and chemical warfare is arrant nonsense. Conscription is the only way to obtain what is called 'free' labour. During the recent dock strike in London voluntary labour could not be obtained and workers in uniform were used.
>
> Whatever disagreements there may be in the trade union movement, this union is confident that there will be a common front against peacetime conscription.

In the demand for peacetime conscription, Fraser was of course only following the lead set by Clem Attlee, British Labour Prime Minister. Like many in New Zealand's Cabinet, Attlee too had once campaigned against such a measure, arguing at one point:

The Cold War Hots Up

> In capitalist countries conscription is confined to persons; wealth is not conscripted, and in practice the wealthy and the industrialists manage to escape from actually serving in the field. The notorious case of the French railwaymen who were called to the colours when on strike shows how conscription can be used against the workers, so that they can be compelled under martial law to blackleg their fellows. Conscription is, in fact, an admirable machine for regimenting workers, hence its popularity with reactionaries.

And just like Fraser and Co in New Zealand, once in office this fine fellow did an about-face, ordering khaki-clad dockers' sons to scab on their fathers in the 1948 port of London lockout.

On 22 September Fraser was invited to address the national council of the FOL and, in the words of Baxter, express his views on 'national defence'. It sounded better than peacetime conscription and was a move by Walsh to stave off the ever-growing opposition. It was obvious to all that this was to be Fraser's next move, and unions throughout New Zealand had been demanding a special FOL conference. Conference was representative of all affiliated unions and was the final authority—not the national council and not the national executive, which consisted of the president (Croskery), vice-president (Walsh), secretary (Baxter) and four others and was completely dominated by Walsh. The so-called national executive was limited to Wellington members and was wide open to pressure from the government of the day.

After listening to Fraser, the council decided to await his return from another London junket and to leave it to him if and when the conference should be called. You did not have to be prescient to know this would never happen. Walsh and Baxter would never allow Fraser to be embarrassed in front of the entire union movement.

Our own WWU national executive, by contrast, was elected on a national basis and was truly representative of the rank and file. It consisted of president, vice-president, secretary and eight members who represented the ports of Auckland, Wellington, Lyttelton, Gisborne, Bluff, Oamaru, Timaru and Greymouth. We requested all our branches to move through their local trades councils for a conference to be held forthwith. The response from the 19 trades councils was overwhelming. Seventeen demanded an immediate conference, the only two prepared to leave it to Fraser being Southland and Walsh's Wellington.

Needless to say, our appeals fell on deaf ears and the Prime Minister was free to attend banquets in London without being troubled by the FOL.

Since the *Mountpark* episode, McLagan's Waterfront Industry Commission consisted solely of Judge Dalglish and the shipowners' nominees, Almond and Anderson. McLagan was happy to leave it that way but our members were not. In particular, we were looking for long-overdue wage increases.

On 16 November a meeting of our national executive was convened and gave McLagan seven days to remedy the situation. Failing this being done, our national council would be called to implement direct action on a national basis. This ultimatum quickly brought results.

A week later a new system of control was set up. On many previous occasions we had claimed that the Waterfront Commission was subject to influence if not control by the government. We also argued that the commission acted as both judge and jury. In the course of the *Mountpark* case, we had proved beyond all doubt that Dalglish took his riding orders from McLagan and that he was determined that his decisions not be appealed before another judge. Partly in response to pressure from our union the government now split the commission into administrative and judicial bodies. The former, the Waterfront Industry Commission, a full-time body, consisted of a chairman and one representative from each side and had sub-committees at each port. Arthur Bockett was chairman and Reg O'Donnell our nominee. The judicial commission of five, the Waterfront Industry Authority, was a part-time body to be convened in Wellington when required to deal with disputes, conditions of employment and wages. Dalglish was again appointed chairman with the status of a judge of the Supreme Court, Toby Hill and I represented our union, and Belford and T.S. Marchington the shipowners.

After the way in which Dalglish was exposed in the *Mountpark* case, his appointment surprised most people, but not those who knew his master. Belford harboured a deep hatred of watersiders that was only inflamed by the hiding that he had taken in the *Mountpark* case. Marchington was an ex-lieutenant commander in the British navy—no more need be said about his attitude to workers! The omens for a relatively long life for the judicial commission were not good.

At the one meeting of the judicial commission held in December 1948, Toby and I succeeded in remedying one major injustice of the Ongley decision and won a guaranteed weekly wage of £5.10.

The Carpenters Caught in the Cold War

Meanwhile, the Cold War Fraser government was not letting up in its attack on the communist-led Carpenters' Union. Roy Stanley, national secretary of this union, was one of the most honest, capable and thoroughly sincere people I ever met in the trade union movement. But Roy was a member of the Communist Party. Automatically, that brought in Bob Semple, who had a personal mission to destroy the influence of the Communist Party. The Carpenters' Union had mounted a claim for 5d an hour increase to their award. After years of so-called stabilisation, the surprising feature was its modesty. On 7 December the Arbitration Court awarded an increase of 2d and for good measure abolished travelling time. In effect, it was a nil decision. This was one penny less than the employers had already offered, with no suggestion of abolishing travelling time. Even for the Arbitration Court this was an astounding decision and provocation in the extreme. That it was inspired by sources outside the court was conclusively proven by the subsequent actions of Fraser, Walsh and Co.

Alexander Croskery, president, Federation of Labour, 1946–52 (*NZ Herald*)

Showing great restraint, the Carpenters' Union put its case before a meeting of the FOL national council. This body unanimously supported its case and recommended to all affiliates to give moral and financial support. A go-slow policy was adopted by the carpenters, and they were immediately locked out.

As was their practice, Walsh and Baxter ignored the decision of the national council and, with outbursts from Fraser, McLagan and Semple, an orchestrated campaign against communist-dominated unions followed. They were accused of being agents of foreign powers and other such tripe.

To the best of my knowledge, Roy Stanley and Bill McAra, the secretary of the waterside branch of the union, were the only Communist Party members holding official positions. Frank Langley, their sincere and most competent president, was a member of the Labour Party, as were most of its members. However, if there had not been one party member in the entire union membership it would have made no difference. Under the Labour government every struggle for elementary justice was a foreign plot. The scenario for '51 was nearing completion. Its authors were a bunch of traitors to the labour movement—Sid Holland only had to write the final pages and supply the cast!

Conscription Referendum

Fraser had returned from his London jaunt and had obviously been well and truly primed by the top brass in London. He was now on the offensive, seeing Russian submarines in Cook Strait and Cossacks in the Waitakeres and on this pretext called a referendum on the issue of peacetime conscription. It was now up to opponents in the labour movement to prevent this rush to militarism. John A. Lee and I wrote a pamphlet, *Resist Peace Time Conscription*, and, among other gatherings, addressed a full house at the Wellington Town Hall.

Hundreds of thousands of pounds of taxpayers' money was squandered on putting the government case for conscription, while the opposition was denied any assistance. Running true to form, the national executive of the FOL refused to be associated with a deputation to Fraser asking for funding. Walsh and Baxter no longer bothered to camouflage their actions and openly campaigned with Fraser and Semple. Little surprise then that the referendum motion was carried. The colossal expenditure of public money, allied with the usual lies, slander and anti-Russian hysteria, rendered the result almost a certainty. It was a Pyrrhic victory for the Labour government, however. This gross betrayal of labour principles made their defeat at the next general election a certainty.

The Cold War Hots Up

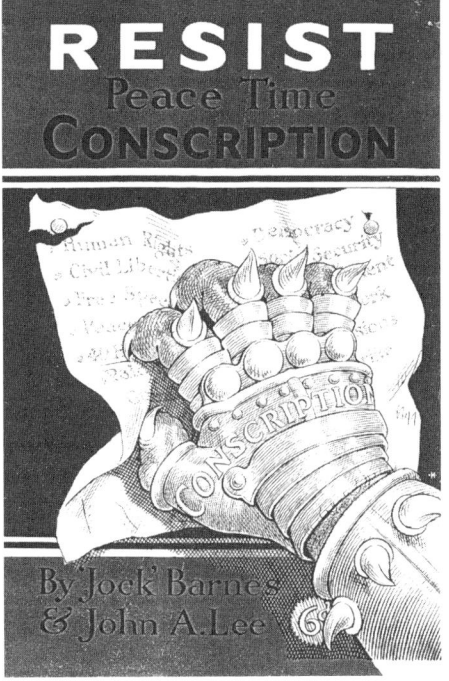

Campaign for a Wage Increase

With the end of the war, all talk of a new order disappeared and both press and politicians resumed their usual role of vilifying workers. New Year 1949 saw grave unrest throughout the trade union movement. Twelve months before, the FOL had requested that action should be taken to control prices so that current wages would have some chance of sustaining a reasonable standard of living. We had been assured by the Minister of Industries and Commerce that if we were patient about wage increases, effective price control would occur and we would be substantially better off towards the end of 1948. The year had come and gone, prices and profits continued to rise and the only people being restrained were workers. To children of the under-privileged, gifts from Santa Claus that Christmas were few.

As usual, the national executive of the FOL pursued a policy of masterly inactivity when it came to prosecuting claims for working people. Even if there had been any desire, their attacks on communist influence in the labour movement left little time for anything else.

By contrast, the Auckland Trades Council, the largest in New Zealand, started to take effective action, demanding:

1. A £2 per week wage increase (equivalent to a shilling an hour).
2. Equal pay for women.

3. Increased pensions.
4. Rigid control of prices and profits.

A manifesto on similar lines, issued by our union, was signed by over 50 officials from the major trade unions. This campaign began to put pressure on the national executive of the FOL, which was forced into taking belated action. Its claim to the Arbitration Court, however, was for a wage increase of only £1 per week or 6d an hour.

Meanwhile, we were pursuing our own claim for a shilling an hour on the waterfront. In early February the Waterfront Industry Authority heard from national vice-president, Alec Drennan, who presented a comprehensive case based on hard economic and irrefutable facts. Confident in the knowledge that McLagan's office boy, Judge Dalglish, and their own two representatives would safeguard their interests, the shipowners did not bother to put up even a sham fight. Their confidence was soon justified.

McLagan had declared the Waterfront Industry Authority to be completely independent and subject to interference from no quarter whatsoever. Its purpose was to give decisions based solely on the evidence before it. However, when Judge Dalglish awarded the sum of 2d in response to our demand for a shilling, he made no secret of the fact that it was in accordance with the Arbitration Court's ruling in the carpenters' case. In case there might be some misunderstanding on this point, Judge Dalglish made his decision interim, pending the Arbitration Court decision on the FOL claim for an increase of 6d an hour. Needless to say, there was no disagreement from the employers' representatives on the Waterfront Authority.

One would have been naive indeed to think that Dalglish would change his spots but here we had two employers' representatives, members of an allegedly free and independent judicial body, happily accepting dictation from the Arbitration Court.

Toby and I recorded our dissent and accused Dalglish of following orders from the government, which was determined that the outcome of our case not exceed that of the Arbitration Court's decision on the carpenters' case. This provoked a storm of criticism from the press, which attacked the wreckers, Barnes and Hill, who had had the audacity to dissent from this legal decision and to make further charges against this impartial body.

McLagan and Dalglish, with no disagreement from the shipowners' representatives, continued to break and violate agreements entered into by all concerned parties. Pursuing his usual tactics McLagan, aided by the press, would then accuse us of the very sins he himself was committing!

When the Waterfront Authority was set up, our full national council made it abundantly clear to McLagan that we would not be a party to, nor have representatives on, any body on which our representatives were denied the right to express dissenting opinion and report back to our union membership. Much against his will, McLagan grudgingly accepted this elementary democratic principle.

On our expressing our dissent at the outrageous wage decision that clearly revealed the independent judicial body to be nothing but an appendage of McLagan and the Arbitration Court, the hymns of hate against us again resounded. Our national executive met and, with its concurrence, we compiled a pamphlet, *Our Union is Attacked*, which was distributed to all members and dealt with each of the accusations made against us item by item (see Appendix 3).

This pamphlet induced a hysterical reaction from Fraser and McLagan and the usual scurrilous lies from the press. No mention of the admission by Belford that he was happy to be a stooge for McLagan while disguised as a member of an impartial judicial body. No mention of Dalglish and Marchington adopting a similar role, but the usual virulent attacks on Barnes and Hill.

The Northumberland

The case of the *Northumberland* further exposed McLagan as an agent of the employers. The national council of the FOL and the Auckland Trades Council had carried resolutions of support for the locked-out carpenters and called on other unions to assist. Many small builders were happy to pay their modest claim for 6d an hour rise, but not so the major construction firms. Secure in the knowledge that they had the full support of Fraser, McLagan, Baxter and Walsh, they decided to deny all supplies to any builder who agreed to pay the increase of sixpence. An instruction was also given to members of the Employers' Federation, many desperately short of labour, to refuse to employ any locked-out carpenters. This was simply a modification of the preference ship idea, with the same goal in mind—starve them back.

One such firm was the Penrose Glassworks, for which No. 6 hold of the *Northumberland* contained a cargo of soda ash. With the glassworks refusing requests to employ locked-out carpenters, the firm was advised that, until it changed its stance, no soda ash would be discharged. A case of tit for tat.

Although only one hold was affected and normal work continued on the rest of the ship, McLagan and his allies ran true to form and declared the *Northumberland* a preference ship. So a dispute that should have been confined to one hold was broadened into one affecting the whole port.

Another field day for the *Herald* and *Star* followed, with an excuse to pillory our union, while extolling the virtues of the bosses and their friends on that impartial judicial body, the Waterfront Authority.

In effect, a demand had been made by the government that we scab on the national council of the FOL, the Auckland Trades Council and our fellow workers of the Carpenters' Union. There was more chance of hell freezing. There then followed one of the blackest acts of treachery ever committed in the history of the labour movement. McLagan deregistered the Carpenters' Union and registered a scab union under police protection.

We were forced to lift our boycott of the *Northumberland* and in protest passed a resolution in which we condemned the FOL leadership as 'agents of the employing class'. We then sent a copy of this resolution to Walsh and Baxter for good measure. The government attacked again, McLagan insisting that we hold a secret ballot of our members regarding our union's position towards the Waterfront Authority: would our members accept and abide by every decision handed down by this authority? What arrogance! Dalglish followed in his master's footsteps on 4 April by suspending the Waterfront Authority. We protested at this action and insisted that it be reconvened. On 27 April we sent the following:

> Judge D.J. Daglish
> Chairman
> Waterfront Industry Authority
>
> Dear Sir
> As you are aware, we dissented from the decision to adjourn the Authority and protested against unwarranted Governmental interference with the affairs of our so-called independent and judicial body. However, it was clearly understood that the position of the Authority would be determined by April 21. As this is now the 27th day of April, in accordance with the regulations of the Waterfront Authority, which empower a meeting to be called by the Authority or by the Chairman, we request that a meeting be held as early as possible to proceed with matters that are at present before the Authority.
>
> We would appreciate an early reply as to your intentions.
>
> H. Barnes, President
> T. Hill, Secretary

We received the following in reply:

> Messrs H. Barnes and T. Hill
> New Zealand Waterside Workers' Union
>
> Dear Sirs
> I return herewith a letter delivered at my office this afternoon. I am not prepared to receive it or answer it.
>
> When I receive a letter from you couched in proper terms and in

particular, excluding the reference to 'our so-called independent and judicial body', I will be prepared to answer it.

D.J. Dalglish, Chairman

Ours was a polite, proper and legal request, despite this Pooh Bah's claim that it was not 'couched in proper terms'. That was his way of saying it lacked servility. From Belford, we received the following:

The President and Secretary
New Zealand Waterside Workers' Union

Dear Sirs
I have to acknowledge receipt of your letter of April 27 requesting that a meeting of the Waterfront Industry Authority be held as early as possible.

At the last meeting of the Waterfront Industry Authority held on April 4 I moved a motion deploring the attitude of your union towards decisions of the Authority and I supported a motion of the chairman that meetings of the Authority be adjourned until such time as the intentions of the Government were clarified in regard to the future of the Authority or until the Authority was reconvened by the chairman.

I mention the foregoing attitude and will be available to attend a meeting of the Authority if and when the chairman convenes such meeting.

K. Belford
Shipowners' Representative

At least Belford's reply lacked the hypocrisy of the chairman's despite his open admission that he was prepared to wait for a direction from the government with regard to the future of this alleged independent judicial body!

Meanwhile, with our pamphlet *Our Union is Attacked* reaching a wide audience, Dalglish and the shipowners' representatives were getting increasingly uncomfortable. When the Waterfront Authority was finally reconvened on 3 June 1949, Dalglish insisted that we tender an apology for the contents of the pamphlet and commit ourselves not to report on deliberations of the authority to our membership. We had had no previous notice of this fit-up and requested an adjournment so that we could suitably reply. This was refused and the motion carried. It would have put any kangaroo court ever convened to shame. Total time of meeting was 45 minutes. Twenty-five seconds would have sufficed. The authority was now adjourned *sine die*.

Solidarity with the Canadians

The campaign against communism was in full cry around the world. At home we had seen a Labour government crush a union simply for the colour of its leadership. We now became involved in a dispute with marked similarities to our own. The following cable was received from Canada:

> National Secretary
> Watersiders' Union
> Wellington
>
> Appeal to you to give full support to striking Canadian crew members as shipowners attempt to change established working conditions—result substantial cut take-home pay and elimination union hiring hall, result unemployment and discrimination.
>
> Harry Davis, President
> Canadian Seamen's Union

Seventy-seven Canadian ships were tied up by seamen and dockers around the world, from Britain and France to Cuba, the British West Indies, and Australia and New Zealand. London and Liverpool dockers walked off and declared that they would pull out the two ports if shipowners tried to use scabs. Rapacious shipowners are the architects of an unexcelled comradeship that prevails between maritime workers throughout the world.

For seven months the Canadian Seamen's Union (CSU) had tried every form of negotiation. Then, on the very day union leaders met the Canadian Minister of Labour in an effort to gain a peaceful settlement, the shipowners signed a contract with a notorious company union—the Seamen's International Union (SIU)—which had no membership in Canada and was not recognised by any Canadian Labour Congress. On the very same day too, the state-owned shipping line signed up with scabs, and seamen were cut off from unemployment insurance, which was administered by the Department of Labour.

On 23 April the crew of the Canadian ship *Tridale*, which was tied up in Wellington by its crew, were arrested for refusing to sail and charged in court for refusing to obey a lawful command of the master. The case was adjourned until 27 April. As all amenities had been denied the crew, it was necessary to make arrangements for their food and accommodation. This was done. Meals were made available at the Wellington branch restaurant and, at all times, by Tony Marinovich at his restaurant. There was no charge. They were not made better than Tony. While solidarity came from our men, vicious attacks were the currency from the shipowners and sabotage that of the FOL. On the morning of 26 April, F.P. Walsh advised the crew to accept the Seamen's International Union agreement and to take the ship home. If they did this, he assured them, there would be no convictions. As the Canadian strike committee was to write later:

Our morale was high, the world's ports were with us, and yet we were being pressed to forget justice and principles, desert the struggle, and become scabs. It was too much for our crew to swallow.

The *Tridale* crew appeared before the courts the following day and were fined 14 days' pay for holding up the ship. On 6 May the captain held a further meeting of the crew to issue another lawful command and once again the crew were arrested, only this time under the 17th-century British Shipping Act. The case was remanded until 11 May when, before Magistrate Hanna, the 27 members of the crew were sentenced to four weeks' hard labour. Their only crime—refusing to scab on their union. While in prison the Canadian seamen were well attended to by members of our Wellington branch, who supplied them with tobacco and helped out with their correspondence and other general matters that needed attending to.

The Canadian High Commissioner's Diplomatic Secretary, Miss Ireland, accompanied by Marchington and the captain, called on the crew in prison in an attempt to intimidate them. Marchington said: 'If you don't work the ship, you'll have to stay here for ever.' To men isolated in jail and in a strange land, such threats can seem very real, but there was no comment from McLagan or Dalglish about Marchington's despicable conduct. Indeed, Baxter, following on the strike-breaking attempt of Walsh, then cabled the *bona fide* union in Canada painting a black picture and asking them to surrender. It was ignored.

On 11 July the New Zealand Transport Workers' Federation held a special meeting to discuss the *Ottawa Valley*, which was due in Auckland on 13 July and manned with scabs. It was declared black and stayed that way for 59 days.

Walsh returned from a visit to Geneva and London and had evidently been well briefed. He declared that the strike of the Canadian Seamen's Union in general and the *Tridale* in particular was a 'Cominform-inspired farce'. It was clear that it was not just the Canadian union that was in the firing line. The *Tridale* was being used in an attempt to force a showdown on the Auckland waterfront and smash our union. Rather than allow any reactionary stooges this opportunity, the New Zealand strike committee of the CSU recommended to the Canadian executive that the ban on the *Ottawa Valley* and the *Tridale* be lifted, to which the Canadian executive agreed. The Canadian seamen held a crew meeting on 7 September, at which there was a unanimous vote of confidence in the union's national officials and the recommendation to return with the ship was agreed to. Negotiations were started between the strike committee and the shipping company, and on 10 September an agreement was signed. The *Tridale* sailed with a full union crew. The Auckland wharfies had made another magnificent stand for maritime solidarity and against the Cold Warriors. But the day of reckoning was drawing closer.

What was interesting about the *Tridale* episode was its close parallels with the carpenters' case:
1. Canadian employers brought in a scab union to worsen seamen's conditions. New Zealand employers did the same with the carpenters, again with full support of the Minister of Labour.
2. A Canadian state-owned shipping company lined up with private employers and signed a scab agreement. New Zealand state-owned railway workshops lined up with the Employers' Federation and refused to employ locked-out carpenters.
3. The Canadian Minister of Labour denied seamen unemployment insurance. The New Zealand Minister of Labour denied carpenters social security.
4. Canadian union leaders victimised the Canadian Seamen's Union. The leadership of the FOL played a similar role in New Zealand.

Toxic cargo on the Barnhill

Meanwhile we were in the thick of a scandal in which commission and shipowners were united in a flagrant breach of safety regulations and a cover-up. The ship concerned, the British freighter *Barnhill*, berthed on 22 June and carried cargo that could have caused horrific casualties, not only to waterfront workers, but also the general public of Auckland. I was working on this job, and the first thing I saw going to the ship was a team of non-waterside workers dressed from head to foot in protective gear, discharging drums of deck cargo. This was watersiders' work, but we had never been consulted and it was obvious something fishy was going on.

On making inquiries, I was informed by one of the gang that the contents were extremely poisonous and that one drop could be fatal. He said a single whiff could kill a man and there was enough in one drum to asphyxiate people over a large area of the city. For good measure, the drums were packed in with cases of acid, which we were asked to discharge in order to free the drums. We discharged some cases but the other workers, who turned out to be a special squad of Shell Company employees, remained in their protective gear, including gas masks. It was time to knock off.

We retired until the Shell squad had finished and the Union Steam Ship Company promptly stopped our pay. The answer was obvious—we left the site. The drums were being discharged by shore crane and reached a height of about 25 metres. If one had dropped, it would have burst. Had we then known just how potentially catastrophic this was, the entire waterfront would have been evacuated.

Further inquiries revealed that the drums contained tetra-ethyl of lead—

the most dangerous lead compound known. All authorities agreed on the extreme danger—the Auckland Harbour Board, the Marine Department, British shipping regulations and medical experts alike—that is, all except the Waterfront Industry Commission. Wartime instructions issued by the British Minister of War Transport had declared:

> Ethyl fluid is an extremely dangerous fluid and its effects on personnel may be fatal, either by absorption through the skin or by inhalation of the vapour. To ensure the most careful handling, the drums must be loaded and discharged singly and lifted by rope slings only—can hooks must not be used. Each drum weighs approximately 900 lbs.
>
> Shoes and other leather articles must be discarded as the fluid cannot be removed from them. The liquid will be absorbed by any wood, dunnage, etc, and as it is not possible to remove the fluid from wood this should be jettisoned.

The Marine Department, acting on the advice of a government chemist, recommended that the *Barnhill* cargo was so dangerous that the ship should not even be allowed alongside a city berth and, if she was put there, said they would insist that everybody be cleared from the wharf.

Alerted by this advice, we wrote to the Auckland Harbour Board demanding that union men, not Shell employees, unload the ship, that they work under proper safeguards and with a special allowance of £1 an hour, to act as a deterrent to the company. The Auckland Harbour Board replied:

> In reply to your letter of June 23, I have to inform you that the matter was considered by the Board at its meeting held yesterday when it was decided, pending additions to the Board's Dangerous Goods By-laws, to apply the following restrictions to the discharging and loading of ethyl fluid:—
>
> (1) No person shall bring ethyl fluid on to any wharf under the control of the Board without the permission of the Traffic Manager and the Chief Wharfinger, and until the vessel about to load same is prepared to receive it at the sling.
>
> (2) No person shall land ethyl fluid on any wharf without the permission of the Traffic Manager and Chief Wharfinger, and such goods shall be removed by the owner, agent, or consignee thereof immediately it being landed on such wharf. Such owner, agent or consignee shall be held responsible for any damage or loss that may accrue from an accident arising therefrom.
>
> (3) Ethyl fluid shall be discharged or loaded only at such times between the hours of sunrise and sunset, as shall be approved by the Traffic Manager and Chief Wharfinger.
>
> (4) During the discharging or loading of ethyl fluid it shall be the responsibility of the owner, agent or consignee to have in attendance a

trained staff, suitably equipped with protective clothing, and decontamination and antidote materials.

(Signed) A.W. Taylor
Chief Executive Officer and Secretary

However, Captain Ryan of the Union Steam Ship Company flatly refused our demands regarding union control of the job at a special premium rate. Accordingly, the Auckland union executive resolved that no further work be performed on the *Barnhill* until an equitable settlement was reached. The Auckland Port Committee met to hear our claim three days later but rejected it outright. We appealed and the letter from Captain Stanich, Auckland port controller, read as follows:

> I have to acknowledge receipt of your letter of even date advising that your Executive wish to appeal against my decision given in relation to the *Barnhill* dispute at a special Port Committee meeting held this morning. This will be placed on the agenda for hearing by the commission. Subsequent to the Port Committee meeting this morning I have made enquiries and find that the quantities of tetra-ethyl lead imported into Auckland are comparatively small, recent shipments comprising 12 drums ex the *Port Macquarie* and 19 drums ex the *Haparangi*. Both of these shipments were handled by members of your Union in the ordinary course of their work.

This letter must surely be a classic and will go down in labour history. Here is an official in the responsible position of port controller blandly implying that because men had once subjected themselves to deadly danger they should do it again and again. The Shell Company had taken extraordinary precautions to protect its men, but nobody—neither ship-owners nor the commission—was concerned to safeguard the lives of watersiders or, indeed, the citizens of Auckland. For them, shareholder dividends came first.

If ever there was a case for headlines and editorials, it was this. It should have been the duty of any responsible newspaper to expose the risk of a major disaster to which the citizens of Auckland had been subjected, but both *Star* and *Herald* were silent. Driven by an obsession to destroy our union, McLagan continued his campaign of lies and vilification. The government produced a pamphlet that stated that 'Mr Barnes' statement that the ethyl cargo was deadly poison was utterly absurd'. This was followed by a speech at Prebbleton on 26 September 1949, during which the minister declared that 'Tetra-ethyl lead was no more dangerous to handle than a sack of potatoes or any other ordinary cargo' (*Christchurch Press*, 27 September).

This flew in the face of all expert opinion. Fresh facts on ethyl fluid

The Cold War Hots Up

now in our possession added to the enormity of the crime of those who dismissed it as harmless. Professor J.B.S. Haldane, FRS, Professor of Biometry at University College, London, Britain's leading scientist of the time, wrote:

> A particularly deadly vapour is that of lead tetra-ethyl, which is used as an anti knock in petrol. A few years ago it killed about 40 men in the United States and others went mad from brain injury.
>
> We are told that workers are now completely protected against it, but as lead may accumulate in the human body over long periods, this may only mean that they are not now being killed as quickly.
>
> Liquids whose vapours are poisonous are continually being introduced into industry as solvents, and unless the workers raise the matter, they are often left unprotected until a number have been killed and many more have had their health ruined.

On this authority, it would be fair to borrow a phrase from McLagan's pamphlet and say to him: 'Your statement is simply a tissue of absurd exaggerations.' But that would not be enough.

Suppose that the danger of ethyl fluid had been overstated by Professor Haldane, the British Minister of War Transport and many others—which is the crime? To make doubly sure that people's lives are safeguarded, or to tell them that a deadly poison is like a sack of potatoes?

Professor Haldane's advice (he knew more than McLagan about trade unionism as well as science) was as follows:

> It is up to the trade unions concerned to do what they can to check the death rate both from poisonous vapours and from dust. Their effects are preventable but they will not be prevented unless the workers take the matter in hand.
>
> I wonder today if a major New Zealand disaster caused by ethyl fluid never eventuated because Auckland waterside workers took the matter in hand.

The union naturally refused to accept the port committee's decision, which was the climax to a long series of one-way decisions against the workers. Furthermore, with the adjournment of the Waterfront Authority *sine die*, we could not even lodge a final appeal. A stopwork meeting on 27 June decided to implement an overtime ban and work a 44-hour week in protest at the response of the commission to the tetra-ethyl issue as well as its stalling on our demand for a decent pay rise and for improved port amenities for the men.

Then, without hearing any representations from the union, without even enquiring into the facts of the case, McLagan suspended the commission in Auckland. With the suspension of the commission and the authority in Auckland, we were in theory free to negotiate wages and conditions of work directly with the employer. An emergency meeting of our national council was called for 12 July to discuss our strategy. Some 34 delegates from 19 ports attended. We sat for three days, with every opportunity given to every delegate to voice his views on our national policy. This was endorsed by a vote of 33 to one. The one dissenter was from Timaru. It was further resolved that all ports would follow Auckland's lead and work a 44-hour week. McLagan, Dalglish and the shipowners got their answer.

As usual, the *Herald* led the attack. We were now working four hours per week more than the 40-hour week that was supposed to be the right of all New Zealand workers. No mention of the *Barnhill* or of the calamity that might well have occurred but for our actions, and no mention of the fact that in Auckland we were breaking no agreement because there was no longer one to break. Just their usual bitter and lying tirades. In a leader of 29 July we read the usual diatribe about 'men who have defied the law' and a suggestion that the government proclaim a state of emergency. On 9 August the shipowners made their move and locked out every wharfie from the port of Auckland, the first time this had ever been done.

We had clearly been targeted as Public Enemy No. 1 in the government's Cold War drive. The US government wanted to ensure unfettered access to Australian and New Zealand ports in the event of a war in Asia, and to do that they had to destroy the power of the waterside unions in the two countries. Both countries had just received visits by delegations of British and American shipowners, and our governments went out of their way to assist the Americans in their Cold War objective. Jim Healy and Ted Roach, secretary and assistant secretary of the Australian Waterside Workers' Federation respectively, had been sacked from the Australian Waterfront Commission for the crime of being members of the Communist Party and militant union leaders. For good measure, they were given jail sentences just before the national ballot for their positions. Despite an extensive campaign against them by the Australian press and the 'Industrial Groupers' (a right-wing faction of the Australian Labor Party, later to split to form the Democratic Labor Party) and despite being locked up in jail, they were returned with sweeping majorities. If New Zealand's parliamentary elections had not been so close, I believe Hill and I would have been jailed too. The government must have realised, however, that this would have killed off their already very remote chance of being returned to office.

The *Herald* continued to spew out its customary diatribes and, while the *Star* was not so irrational and vindictive, it followed suit. Logical argument with both on matters concerning watersiders had long since gone overboard. It was notable that no other daily paper in New Zealand pursued

The Cold War Hots Up

this campaign of hate to anything like the same extent. This was evidence of the conspiracy by press, shipowners and government to smash the Auckland branch first, and then pick the rest off at their leisure.

We set wheels in motion from our side as well. We established a lockout committee, picketed the wharves, and issued leaflets pointing out why we were being victimised. We also organised a meeting at the Auckland Town Hall to put our case. On 14 August more than 3000 citizens turned up to hear our side of the story. Both main hall and concert chamber were packed and a large overflow audience in Grey's Avenue listened to proceedings by medium of loudspeakers. This on a cold winter's night. It ended by calling on the government to direct the shipping companies to end the lockout so that community supplies and facilities could be maintained.

The success of the meetings, with little advertising, was indicative of the fact that the venom of McLagan, Fraser and the *Herald* was creating a reaction, but the opposite to what was intended! People were starting to ask questions and whenever we had the opportunity of answering, the result was the same—overwhelming support.

With the coming election's warning bells ringing in his ears, Fraser decided to intervene. On 18 August our national executive had a meeting with him and McLagan. I stated our case in comprehensive detail. I pointed out that the excuse offered by Dalglish and the two employers' representatives in adjourning the commission *sine die* and refusing to arbitrate on outstanding and urgent matters was that no member should publish

Ships in berth at Auckland wharves, 1949 (*NZ Herald*)

comment on its deliberations as we had done in our pamphlet *Our Union is Attacked*. In the first few months we had settled some longstanding grievances and these had been reported in detail to our members. Favourable comment, it appeared, was quite acceptable, but when we had occasion to criticise what, in our opinion, was an iniquitous decision on our wage claim, Hill and I committed an offence that must be purged by unqualified apology. This we would not do, nor would our union accept that comment on or report from its representatives must be favourable to and censored by Dalglish, Belford and Marchington.

In his reply Fraser said:

> I have listened with interest to the statement of the Union's case by Mr Barnes. The Government will after a thorough examination and an analysis of the statement, give it full consideration. On full working hours, including overtime, being resumed, discussions can be commenced with a view to achieving satisfactory administration and conditions on the waterfront throughout the Dominion. We want peace on the waterfront of the country. We want normal work to commence at all ports, and discussions can be started as soon as possible afterwards.

Accepting Fraser's assurance in good faith, the national executive directed all branches to resume overtime work. However, we did not have long to wait for another betrayal by McLagan. Just a few days later, even before discussions had begun, McLagan issued a 27-page pamphlet of which 20 pages were devoted to an attack on me, while seven pages were given over to our statement and Fraser's remarks. This was printed by the Government Printer and distributed to watersiders throughout New Zealand.

It is inconceivable that this was done without Fraser's knowledge, and it indicates that when they could not break the overtime ban by force and intimidation, they would endeavour to do by treachery.

Once again, the rank and file gave the answer. Branches throughout the country were to advise Fraser and McLagan by telegram of the only practical value of McLagan's 20 pages. It was noted that, along with a host of other goods, toilet paper was in short supply!

Sacked from the Waterfront Authority

If further evidence were required of the duplicity of Fraser and McLagan, it was soon provided. With no discussion having eventuated, Toby and I received the following from the Minister of Labour:

> In the Matter of the Waterfront Industry Emergency Regulations 1946
> I hereby give you notice that his Excellency the Governor-General will be asked to consider whether he should exercise his power of removing you from your office of a member of the Waterfront Industry Authority upon the grounds—

(1) That you have caused or permitted to be published two pamphlets entitled respectively 'Our Union is Attacked' and 'The Attack Continues' containing animadversions for which you are responsible upon the judicial actions of the Waterfront Industry Authority and certain of your fellow members of that Authority.
(2) That your action in so doing amounts to misconduct within the meaning of the above mentioned regulations justifying your removal from office.

And I hereby give you further notice that any reasons you may wish to submit to the Governor-General setting out why you should not be removed from office should be set out in writing and delivered to me, or at my office in Wellington not later than five o'clock in the afternoon on the 30th day of August 1949 and I inform you that any reasons so delivered will be submitted to the Governor-General for his consideration.

Dated at Wellington this 25th day of August 1949
(signed) A. McLagan
Minister of Labour

This gem of English literature was hotly pursued as follows:

2nd September 1949
Parliament Buildings
Memo 47/1

I have to inform you that his Excellency the Governor-General has this day removed you from office as a member of the Waterfront Industry Authority because of your misconduct as a member of the Authority.

(signed) A. McLagan
Minister of Labour

So, while neither he nor Fraser was prepared to claim that we did not have the right to criticise, when we exercised that right, it became a heinous offence. Had they made it clear that the appointees' only role was as frontmen for McLagan, they would have still been waiting for union representatives. In fact, it was an honour to be sacked from this 'independent' judicial body, made doubly so by the fact that he had to get a scab to sack us. Many watersiders still had vivid memories of the Governor-General, Sir Bernard Freyburg, scabbing on the Wellington waterfront in 1913.

The success or failure of McLagan's efforts to be prosecutor, judge and jury had yet to be determined. Our union membership, the real jury, had yet to return its verdict, and the prevention of this was beyond his dictatorial powers. It was decided that Toby Hill and I should be counsel for the defence of our union policy, and visit all branches.

The hectic pace of the last five years had left us little time for visiting branches, all of which had been subject to a surfeit of lies from Fraser,

McLagan and Semple of the political wing, Walsh and Baxter of the industrial, plus the press for good measure. This, together with the activities of a handful of stool pigeons within our own ranks, no doubt led them to believe that considerable success had been achieved. Any illusions they may have held were soon shattered.

Too many in our ranks had grown up in the trade union movement. Too many were veterans of past strikes and lockouts. Too many, from long experience, were familiar with the foul smell of Labour fakers and union scabs.

Unlimited time was given at all stopwork meetings, with no limit on questions. It was an inspiring tour. Complete confidence was expressed in the national officers of the union and no confidence in McLagan.

Here are some of the resolutions that were carried:

> We reaffirm our confidence in our National Officers and view with the utmost concern the undemocratic action of the Minister of Labour in deposing the constitutionally elected representatives of our union on the Waterfront Industry Authority.
>
> *Port Chalmers*: carried unanimously.

> This branch condemns the action of the Minister of Labour in removing our officers from the Waterfront Industry Authority. We point out that our officers have at all times conducted themselves in the best interests of the Union. We resent the Minister's unwarranted interference in our Union affairs.
>
> On matters of secret ballots, we will determine when such are necessary. Our rules are democratic, our officers elected by democratic vote, therefore, we view the attack on them as an attack on the Union. We unhesitatingly reaffirm our complete confidence in our National President, Mr Barnes, our National Secretary, Mr Hill, and express our appreciation for the gains that have been obtained due to their untiring efforts on behalf of the membership.
>
> *Dunedin*: carried unanimously.

> This Branch expresses full confidence in our National President and National Secretary as Union representatives on the Waterfront Industry Authority and asks that the National Executive reply to the Minister of Labour to this effect. Further, we have full confidence in the policy of our National Union and its ability to fight as a trade union and resist all attacks from whatever source they come.
>
> *Auckland*: carried by an overwhelming majority, with only two dissentients.

> *Nelson* Branch unanimously reaffirms its loyalty to our National Executive and deprecates the attitude of the Minister of Labour in removing our representatives from the Waterfront Industry Authority.

> This Branch expresses a vote of thanks to the National Officers for their

addresses and has full confidence in them, the National Council and the National Executive. Further, we deplore the attitude of the Minister of Labour in his interference with the democratic rights of our Union.

Bluff: carried unanimously.

This Branch expresses its complete confidence in its National officers and the National Executive and condemns the action of Mr McLagan in dismissing its representatives from the Waterfront Authority.

Oamaru: carried unanimously.

That the *Lyttelton* Branch retains full confidence in our National officials and protests at the action of the Minister of Labour in removing Messrs Barnes and Hill from the Waterfront Industry Authority for carrying out their obligations in reporting back to the Union on decisions of the Authority.

Further, we again confirm the decision of our National Council that no member of our Union, whilst Amendment No 1 (1946) remains in force, will sit upon the Authority.

Carried unanimously.

That this Branch expresses full confidence in the National Executive and our Representatives on the Waterfront Industry Authority.

Picton: carried unanimously.

A vote of confidence was passed in Messrs H. Barnes and T. Hill and disgust at the actions of the Minister of Labour.

Wanganui: carried unanimously.

(1) That this Branch has no confidence in Mr McLagan, Minister of Labour. We strongly resent his interfering in the domestic rights of our members. At all times we claim the right to representatives of our own choice. We declare his attacks on our President, Mr Barnes, and our Secretary, Mr Hill, to be attacks on this right.

Recognising that Trade Unions that submit to domination and control by a Minister of State are no longer free Trade Unions, we reaffirm our confidence in the National Union and our National Leaders and pledge them full support.

(2) This Branch also calls on the Prime Minister to fulfil the assurances he gave the National Executive of our Union when overtime work was resumed and to cease condoning attacks on our Union.

Whangarei: carried unanimously.

(1) That we thank the National President and Vice President for their addresses and we continue to place our confidence in our National Officers and Executive and will abide by their decisions and instructions.

(2) That this Branch has no confidence in the Minister of Labour and calls upon the Prime Minister to implement his promise to our National Executive to arrange discussions in order to effect a settlement of matters in dispute.

Onehunga: carried unanimously.

Such were the feelings of our branches. Prior to our visits, McLagan had said that after our next elections the union would have different national officers. We had replied that that was debatable, but one thing was sure and that was that after the forthcoming general elections, New Zealand would have a new Minister of Labour!

Mention should also be made of a public meeting held in Christchurch. Arrangements had been made that, following the Lyttelton meeting, I should speak there. McLagan's being member for one of its electorates increased the significance.

The mayor, Mr E.H. Andrews, chaired the meeting, which was classed as one of the largest held in Christchurch since 1935. The Christchurch *Star-Sun* of 26 September reported the attendance at over 1000. A resolution stating that the union case was based on valid reasons and should not have been aggravated by actions of the Minister of Labour was carried, with only three or four dissenters.

The meeting was headlined as the main story on the *Star-Sun*'s local news page, and featured on the leader page of the *Christchurch Press*. North Island papers, however, could not spare a line. The result was complete vindication for the union and condemnation of McLagan. This latest rebuff for the minister, and in his own patch, called for immediate and increased action from his fifth-column chiefs—Walsh and Baxter.

In Walsh we had a fine opponent. This man, who had accumulated a string of union positions, being simultaneously president or secretary of the Fish Workers' Union, the Clerical Workers' Union, the Wellington Biscuit and Confectionery Workers' Union and the Seamen's Union, also owned several rural properties and was a wealthy man. Those who were now his friends were once his enemies, united by their support for Fraser and the Labour government. Baxter, the FOL secretary, for example, had commented in an illegal pamphlet published in 1940 that: 'This white livered autocrat, this shipowners' pimp, has access to the Police Gazette, and he picks his thugs accordingly. Provided they play ball they are guaranteed good jobs and nomination to official positions.' Similarly, Jim Roberts, as president of the New Zealand Labour Party, had said in 1937 that: 'Walsh is a supporter of the capitalist system . . . A three hundred pounds banquet would only be a flea bite to his bank account' (*Evening Post*, 27 February 1937). However, these scoundrels now closed ranks to defend Labour in its dying months in office.

Taking Action Over Safety, Again

Watersiders throughout New Zealand had shown in no uncertain manner that they were fed up to the back teeth with McLagan and Fraser. Nowhere was this more apparent than in Auckland, which for so long had been their

The Cold War Hots Up

primary target. A longstanding dispute was the discharging of bulk wheat. The high percentage of silica dust in Australian wheat was a very real menace to health, and our enquiries from Canadian and United States sources elicited information of a most alarming nature. There had been explosions of wheat dust, particularly in silos, with heavy casualties, and it was an ever-present danger, rendered even more so by the antiquated method of discharging in New Zealand ports.

Once again, it was necessary for our union to draw the attention of authorities to another very real danger, not only to watersiders, but also the general public. The issue was first raised with the Auckland branch of the Waterfront Industry Commission in February 1947 when we were advised that it would be dealt with by the commission and, if any extra payment were allowed, it would be retrospective. For nearly three years, while awaiting this promised decision, ships carrying bulk wheat had been worked. In October, however, with the arrival of the *Glenpark* with another shipment, that patience was finally exhausted. An ultimatum was given to the Union Steam Ship Company that the *Glenpark* would not be worked until a settlement was reached of this outstanding claim. The response was immediate. An extra 1/6 an hour was awarded, retrospective to February 1947. Like the press, McLagan and his stooges maintained a discreet silence.

Back on the Attack over Wages

We now had to return to the issue of the pay increase. We had called off our overtime ban on the basis of Fraser's promise that immediate discussions on longstanding grievances would immediately take place. This promise was not honoured, and there was no indication that it ever would be. We had tacitly accepted the situation but now decided to take action. An ongoing sore on the waterfront was the shipowners' habit of engaging men late in the afternoon to work overtime. They simply refused to employ enough men on a permanent basis through the Bureau system, despite our continuous requests to do so, the idea being to restrict union membership to the lowest possible level and, at the same time, create a potential reserve of scab labour. Now we too decided that no leeway was to be given. Two hundred of our men walked off the job at 5pm, as was their entitlement. The shipowners now put out a call for non-union men to replace our members who had walked off. However, due to the excellent and close relations we maintained with non-union men, these efforts to recruit them were a dismal failure. I told the shipowners that they would have to obey the terms of the Commission's Order and engage all labour at the correct times.

The employers then elected to stop all work in the port at 5pm and from undisclosed sources they also recruited a mere handful of non-union men. When our men refused to work with them they were put on penalty. This was pure hypocrisy: when the shipowners openly flouted the Commission's Orders concerning manning practices no action was taken, but when our men refused to work with illegally engaged scabs they were penalised.

All work in the port was rapidly shutting down, but we waited in vain for press comment on the cause. Even the imaginative powers of both the Auckland dailies could not conjure a case against the union.

The question of non-union labour was almost wholly an Auckland one, as the situation in Wellington had been resolved by a Waterfront Commission ruling that only casual replacements, but not full gangs, could be engaged after 10am. In Auckland the question was one for the Waterfront Authority, from which Toby Hill and I had been sacked, and in no way was it the concern of the Waterfront Commission. But with the general election looming, and with neither employers nor commission having the semblance of a case, McLagan had to concede. We were permitted to enrol more men and the need for extensive overtime was thereby lessened.

Electoral Defeat for Fraser Government

This was McLagan's final stand, however, for in November he lost his job when the Fraser government was voted out of office. This had become inevitable, for the government had defeated itself. To an ever-increasing degree, the passing years had witnessed the jettisoning of fundamental principles of the Labour movement. Scab unions, peacetime conscription, union bashing—Labour had usurped the role of the Tories.

And all that talk of a new order: ever-increasing profits for the privileged few and worsening living standards for the many. Workers everywhere found falling purchasing power, coupled with slanderous attacks from their alleged representatives, just too much to stomach. In attacking Roy Stanley, the government had attacked the rank and file of the Carpenters' Union. In attacking Jock Barnes and Toby Hill, they had attacked 7000 waterside workers. And of still greater moment, they had attacked their wives and families and those of *bona fide* unionists everywhere.

With very few exceptions—Frank Langstone was one—we witnessed the defeat of a few bureaucratic despots whose souls had been stripped of conscience. The rest were the usual collection of no-hopers and party hacks. Frank campaigned against peacetime conscription, divorced himself from the party machine, and became Independent Labour. However, he too lost his seat in the massive swing to Sid Holland and his National Party cronies, who were voted into office for what was to become nearly a quarter of a century of almost uninterrupted Tory rule.

We had no illusions that our struggle would be any less with Holland

and his gang. However, they did not need to build a union-bashing platform from scratch, as McLagan and Fraser had already built it for them, and Walsh and Baxter were still available. Overnight, McLagan's minions became Holland's hoods.

The WWU biennial conference was held a week after Labour's defeat. Thirty-eight delegates from the various ports attended, together with Jack Lonergan and Jim Healy, president and secretary of the Australian Waterside Workers' Federation. For the first time, conference voted not to seat one particular delegate, from Timaru. This port was the only branch in our national union that responded to McLagan's call to defy national union policy in July regarding our overtime ban. For some time it had been a fertile breeding ground for termites and its delegate was high on the list of McLagan's stool pigeons. A resolution was successfully moved that he be suspended from conference.

In nominations for national president and secretary I had two opponents, as did Toby Hill. That Labour Party political scheming was paramount in this was beyond all doubt, but the defeat of the Labour government effectively destroyed any plans that may have been hatched. Our opponents withdrew and Hill and I were returned unopposed. One of my scheduled opponents, Noel Donaldson, showed his true colours when he was quick to scab on the Auckland waterfront in '51, an action that was followed by members of Timaru branch. At this conference I also became a full-time national official for the first time and consequently resigned the branch presidency in Auckland. This position was subsequently won by Alec Drennan in April the following year.

The national officers' reports were adopted unanimously, as were all actions and decisions of the national executive. Retiring vice-president Alec Drennan presented a comprehensive and outstanding report which, in its turn, was also unanimously endorsed.

McLagan had stated that, after the elections, our union would have a change of both president and secretary. In this direction, all his machinations and those of his stool pigeons had been a disaster. However, with Holland now in power, delegates left for their home ports with no illusions about the struggle that lay ahead.

7 THE RUN-UP TO THE '51 LOCKOUT, 1950

The new decade brought new attacks. Not from government or shipowners this time but from the national executive of the Federation of Labour. On 19 January 1950 our union received a letter from the national executive that signalled the start of the biggest showdown in New Zealand union affairs since the destruction of the Red Federation of Labour in 1913. The executive demanded that we apologise for what they called the 'insulting, abusive and disruptive letter' that we had sent nine months earlier in which we accused them of being 'agents of the employing class' for their actions during the Carpenters' Union deregistration. This had been drafted by the Auckland branch, endorsed nationally and forwarded to Baxter on 17 March 1949. The FOL executive also insisted that we disaffiliate from the maritime section of the World Federation of Trade Unions, the Moscow-aligned international union body, or face expulsion on both these counts.

After full consideration of the letter we felt that, far from being 'insulting, abusive and disruptive', it was too mild given the enormity of the sell-out of Baxter and his national executive over the carpenters. The FOL executive had usurped power it did not possess, ignored its national council decision, and actively scabbed on the union. As for the WFTU, this demand was rank hypocrisy. The Miners' Union was affiliated to the Australian Miners' Federation, which was in turn affiliated to the Miners' Trade section of the WFTU. Walsh and Baxter appeared to have no concern about this. Further, the Australian Waterside Workers' Federation was also a member of the WFTU. The decision to affiliate had been taken unanimously at our 1949 conference after strong dissatisfaction with the operations of the International Transport Workers' Federation. This organisation was chiefly concerned with the interests of road transport but more important was the fact that even when it took an interest it had been of no help. This peak body certainly never helped the Canadian seamen and, furthermore, it was allied with the International Confederation of Free Trade Unions, Washington's Cold War union alliance. This federation was a hollow shell, dominated by the US. Many of its affiliates were small, extremely right-wing or completely unrepresentative of the labour movement of their own countries. Furthermore, it had shown no interest in the growing anti-colonial struggles, for in many cases demands for independence by countries such as Cyprus threatened US or British Cold War interests. By contrast, the overwhelming mass of seamen, waterside workers, dockers and longshoremen of the world were affiliated to the maritime section of the WFTU.

In response to the executive's ultimatum we fired off a reply on 17 March which condemned Walsh and Baxter in no uncertain terms. Unionists around the country rallied to our defence. The president of the Auckland Hotel, Restaurant, Hospital Workers' and Related Trades Association, I.M. Wilson, declared:

> To expel the Waterside Workers' Union from the Federation is, in my opinion a grave act, and will have a detrimental effect on the whole trades union movement in New Zealand . . .
>
> The reason for the expulsion, as I see it, should be made known to the public—that Mr H. Barnes, president of the Waterside Workers' Union, has been approached by a number of unions to accept nomination as president of the Federation of Labour. He is a hot favourite, and attempts have been made to nobble a favourite the night before the race.
>
> As a trades unionist of 26 years standing in New Zealand I say it is the duty of every member to resist, through his organisation, this further attempt by a small group to destroy the fabric of the whole Labour and trades union movement.

Similar sentiments were expressed by the majority of trades councils, which continued to admit delegates from our union. In particular, Canterbury and Otago voiced exceedingly strong criticism of Walsh, Baxter and their executive, with the Belfast branch of the Canterbury Freezing and Related Trades Union unanimously calling on its national association to suspend affiliation to the FOL.

Such resolutions of support for our union caused Walsh and Baxter to think again. They now submitted a very different proposal to the 17 February meeting of the FOL national council, as follows:

> This National Council urges the New Zealand Waterside Workers' Union to withdraw its letter to the National Executive of the FOL and apologise for it; the matter of the affiliation of the Union to the Maritime Section of the World Federation of Trade Unions to be referred to the annual conference for decision whether an organisation can affiliate or not with any organisation from which conference has decided to disaffiliate.

This was something of a backdown, but even though they won the endorsement of the council by 13 votes to 11 after an all-day debate, we won the moral victory. Seven of the 13 votes were from president, vice-president, secretary and four members of the national executive, which meant that the trades councils of New Zealand had rejected their motion by 11:6. Eleven of the trades councils were not even prepared to 'urge' our union to reconsider our letter. In effect, they endorsed it.

Not content with the rebuff administered by their national council, the Walsh machine then directed all efforts at organising for the forthcoming national conference. The first step was to issue to all affiliated unions a three-page circular that was a gem of deceit, misrepresentation and deliberate lies. The opening contents were as follows:

> A threat to the unity and strength of the New Zealand Federation of Labour, indeed to our whole Trade Union movement, had been developing during recent years.
>
> In mid-1948 for instance, during a lengthy stoppage on the Auckland waterfront, an abusive attack upon the officials of the Federation and upon our Labour Government was launched by individuals in the Watersiders' National Council, in spite of the fact that by direct negotiations with the Government the Federation obtained a satisfactory settlement of the dispute. On this occasion the Federation Executive was content to ask for an apology for the abuse heaped on its officials, and when this apology was denied, took no further action.
>
> In early 1949 during a dispute in the building trade in Auckland, the Auckland Branch of the Watersiders' Union passed a resolution which was conveyed in a letter to the Federation Executive. This letter accused the Federation's Executive, elected as your representatives by the 1948 Annual Conference, of a 'betrayal of the affiliated members' and of acting as 'agents of the employing class'. Your Executive very naturally took strong exception to this and again asked for an apology and the withdrawal of the letter. Once more this was denied.
>
> At the 1949 Annual Conference therefore, representatives of every union in the country, after hearing Mr Barnes speak for an hour and a half in defence of his Executive's action, will recollect that he said he would recommend his Union to withdraw the letter, agreed to leave the matter in abeyance. This undertaking has never been honoured, and the Secretary of the New Zealand Waterside Workers' Union (Mr T. Hill) has advised the Federation that the letter will not be withdrawn, and the charges stand.
>
> The New Zealand Waterside Workers' Union also in December 1949, in direct defiance of a decision of the 1949 Annual Conference, broke from the agreed policy of our New Zealand Trade Union movement as decided in Annual Conference, and affiliated with the Communist World Federation of Trade Unions.

This was a complete farrago of lies, and the continuing gall of Walsh and Baxter was incredible. The first section referring to mid-1948 concerned the *Mountpark*. That case has already been covered. Despite the treachery of Walsh and Co, our union won a resounding victory in the Auckland Supreme Court before the Chief Justice, Sir Humphrey O'Leary. One would have thought that on this they would have been only too anxious to bury for all time the record of their infamy. But no, they claim to have been responsible for a satisfactory settlement. This was the very acme of hypocrisy.

The second section was also a deliberate lie. I made the union position crystal clear. Our union, contrary to a widespread belief, was no one-man band. Its democracy was its strength. The comment concerning the carpenters' dispute was the expression of 2200 Auckland watersiders. I said that I would ask them to reconsider it but in no way was I competent to make a recommendation, nor would I. The members of the Auckland branch reconsidered it and their decision was that it was far too mild and in no way expressed their contempt. To say I did not honour my promise was just another of their insidious calumnies. On the affiliation to the WFTU, the Walsh clique again defied the national council, which had decided that the question should be resolved at the forthcoming conference.

Their diatribe of falsities concluded with this epic:

> Your Executive and your National Council have therefore with patience, tolerance and moderation endeavoured to maintain the unity of our movement in the face of spiteful, abusive personal attacks. They pledge themselves to continue to sink their personal feelings in the prolonged effort to obtain a workable healthy and happy relationship with our fellows on the waterfront and their elected officials.

This would have caused Dr Goebbels to blush. The 11 national council members who voted against them did not relish being bracketed as fellow shysters. A major stoush at the forthcoming FOL conference was clearly on the cards. The March 1950 issue of the *Transport Worker* published an article in which I spelled out the problem that we faced in the bluntest terms:

> Our affiliation [with the WFTU] is now the subject of an attack on us by the National Executive of the FOL. Well, let us be realistic.
>
> I challenge anyone to name one dispute in the last few years where the National Executive of the FOL has lined up on behalf of the workers. Take them all:
> Freezing workers,
> Gas workers,
> Drivers,
> Railway workers,
> Dairy workers,
> Waikato miners,
> Carpenters,
> Waterside workers,
> Mangakino workers,
> Canadian seamen.

True, in some they have given nominal support. In the carpenters' dispute of last year they became ultra militant. They appealed to all affiliations to give full moral and financial support to Auckland carpenters. And they then tried to assassinate any union that responded to their appeal.

Through our affiliation fees we have purchased for them bludgeons with which to attack us. Let this tragic nonsense cease.

The FOL today is comprised largely of products of compulsory unionism. If compulsory unionism was abolished half of them would fade away over night.

If you sleep with pigs, you too will stink. The issue is crystal clear. Either the Federation of Labour is cleansed or else no self-respecting trade union can any longer be associated with it.

Without a few unions such as ours they would have no significance. By continuing to function as part of a reactionary machine we and all other unionists who are prepared to accept the present position are playing a reactionary role.

One of the oldest lessons of history is that what the boss class cannot prevent it endeavours to control. The present National Executive of the FOL is not and never has been of value to us. They are shackles on our ankles.

Our international affiliation is of real value to us. It was a unanimous decision of our Conference. We will continue with it.

Back on the Waterfront

Apart from the scheming of Walsh and his followers, we also had to deal with domestic issues on the waterfront. At Whangarei, a dispute had been simmering for some months over cement cargoes. The Waterfront Commission had given its decision in favour of the Whangarei branch but this was not accepted by the employers, who then appealed to the Waterfront Industry Authority. Since Hill and I had been sacked, this now consisted of Dalglish, Belford and Marchington. Whangarei watersiders were not prepared to accept rulings from this entirely boss-oriented body, nor were they going to accept employers appealing to their own representatives. They resolved to discharge no more coal or gypsum at Portland, thereby effectively stopping production of cement.

Prior to their doing this, however, a meeting had been held with Bill Sullivan, the new Minister of Labour. At this we advised him that until amendment No. 1 of the Waterfront Industry Regulations was repealed, which stated that the minister could reject any decision of the authority at any time, no union representative would sit on that body. We would not be a party to an allegedly independent judicial body whose decisions could be overturned at the whim of the Minister of Labour. With no McLagan to endorse their every attack and Sullivan still feeling his way, the employers were compelled by Sullivan to accept the Whangarei decision. Once again,

Bill Sullivan, National Party Minister of Labour, 1949–57
(News Media: *Auckland Star* collection)

it was demonstrated that direct action was the only way to stop shipowners' attacks.

Early in March, another dispute reminiscent of the *Mountpark* arose in Auckland. The hatches on the ship concerned, SS *Defoe*, were of a type not previously seen in New Zealand. They were of steel, with the beam having flanges on which hatches had to be placed by sliding along over an open hold. With very little room for men to manoeuvre, they constituted a real risk at any time but a still larger one at night. The Auckland branch executive, after meeting with the usual employers' reaction, ruled that no work would be performed after hatches had been fitted at 5pm.

The *Defoe* moved on to Wellington to complete discharge. A similar attitude was adopted by the Wellington branch, where men ceased work at 5pm and were then sacked. Not satisfied with flagrantly disregarding the decision of Sir Humphrey O'Leary relating to the *Mountpark*, the employers then followed their customary tactics and endeavoured to have the *Defoe* declared a preference ship.

Sullivan ordered a conference of the parties. Present were union representatives, two from the Marine Department, and Bockett from the Waterfront Commission.

As was to be expected, the Marine Department had ruled that the hatches were safe to handle at any time, day or night. Bockett, of course, agreed. It was made abundantly clear by us, however, that on questions of safety, our union would under no circumstances depart from the *Mountpark* verdict and that at all times our members would be the final arbiters on questions of safety. Sullivan referred it back to Bockett, who then upheld the union stand. That Wellington, not Auckland, was the port involved, allied with the fact that Sullivan was still new to the job, was undoubtedly the underlying reason the shipowners gave in.

At about the same time another dispute erupted in Lyttelton. It concerned the SS *Leverbank* and one of the most obnoxious cargoes known—lampblack. Previous disputes on the handling of this particularly filthy freight had been settled in a reasonable manner, with employers recognising the need for some protective clothing.

On this occasion the employers refused to supply overalls, gloves and boots and the Lyttelton men refused to work. With the Waterfront Authority still suspended, the usual role of declaring the *Leverbank* a preference ship was not pursued. Toby Hill and I argued the case before the Waterfront Commission at Lyttelton, while the *Leverbank* was not worked. Employers' representatives, apart from saying 'no' to our claims, were devoid of argument.

They were aware, as were we, that stoppages over lampblack had occurred in ports throughout the world. After a lengthy dispute in the port of Melbourne, the matter had been referred to analysts for a report. The analysts' report stated that they had received some specimens of clothing contaminated by carbon black during unloading operations of less than two hours. Each article had already been laundered. Their report concluded that 'the contamination of clothing by carbon black is an abnormal one and calls for special consideration or compensation'. This report concerned clothing that had been exposed to lampblack contamination for a mere two hours. Consider the effect on clothing when exposed for 11 hours a day. And the effect on human bodies, as might be expected, was never subjected to expert analysis but was known only too well to our members. It was incredible that it continued to be shipped in paper bags, often broken, instead of sealed containers. Without political interference from the Minister of Labour, however, we obtained a reasonable settlement at the Lyttelton Commission. Belford was his usual dogmatic self, but without Dalglish, Marchington and McLagan, he found the lack of the usual automatic majority of the Waterfront Authority somewhat disconcerting.

The outcome was that shipowners were required to provide boiler-suits, gloves and boot covers. Washing time of 10 minutes at one-hour meal breaks and 30 minutes at the end of the working day was allowed, with employers to provide soap and towels. Pursuing their customary short-sighted attitude, however, shipowners made no attempt to provide suitable containers for this dirty cargo.

The Break from the FOL

Came 18 April 1950 and with it the annual FOL conference. When Walsh and Baxter spoke of decisions by a democratic vote of conference delegates representing the workers of New Zealand, it was typical of their hypocrisy. The card system of voting in force could not have been more undemocratic and was only possible because of compulsory unionism. In its annual report for 1950 the FOL executive reported the following among its affiliates:

Greymouth Laundry Workers	16 members
Green Island Iron Rolling Workers	29 members
Kaitangata Deputies and Underviewers	7 members
Taranaki Picture Projectionists	12 members
Cable and Wireless Employees	30 members
Oamaru Grocers	30 members
Dunedin Transport Officials	25 members
Gisborne Gas Workers	24 members
Otago Paint and Varnish Workers	26 members
Wellington Sports Goods Workers	25 members
Auckland Hatters	60 members
Auckland Coopers	39 members
Wellington Fishworkers	25 members
Dunedin Waxworkers	36 members

Each of these tadpole unions had one vote. With a total membership of 384, they carried 14 votes, five more than the waterside union with its 9000 members. Not just our union, but also the freezing workers, the miners and the drivers were all woefully under-represented, to the benefit of the unions that relied entirely on compulsory membership to make up their ranks. Compulsory unionism also meant that Walsh's clerical union had 16,000 members rather than the 1600 that it would have had without conscription. With few exceptions, the membership of such products had not the vaguest idea of the birth and struggles of the trade union movement. If they had any at all, it was coloured by the columns of their daily papers.

Their union ticket was an annual licence to work which, more properly, should have been purchased at any post office. In most cases their office seat-warmers, masquerading as workers' representatives, did not even collect their subscriptions. These were collected by the boss and guaranteed by government. With most of these conscripts, unionism was a dirty word. Years of propaganda had conditioned them to regard militant workers as denizens of a lower social order, with a collar and tie the badge of a superior race.

At the conference itself all 34 of the tadpole unions were represented—salon hostesses and all—by one of Walsh's dupes, who exercised 34 votes.

Conference opened in the morning with Croskery, Walsh, Baxter and their four executive members on the platform. After formal proceedings the executive moved the suspension of standing orders to allow the watersiders' case to come up. On this being carried, the executive demanded that we withdraw our letter on the carpenters' lockout by 31 May. We rejected this ultimatum and called for a decision by conference. In this we were supported by other unions, which demanded that conference and not the executive should decide. We were defeated in this, however, and the executive's motion was passed.

During the luncheon adjournment we held a meeting with supportive unions. Walsh had made it clear that after 31 May he intended to have our expulsion carried out by his executive. Under the voting system operating, any motion his gang moved would automatically be carried, but it was already abundantly clear that a resolution by conference to expel our union would be followed by an exodus of others.

If expulsion were carried out by the national executive after conference delegates had dispersed, it had a far greater chance of isolating the Waterside Workers' Union. It was agreed that, on return, I would force the issue and move the expulsion of our union. This was the only way of getting a conference vote. We would not then be isolated and a walkout would follow.

It was appreciated by all that the issue had ceased to be one for the New Zealand Waterside Workers' Union alone. It was now a question of any *bona fide* trade union docilely walking into Walsh's industrial gas oven or fighting back.

I attempted to move the resolution, but was barred from doing so by Croskery. A motion that the morning's motion by recommitted was lost and I then told the conference that 31 May had arrived. The walkout followed and the resistance movement was born. Delegates representing 80,000 industrial workers walked out with us.

A meeting the following morning was attended by still more delegates who had decided to vote with their feet and left the FOL conference. After very full discussion, a programme of workers' rights was adopted and a delegation consisting of Messrs Fred Young, Sid Giles and John Roberts elected to present it to the FOL conference in an endeavour to get one united and genuine trade union movement. Walsh promised a reply by 2pm. None came. It was then decided to form the New Zealand Trade Union Congress and the following officers were elected:

Chairman	Fred Young	New Zealand Hotel Workers
Vice-chairman	John Roberts	Canterbury Clothing Workers

Secretary	Percy Hanson	New Zealand Tramways Union
Committee	A. Melville & F. Muller	New Zealand Drivers
	H. Kay & T. Potter	New Zealand Labourers
	S. Giles & H. Kilpatrick	New Zealand Freezing Workers
	H. Barnes	New Zealand Watersiders
	W. Richards	New Zealand Tramways
	F. Langley	New Zealand Carpenters

The above facts were fairly reported in the Wellington *Dominion* of 19 April, and the *Evening Post* of 20 April also said quite correctly that:

> Although many have gained the impression that the watersiders were the dominant force in the new organisation, this is not so. The union certainly supplied the motive which precipitated the break, but it is sure that many unions were only waiting for an excuse for a showdown.

Our union was not one dominated by one or two men, and the revolt against Walsh and his gang was not ours alone. Not only had the move to isolate our union been a dismal failure, but we were now united with fellow workers—not conscripts, but unionists with a background of struggle and solidarity. We were in a position to resist and we would.

Business as Usual

Work was proceeding normally in the port of Auckland but there was an acute shortage of berths to handle the increasing traffic. Many ships were anchored in the stream and there was wholesale congestion in wharf sheds. Cargo delays placed many of our habitual detractors in an invidious position. Faced with a situation in which watersiders could not be used as whipping-boys, they had to face the truth. A most unpleasant predicament. With so many of its friends suffering financial losses, the *Herald* had no option but to present a factual report. 'More Port Berths Needed Urgently' was the heading for a two-column article. A committee representing the affected interests met with the Auckland Harbour Board and reached full accord in concluding that lack of sufficient berths and port facilities was the reason for the congestion. However, from this point unity ceased, with everybody blaming everybody but waterside workers for the crisis. Truly a case of when rogues fall out, honest men come into their own.

On 17 April we received a conciliatory letter from the Minister of Labour advising that, following representations from our national executive, the government had agreed to reconstitute the Waterfront Industry Authority on the same basis as formerly. It also agreed to revoke Waterfront Authority Emergency Regulations Amendment No. 1, which gave the Minister of Labour power to overrule the authority.

In the elections for union representatives on the Authority, Toby Hill and I decided not to stand and Archie Dellaway from Wellington and Jack Flood from Lyttelton were elected instead. However, with Dalglish still chairman and Marchington and Belford shipowners' nominees, the meanest of bookmakers would have laid 100 to one against its longevity.

In late April a dispute arose on the freighter *King Neptune*, under charter to the New Zealand Shipping Company and carrying a cargo of cement. Our contract of employment provided for 15 men in a crane gang, six men below, one hatchman and eight on the wharf. With no discussion and flagrant disregard for their contractual obligations, the company reduced the wharf gangs from eight men to four. An appeal was made to the Waterfront Commission, which endorsed this barefaced violation. Here was a classic example. Our union followed every constitutional procedure, while employers, who had broken the terms of a longstanding contract, were upheld by the commission.

Work ceased on the *King Neptune*. That it was not declared the usual preference ship can only have been because, excepting the New Zealand Shipping Company, this piece of banditry was too strong even for the employers to stomach.

Minister of Labour Bill Sullivan was in Auckland investigating waterfront facilities, and after the *King Neptune* had been idle for seven days he appointed a special disputes committee. Dalglish was chairman, with Tom Marchington representing the employers and Toby Hill for the union. I presented the union case and Captain Holm the employers'.

We got the usual: Dalglish and Marchington against Toby. A two to one decision endorsing the company's open and shut breach of contract. After this one, the meanest of bookmakers would have upped his odds to a 1000 to one.

Anxious to demonstrate their fealty to both shipowners and their new political masters, Dalglish and Co had by now completely abandoned any pretence at being either independent or judicial.

Lampblack Again

After the settlement of the lampblack dispute in Lyttelton, nobody would have envisaged any responsible body provoking another one on the same issue. However, the arrival in Wellington of the *Myrtlebank* in June 1950 proved us wrong. In view of the particularly filthy state of its cargo, even for lampblack, we claimed an additional penalty rate, which was provided for by clause 6 of the Commission's Order. However, acting on orders from Waterfront Commission chairman A.E. Bockett, the Wellington port controller refused any extra payment. Our members stopped work in protest.

Without hearing one word from our union and without inspecting the job, Dalglish then bowed to the employers' request and declared the

Myrtlebank a preference ship, in effect locking out the entire membership of the union. Our request to confine the dispute to the *Myrtlebank* was refused. They were determined to starve us back.

We had had a gutful. All work ceased on the Wellington waterfront and pickets were mounted. Our national executive was summoned and Sullivan convened a meeting with us on 20 June. Here it was clearly revealed that Bockett had been behind the denial of our legitimate request. Sullivan was decisively told that if the commission were to declare another ship in any port a preference ship with a view to locking out our members, national action would follow. Faced with this threat, Bockett and his commission decided to back off and inspected the job. Clause 6 was duly invoked and an award of an extra 2/6 an hour was then made, plus an allowance of 10/- for damage to clothing. An assurance was also given that efforts would be made to have this filthy and obnoxious cargo packed in proper containers. In further violation of the Lyttelton agreement, employers had also refused to supply towels and soap. This too was remedied. It was now up to the Waterfront Authority to endorse or amend this agreement.

At the subsequent hearing, evidence was given by port controller Captain Vandenberg and assistant controller Harding, who both attested to the noxious state of the cargo. Captain Vandenberg stated that men came off the job and, after stripping, were as black as negroes. He did not think it was possible for men to get into such a state. Mr Harding stated that even the men's underclothing would be of very little use after working with lampblack. These were the people who were instructed by Bockett to give nothing by way of compensation to men working in such dreadful conditions. In the end the Waterfront Authority determined that protective clothing was to be supplied and 15 minutes allowed for washing before every break.

While the hearing had justified our stand, this did not stop the press going on the attack. On 20 June the *Herald*'s lengthy leading article abused waterside workers as part of a complete misrepresentation of the facts, and its leader of 21 June was headed 'Waterfront Surrender'. This was its stock role. When the final settlement revealed that the union was 100 per cent justified in its stand and Bockett was 100 per cent wrong, unable to refute our case by logical argument, it reverted to its time-honoured policy of preaching class warfare. In this respect it left any communist production for dead!

All daily papers were united in condemning any action taken by workers in an endeavour to obtain some semblance of natural justice. We were in the forefront of that condemnation. Wellington's *Dominion*, for example, started its leader of 22 June as follows:

The public will not, we think, begrudge the waterside workers the extra payment they have extracted from the Waterfront Industry Commission, as the price to complete the unloading of a particularly dirty cargo from the *Myrtlebank*. We are of the opinion also that the Port Committee and then the commission erred in the first instance in refusing the men's demands for the additional 2/6 which had been awarded as a result of the commission's 'reconsideration' of the case. But the fact that the Waterside Workers' Union was able to present a strong case and got what it wanted is an issue of secondary importance. The crucial point is the means by which the watersiders gained their objective.

Jock Barnes (back), Toby Hill, Eddie Napier (centre), Jim Napier, Tommy Wells (front) (Jock Barnes)

Fair comment initially and in marked contrast to the *Herald*. But it then proceeded to criticise the way we obtained that settlement. As with the rest of our critics, it could suggest no other way short of the usual nonsense of 'ample means being readily available for the settlement of industrial disputes' etc. When these procedures had been followed and the result was gross violation by commission and shipowners, we had one course open and one only—acquiesce or resist. Our policy was to resist and so it would continue to be. If in resisting we sustained casualties, the master class would sustain them too. For all workers, the formula is the same and very simple—fight back. There will be temporary setbacks, but no workers' fight is ever lost. But when workers quietly submit to injustice, all hope can be abandoned.

The Authority Hears Our Wage Claim

On 27 June 1950 our case for a substantial wage increase was finally heard by the Waterfront Authority. The claim was now for a two shilling rise, from 4/-, to 6/- per hour, retrospective from 1 June 1949, the increased claim being justified on the following basis:

1. A major decline in the wages share of national income, from 55 per cent in 1938–39 to 47 per cent in 1947–48, with wages increasing by 103 per cent, other personal income by 144 per cent and company income by a massive 151 per cent.
2. A significant increase in the tax burden, both direct and indirect, imposed on workers' wages in the same period.
3. To adjust wages to the level offered by employers back in 1938 but which was overridden by the Waterfront Commission in 1940.
4. To restore relativity with the wages of other New Zealand workers who were consistently paid over-award wages.
5. To restore relativities with Australian waterside workers, whose margin over our wages had increased from 1d or 2d per hour in 1938 to 1/5 by 1950.
6. To allow wharfies to sustain a decent standard of living without being reliant on overtime pay, penalty rates and bonuses.
7. To take account of increased skills required for the job, in line with an Australian precedent.
8. To compensate for the devaluation of the New Zealand pound and the recent withdrawal of subsidies.
9. To restore industrial equity within the maritime industry, in the light of massive profits being made by shipowners.

The employers' advocate at the Waterfront Authority was Captain Holm. Here was a classical case of the old boys' network looking after its own. When you know beforehand that the bout is a fix, you don't have to worry about the capabilities of your boy. Holm filled the required criteria admirably. If he had any ability as an advocate he was successful in concealing it. He was a master mariner whose word at sea was law and could not be questioned. He was therefore quite incompetent at the job he now faced.

After a series of attempts at cross-examination, the farce was over. And yet it was one in which we had to participate. For so long we had been faced with press propaganda about overpaid wharfies. And now that we had put up a comprehensive case justifying an increase, one would have expected headlines and editorials ripping our case to pieces. That they did not appear and that our case received so little publicity would be the biggest tribute that could be paid to the validity and justice of our claims. However, validity and justice never worried the minds of Judge Dalglish and the employers' representatives Belford and Marchington. They were the Waterfront Industry Authority. With all due respect to our two members, they might as well have been out fishing. Their presence was only perpetuating the farce.

A feature of our hearing was the attitude of the officer and gentleman T.A. Marchington. The only visible qualification for that title was the plum in the mouth. Following the visit to New Zealand and Australia of American and British shipping combines, we saw the same pattern being developed in both countries. The storm clouds of '51 were starting to appear. Any veneer of fairness the ex-lieutenant commander may have shown had gone. It was back to the best traditions of the navy—100 lashes and then hang them from the yardarm.

The following exchange on our margin for skill was reported in the September issue of the *Transport Worker*:

> The congratulations received by the Auckland Branch from Commodore Jupp, US Navy, for the efficient handling of military supplies during the war were referred to by Jock Barnes during the course of the margin for skill case.

The union had supplied all the personnel and completely supervised this major undertaking, he said. Of course part of the efficiency was due to the fact that we were free from professional troublemakers employed by the shipping companies.

> Marchington: Would you like to name one of these troublemakers?
> Barnes: No. I was just making a general reference.
> Marchington: So you are not prepared to name one.
> Barnes: No. I didn't name any, but if the cap fits wear it.

While Judge Dalglish admitted that experience, knowledge and skill were required for the job, the decision was the usual. In an endeavour to create the illusion that he was considering submissions Dalglish delayed his verdict for a few days. On 4 July he announced an increase of 3d per hour. In his typical long-winded and vacuous style, any valid rebuttal of our claims was conspicuous by its absence. Not a line on shipowners' profits, financial position or ability to pay. That the 3d per hour had been agreed upon before the hearing is a certainty. After the depth and strength of our case the iniquity of it surprised even the press. Comment was minimal. We protested, even staging a one-day protest strike, and our branch resolved thenceforth to use direct negotiations with the shipowners for all future wage demands.

The Rangitoto Dispute

With Marchington now usurping Belford's job as hatchet-man No. 1, more trouble was inevitable. Waterside workers, in common with all others, had the legal right to morning and afternoon tea breaks. To provide for continuity of work, the Commission's Order required the employment of relievers.

On Monday 24 July two men at No. 1 hatch on the *Rangitoto*, owned by Marchington's New Zealand Shipping Company, asked to be relieved so they could have their morning tea. Hamblyn, shipping company foreman, refused and said he would sack them if they went. More barefaced provocation would be hard to imagine.

The two exercised their legal right and on their return were sacked. In Hamblyn, Marchington had a good understudy with the necessary qualifications of old school tie and plum in the mouth.

Needless to say, while the men were having their tea break and Hamblyn refused to supply relievers, the rest of the gang refused to work shorthanded.

Auckland branch president Alec Drennan then intervened and the company agreed there would be no docking of wages.

The following morning Hamblyn dishonoured this agreement. Work at No. 1 hatch then stopped. Captain Stanich, port controller, decided to call a port committee meeting to resolve the situation. Alec and Johnny Mitchell attended for the union. Both had too much experience in the trade union movement, and too much ability, to be hoodwinked by either Captain Stanich or the shipowners.

Recognising that they had not the slightest vestige of a case, the New Zealand Shipping Company representatives made no attempt to justify their action. Relievers would be supplied. On wages, Stanich ruled that men would be paid for the tea break, but no more. Being left with no alternative but to concede that the men had been wrongfully dismissed, Stanich was then reminded that the question of payment under such circumstances had been determined by the Chief Justice in the *Mountpark* case, in which the judge determined that men who had been wrongfully dismissed were entitled to full monetary recompense. However, this meant nothing to the man, who refused to review his decision. At 1pm Drennan advised Mr Downie, New Zealand Shipping Company superintendent, that the union was viewing the matter with concern and demanded payment for the gang because of the company's violation of the Commission's Order regarding relief breaks. Downie replied that the port committee had made its decision and that was the end of the matter.

At 3pm, aboard the *Rangitoto*, Drennan again met Downie and told him that unless the men got what was rightfully theirs, there would be reprisals. Furthermore, the union would be justified in asking for the removal of Hamblyn. Hamblyn flew into a rage and butted Alec in the face. The old Liverpool kiss! If a watersider had committed such an offence, it would have meant immediate suspension, followed by a prosecution for assault. Downie's response was to sack the gang at No. 1 hatch.

At 4.45pm in the Labour Bureau, Alec disputed a requisition for a new gang at 8am in the morning and the penalising of the original gang for three days. Port committee rules were that this should then be held in abeyance pending a meeting of the committee. This was not done.

At 5.30pm Drennan advised Stanich of this request. Stanich did nothing. On 26 and 27 July men refused to lift discs to work on the *Rangitoto*. Over time first 25, then 50, then 200 were suspended and placed on penalty. At all times the Auckland branch acted in accordance with the provisions of the Commission's Order and with established procedure. By contrast, both the Waterfront Commission and the New Zealand Shipping Company treated and continued to treat these provisions with utter contempt.

Once again, it had been shown that if justice were to be obtained, and if we were not to become abject slaves of the shipping combines and their enforcing agencies, the commission and the Waterfront Authority, we had but one recourse. A stopwork meeting was called for 1pm on the following day, at which the following claims were unanimously approved:

1. Full payment for all workers of No. 1 gang on the *Rangitoto* until 9pm July 25.
2. Disciplinary action against the stevedore of the New Zealand Shipping Co for: (a) violating the Order of the Commission by making deductions in pay for time taken for tea breaks, (b) assault on an officer of the union on board *Rangitoto*, 25 July 1950.
3. Employers to be subject to the same penalties as workers.
4. Payment for all men wrongfully penalised in connection with engagement of labour for No. 1 hatch on the *Rangitoto* from July 25-28.

The meeting then decided to cease work on all ships in the port and on Friday 28 July discs for two more gangs for No. 1 hatch were hung out

The Run-Up to the '51 Lockout

with no takers. Some 250 men were now on penalty and still no action was taken against the New Zealand Shipping Company. We voted to take decisive action and called a strike. Picket lines were deployed. A bulletin was immediately produced and distributed to fellow unionists and citizens of Auckland. The response was immediate. Seamen, harbour board workers, drivers, the Transport Workers' Federation and the Auckland Council of the Trade Union Congress all pledged full support with assurances that under no circumstances would picket lines be broken.

With officers of the Auckland branch I had a further meeting with the New Zealand Shipping Company. We were advised by their Auckland manager that Marchington had advised him that the dispute was not one for the Waterfront Commission or the Waterfront Authority, but a matter for negotiation between the union and the New Zealand Employers' Association.

On Tuesday 1 August at 4pm Dalglish read a letter from shipowners' representative Captain Holm, in which the employers asked the Waterfront Authority to order the Auckland men back to work. He also stated that the authority would consider our complaints in the morning and asked Toby Hill and myself to hold ourselves in readiness.

From left: Roly Tate, Jock Barnes, Alby Whowell (back turned, no hat), George Samways (facing) and Alec Drennan (far right) outside the Auckland Town Hall after stopwork meeting (Jock Barnes)

We were in our national office from 8am until noon and received no communication. In the afternoon we were handed a copy of the authority's decision. Accustomed though we were to Dalglish's role of denying waterside workers any semblance of justice, the decision was incredible. In his usual long-winded diatribe, Dalglish ordered the Auckland branch to resume work. If this order was not immediately obeyed the judge threatened to 'take steps against the whole membership' and quoted penalties of fines and imprisonment. Under any circumstances, such a decision would have been iniquitous even for this 'independent' body. But for it to be published throughout New Zealand that this was arrived at after hearing submissions from our union was the last straw. Not only had they not heard any submissions from our union but, at the request of Dalglish, Toby Hill and I had awaited a call all morning with no result.

On Thursday 3 August all ports from Awanui to Bluff ceased work for the first time since 1913. Watersiders everywhere were not prepared to submit passively while their union was slaughtered. Our branch had a very efficient publicity committee and thousands of bulletins were soon distributed. Support was volunteered, not only from fellow unionists but also from the general public. Conscious that many Auckland residents would be getting the truth from our bulletins, the *Herald* published two editions on 4 August, one for city and urban consumption and one for country. The city edition had its usual biased leader, but little else. But in the country one, with most people's knowledge of union matters limited and governed by *Herald* propaganda, it was open season. How vicious and bad could this paper get? Screaming headlines and a cartoon that marked an all-time low even for them. These were not in the city edition and the country editorial was completely different and much longer. Not one line was devoted to the cause of the dispute or open violation of the Order by both shipowners and Waterfront Commission. The editorial urged the government to use the provisions of the Public Safety Conservation Act 1932, which was a disgrace both at home and abroad. This leading article was a doctrine of sheer hatred and barefaced lies.

Seamen wasted no time. They were behind us 100 per cent. At Greymouth for instance, when watersiders walked off the *Gabriella*, hatches were left off. Seamen refused to put them on and the *Gabriella* could not proceed to sea. They did not wait for instructions from their union's leader, one F.P. Walsh.

Alarmed at this development and the support we were getting from kindred unions, Walsh wrote on behalf of the national executive of the FOL asking us to hand the dispute over to this body. Our reply can be imagined.

Next came a request to meet Holland and Sullivan at 9pm that night,

4 August. We replied that we would be there, together with representatives from other unions. It was a good muster: engineers, seamen, plumbers, miners, drivers, railwaymen, freezing workers, hotel workers and labourers. I stated our case and Toby Hill elaborated. Holland, Sullivan and Bockett then retired. There was no Dalglish.

Upon their return, Holland stated that if normal work was resumed, he would give his assurance that matters would be fairly settled. They then adjourned to allow the delegation to deliberate. And what a circus performance we saw from the national executive of the FOL. Walsh jumped to his feet and said, 'You've had a mighty victory.' We told him pretty sharply that neither Toby Hill nor I could talk well enough to convince wharfies in any port that this was a mighty victory. If he thought he could, he was invited to start on the Wellington waterfront at 8am in the morning. The invitation was declined.

Further discussion took place and the following wording was agreed upon:

> That the Prime Minister should appoint a tribunal forthwith to investigate the charges made by Mr Barnes and that the tribunal have powers to act on its findings.

Holland, Sullivan and Bockett again retired. On their return, Holland offered to set up a Royal Commission to investigate 'all aspects of waterfront work and before which we could present all our grievances'.

We accepted this, pleased that at last we were to have the unrestricted right to state our case before the bar of public opinion and, of more importance, cross-examine Dalglish, Marchington and the shipping combines.

The Wellington *Evening Post* was most perceptive in its comment later that day:

> The value of the Commission's work will depend very largely on its order of reference. It may be presumed from Mr Holland's statement early this morning that it will be as all-embracing as it is possible to make it. Certainly anything less than this will not satisfy the public.

However, the paper omitted to say that anything less would also not satisfy the watersiders!

Yet Another Lampblack Dispute

The last preliminary bout to the 1951 main event took place on 7 September. The ship was the *Ascunsion de Larinaga*, the cargo again lampblack. Prior to its arrival in Wellington, we received a letter from Judge Dalglish advising that as it was a particularly large cargo it would be inspected by the

Waterfront Authority before and during working. Arising from the *Myrtlebank* dispute, on 25 June the Waterfront Commission had awarded an extra payment of 2/6 per hour for working this noxious cargo, and we looked forward to this being paid in this case. The authority had a look before work started and adjourned. However, there was to be a second inspection, prior to which Marchington ordered that the ship's crew clean the holds thoroughly in order to give a false impression of the dirt and filth associated with the operation of unloading the lampblack. Our crew obeyed his orders but advised us and Pat McGavin, one of our two Wellington lawyers, who obtained affidavits from some of the men.

In view of complaints from the crew, it is hard to believe that the judge was not aware of Marchington's dirty deed. However, after viewing the hold a second time, the Waterfront Authority then adjourned to give its decision, which reduced the penalty rate for lampblack from 2/6 to 1/6 per hour. It was the usual three to two vote, with Marchington one of the three. An incredible decision, made even worse by Marchington's scandalous move to frustrate the course of justice.

This low and contemptible action should have been followed by calls for Marchington's instant dismissal. However, this would have meant the press telling the truth and they were not about to change their habits. In its leader of 13 September the *Evening Post* (milder than most) stated *inter alia*:

> Whatever case they may have for a higher rate of payment has been destroyed by their refusal to abide by the result of a proper investigation.

If that travesty was a proper investigation, we prayed to all the gods that we should never have to suffer an improper one! In line with its normal role, the *Herald* led the baying pack. Its leader of 16 September, headed 'Watersiders Defy the Nation', was a diatribe of hate and distortion of fact, well up to its usual vitriolic standard. As an example of deliberate distortion its leader of 20 September was superb. Look at this gem:

> The public has lost patience with a group of self confessed malcontents who have shown themselves scornful of the public interest. If it has not been the weight of hatch covers, it has been a quarrel over a cup of tea; if it has not been dirt money, it has been smell money—any excuse has been better than none for these men to make the ports of New Zealand, and particularly the port of Auckland, a by-word for fractious sloth.

On hatch covers, the Chief Justice of New Zealand, in the *Mountpark* case, had ruled that we were justified and correct in our action and awarded substantial damages. Both the Waterfront Commission and shipowners were severely criticised. The *Herald* blamed watersiders.

The Run-Up to the '51 Lockout

The illegal action of the New Zealand Shipping Company in denying men their legal tea break became a 'quarrel over a cup of tea'. The *Herald* blamed watersiders.

On dirt money, our attitude had again been upheld, with employers being ordered to provide protective clothing and adequate washing facilities and to pay a substantial penalty rate. The *Herald* blamed watersiders.

On smell, we had a legitimate complaint—the *Herald* itself. It stank to high heaven!

Our national executive met on 14 September and unanimously agreed on the following:

> This National Executive states that no lampblack will be worked in any New Zealand port except on the terms laid down by the Waterfront Commission in its decision of June 20, 1950.
>
> Further, this National Executive requests the Government to:
> 1. Immediately take steps to wind up the Waterfront Industry Authority and leave the way clear for the Union to negotiate directly with representatives of the shipowners with a view to obtaining a satisfactory agreement

Lampblack dispute, Wellington. From left: Eddie Napier, Toby Hill, Jock Barnes, Tommy Wells (Jock Barnes)

on the question of wages, a marginal rate for skill and other matters that are in dispute.

2. Revoke decisions of the Waterfront Industry Authority that conflict with the terms of the Main Order of the Waterfront Commission.

3. Investigate the actions of Mr T.A. Marchington in the current lampblack dispute with a view to a prosecution on a suitable charge. We suggest it should be 'conspiring to defeat the ends of justice'.

4. Investigate the conduct of the Waterfront Commission with particular reference to the management of the various Bureaux and imposition of penalties.

Failing an equitable agreement on the above the National Executive directs all Branches to cease work until advised to the contrary.

The following day we had a five-hour meeting with Holland and Sullivan. Bob Adams, executive member of the TUC, was also present. Neither Holland nor Sullivan could defend this latest monstrous act of the Waterfront Authority and, overall, the meeting was harmonious. It was agreed that we would bypass the authority and next day make a direct approach to the employers.

Our meeting the following morning with a request for discussions met with the usual response. They were more than happy with the Waterfront Authority and would discuss nothing. All ports were now out.

On 19 September Holland decided to follow the urging of the *Herald*. In a statement to Parliament, fully reported in the *Evening Post*, he stated:

> Unless normal work is resumed on all waterfronts tomorrow morning the Government will, under the provisions of the Public Safety Conservation Act, declare a state of emergency to exist.

The following three columns were the usual propaganda to which we had been subjected for so long, and might well have been taken from McLagan's pigeon-holes. Unsubstantiated accusations with no semblance of truth, while at the same time blaming our union for the sins of employers. Of course he followed the boss-class golden rule. When you have no case, trot out the red bogey. This masterpiece was included: 'In the opinion of the government the present hold-up is part and parcel of the Cold War being waged throughout the world and must be treated on that basis.' The first smell of Pentagon riding orders was starting to pollute the air of New Zealand.

Reaction was immediate. The TUC had already pledged full support and its secretary Archie Grant had been sitting with our national executive. A special meeting of the TUC national executive was called. West Coast, Buller and Waikato miners were ready to strike in support. Auckland and Wellington drivers declared all wharves black.

That night a further meeting was held with Holland and his Cabinet. We related our experience with the employers and their refusal to enter into any discussion, being content to shelter behind the protection of the Waterfront Authority. We would not accept that decision and we would not tolerate Marchington's despicable underhand conduct in ordering the crew to clean up the holds prior to their being inspected by him and the rest of the Waterfront Authority.

At nine the following morning, after a Cabinet meeting, Sid Holland called a compulsory conference with J.A. Gilmour SM as chairman. Mr Gilmour had presided over the Kelly–Murray case and we respected him as his own man. Holland's proposal was for four representatives from the employers, two from our union and two from the FOL. Irrespective of the chairman, this would have been another sell-out. We refused to sit with anyone from the FOL.

It was then accepted by Holland that we would have four from our union. Toby Hill and I, with Tom Wells and Eddie Napier, president and secretary of the Wellington branch, would represent our union. Employers' representatives were K. Belford and H. Dobbie (USSCo), D. Robertson (Shaw Savill) and T. Marchington (New Zealand Shipping Company). That afternoon, while we were sitting, Holland declared a state of emergency.

At our meeting Marchington was strangely silent. It was obvious that his deceitful act on the *Ascunsion de Larinaga* was not appreciated by his colleagues. The old school tie was looking somewhat tatty. It wasn't cricket, you know. The act of a cad and bounder, bringing them all into disrepute. But his real crime was in being found out.

We now saw a complete turnabout by the shipowners' representatives. Having no chairman in the bag and compelled to present reasoned argument was a new experience and they were hopeless. We were even congratulated on our case. The outcome was as follows:

> 1. The authority's 1/6 lampblack decision was repudiated and a new penalty rate of 4/- per hour gained.
> 2. Shipwork carpenters were given an interim pay increase and a new agreement would be negotiated.
> 3. Our transfer clause would be maintained and the authority's ruling on this also repudiated.
> 4. A further meeting would be held over our wage claim. It would be renegotiated.

But of more importance than these decisions was the fact that we had exposed the Waterfront Authority as an agency of both government and shipowners and forced the employers to negotiate directly.

Dispute over Order of Reference for Royal Commission

Work resumed at all ports. Headlines, editorials and the state of emergency disappeared. However, we were left with no illusions. This was another bout they had lost, but the conspiracy against our union would continue.

We were not kept waiting; it was immediate. Once again, it was occasioned by a complete breach of faith by the law and order choir. On 19 September Holland had repeated a pledge made to us when announcing the Royal Commission:

> We have invited the watersiders to put forward to the Royal Commission their proposals for running the wharves. We have promised them that the present, and any future disputes, can be considered by the Royal Commission.

We had written to the Minister of Labour on 14 September and submitted a series of proposals regarding the Order of Reference for the Royal Commission. We rejected the minister's proposal to appoint a Supreme Court judge as chairman, together with two independent persons of repute and standing in no way connected with the industry. We held that in order to hand down a report that would be of value not just to the waterfront but to New Zealand industry more generally, any such chairman would have to be advised by men with a practical knowledge of the industry. In particular, we suggested that the chairman should have associated with him one or two nominees each from the Waterside Workers' Union and the New Zealand Port Employers' Association. Further, we insisted that the Royal Commission be required to look not just at wages and working conditions but also pricing and profits of the shipowners since this was required in order to judge the truth behind the frequent assertions of high costs being the result of extravagant wage claims by wharfies.

In our correspondence we contrasted the highly successful 1911 Sankey Commission which had reviewed the British coal industry, taking into account a wide variety of matters including the possible nationalisation of the industry, with the highly provocative 1925 Samuel Commission, whose rejection by the British National Union of Miners had occasioned the 1926 General Strike. The difference was that the first had involvement of coalminers and colliery owners, while the Samuel Commission consisted of four persons totally unconnected with the industry. As to the request to look into freight charges and company profits, we argued that in the absence of this requirement, the Royal Commission could only be interpreted as a set-up, which would cover up the shipping companies and attack the workers.

We also insisted that the Royal Commission investigate the operations of the Waterfront Commission and the Waterfront Authority, with particular reference to Judge Dalglish and Marchington; the attitude of the press, with particular reference to the *Herald* and *Star*; the government's use of the publicly owned radio service to attack waterside workers; discriminatory treatment of Ports by Waterfront Commission, Waterfront Authority and employers; the application of penalties; and the use of police methods against members of the union and their families.

Needless to say, the minister set out the Order of Reference without taking into account any of our concerns. In particular, the Royal Commission would not be required to include any consideration of profitability and freight charges.

We fired back a reply to the minister on 29 September, accusing the government of reneging on its promises:

> The only conclusion we can draw is that the Government intention is not to have a full inquiry into all matters but rather to place an iron curtain around some parties and their actions while declaring an open season on waterside workers. In short we say, if all relevant matters were to be investigated, then we believe that report would be of inestimable value. Clearly such is not going to be the case.
>
> In view of all the talk on honouring pledges and promises we want to make the position perfectly clear. We believe the Order of Reference is drawn up to protect shipowners and other interests. We cannot accept that.

On this basis we therefore pledged not to co-operate with the Royal Commission or provide it with any assistance until such time as the government amended the Order of Reference to specifically include such items as freight charges, shipping companies' profits and their financial ramifications.

This breaching of Holland's commitment brought even the Labour opposition onto our side, with an attack on Holland and Sullivan by, of all people, Angus McLagan! The shipowners now went on the offensive and tore up the agreement entered into before Mr Gilmour SM and signed on their behalf by Belford, Marchington, Dobbie and Robertson. In a press statement they announced they would no longer continue direct negotiations with our union. When we referred this to Sullivan he refused to take any action. Such brazen repudiation of earlier commitments by both government and shipowners, no longer covered by the usual camouflage, signalled storm clouds ahead. Even some sections of the press supported our stand, with the *Star* calling on the government to honour its undertaking of an inquiry into 'every aspect of the waterfront industry'.

8 THE LOCKOUT BEGINS

The Royal Commission Begins

And so the witch-hunt was intensified and it was full speed ahead for the great conspiracy. A Royal Commission with Sir Robert Kennedy, chairman, and Messrs T. Bloodworth and J. Sawers, his associates. With due respect to them, none would have known a cargo hook from a soup spoon.

Counsel for the Port Employers' Association, S.G. Stephenson, lost no time in presenting shipowners' views. Heavy fines on the union and criminal proceedings against its leaders was his theme. Marchington was the first witness called. After his exhibition on the *Ascunsion de Larinaga*, one would have thought he would have dived into his funk hole. But no, there he was with the usual 'dishonouring agreements' etc. He had done everything possible to promote better relations, including organising a cricket match between the employers and the men!

Next up was Belford. His testimony, too, called for severe and punitive legislation against our union. Really, the Royal Commission was a gross waste of taxpayers' money—the *Herald* had said it all so many times before. The one connection Belford omitted to mention was Senator McCarthy, without whom the anti-union Taft-Hartley Act that he envisaged for New Zealand was not complete. Sid Holland and his government were now clearly dancing to the tune set by Washington. President Truman, with John Foster Dulles as his frontman, was endeavouring to destroy all potential opposition to his Cold War drive in the Asia-Pacific area. First on his list were trade unions aligned with the World Federation of Trade Unions. Both Australian and New Zealand waterside unions had already proved in the pig-iron disputes back in 1938 that we could stop our governments aiding and abetting militarism in the region. We were therefore to be crushed. Thus it was that 1950 and 1951 were marked by increasing pressure on the conservative Menzies and Holland governments of Australia and New Zealand, pressure which these governments were happy to accede to. Late in 1950 Menzies and Holland attended the Conference of Commonwealth Prime Ministers and, apart from committing the social gaffes for which he was notorious, Holland's main activity was extolling the virtues of the US. Both returned to their capitals via Washington, where they received their

The Lockout Begins

Harry S. Truman (US President), Dean Acheson (US Secretary of State), Sid Holland (Prime Minister) and Carl Berendsen (NZ government representative in Washington D.C.), signing an agreement on military and economic co-operation
(News Media: *Auckland Star* collection)

riding orders. Both were the US, right or wrong. Both were in complete agreement with Truman and the Pentagon. An alliance with the US was vitally necessary to halt the 'scourge of communism' already endangering the Pacific. Further instructions, both civil and military, would be faithfully obeyed.

Negotiations for a Pay Rise Continue

Meanwhile, attempts to win a decent wage rise were still on our agenda. In April 1950 Walsh and his FOL executive had applied to the Arbitration Court for a general wage increase. The FOL's claim was for a general wage rise of £2.18/6 per week and that of the TUC was for £3.10/0. These were the equivalent of approximately 35 per cent and 43 per cent. Months dragged by with no response from the court. Meanwhile, the Korean War was pushing up prices at an alarming rate and by then inflation in New Zealand was the highest in the Commonwealth. Subsidies had been removed from many goods and industrial trouble was rife. Freezing workers, hydro-electric workers, cement workers and carpenters were all taking protest action and there was a national railway strike.

In these circumstances, the WWU national executive met at the end of November and vowed to force the employers to the bargaining table, in line with the recommendations of Mr Gilmour SM. The employers, however, flatly refused to meet, preferring to fob us off, telling us that when the Arbitration Court handed down its decision, the defunct Waterfront Industry Authority, a body that no longer existed, would give it its full consideration! Safe in the knowledge that the government would crack down on our trade union, in line with Washington's instructions, shipowners were content to sit back to watch the Holland government in action. A wonderful excuse to avoid a wage increase and, at the same time, increase freight rates.

The Arbitration Court decision, for award wages to be increased by 15 per cent, was finally handed down on 31 January and occasioned protests throughout the labour movement. Even Walsh was compelled to voice some gentle protest. That of the TUC was, as can be imagined, anything but gentle. National secretary of the TUC, Archie Grant, was trenchant in his criticism and in a press statement said:

> I am more confirmed in my opinions. The working class has nothing to gain from the Court. The FOL, which professes belief in legal action and arbitration, today supports my opinions by demanding the resignation of its spokesman from the Court. If the FOL, with its belief in arbitration was now dissatisfied, how much more angry would Congress affiliates be?

Such was the discontent that Walsh and his executive went as a deputation to Parliament and protested to the government about the pathetic increase. A sham that made professional wrestling look good.

Freezing companies, none of which would ever win an Oscar in the role of benevolent employers, paid the 15 per cent plus an extra 6d per hour. This was equivalent to a wage increase of about 25 per cent. Clearly they were seeking to buy off potential support for our union if we were left to fight for our share.

After continuing to repudiate their agreement of the previous September, the employers condescended to meet our negotiating committee on 8 February. If we were to maintain parity with Australian watersiders (a situation that had obtained until the arrival of the Waterfront Commission), our hourly rate would have to increase to 6/3d. To maintain parity with New Zealand freezing workers our wages would have to rise to 5/2d. The Arbitration Court award would have taken us to 4/10d. As it was, even the court decision was too much and Messrs Belford and Marchington made us an insulting 'final offer' of 9 per cent, taking our hourly rate to only 4/7½d.

Adding insult to injury, Marchington claimed that our negotiating committee did not represent the views of our membership. They wanted

The Lockout Begins

to meet our national executive. Still endeavouring to get a reasonable settlement, we agreed to meet on the following Tuesday, 13 February. In the meantime, we sent the following wire to all branches:

> Re wages employers' final offer 4/7½d per hour. We consider this inadequate. Request you to call special branch meeting and advise of their decision before Monday. National executive meeting Tuesday.

And back they came. All branches from Awanui in the far north to Bluff. The decision of the rank and file—not Barnes and Hill—and they were unanimous. The offer was an insult and they pledged to implement any decision of the national executive. While pledging to obey any national decision, New Plymouth and Wellington immediately banned overtime and introduced a 40-hour week. Addressing the Auckland branch, I told members we would not vote until the following morning. This is the big one, I said. Discuss it first with your wives and families. Auckland, perhaps more than any other branch, knew what to expect.

It was with the knowledge that we were not alone in our protests against the miserable Arbitration Court decision that our national executive met with the employers on 13 February.

The meeting was short. They were adamant that 4/7½d was generous and was their final offer. Although accompanied with the cant and hypocrisy that was their norm, it was a declaration of war.

A couple of executive members argued for an immediate strike, but we finally agreed unanimously on an overtime ban. A 40-hour week was not only the right of every watersider under the terms of the Commission's Order, but was supposed to be the right of every New Zealand worker.

From 5pm the next day a 40-hour week operated at all New Zealand ports. The employers put out a statement on 14 February: 'That men refusing overtime will be dismissed for a "breach of the law" and under Bureau rules will be subjected to automatic penalty of two days' suspension.' It was on again. The law as laid down by shipowners and subject to change from hour to hour.

Overtime was now compulsory and penalties automatic. Before such penalties could be imposed, they were supposed to be the subject of port committee discussion and decision. By sacking men at 5pm and then penalising them with suspensions, shipowners were reducing the working week to a maximum of 16 hours. We had been prepared to work 40. Politicians and press alike were already screaming their usual drivel about defying law and order and holding the country to ransom. This was watersiders, of course, who wanted to work a 40-hour week; not shipowners who restricted it to 16.

On the afternoon of Friday 16 February the union's negotiating committee was called to a meeting with Cabinet and employers. Keith Holyoake, acting Prime Minister, Sullivan and Webb represented Cabinet and the shipowners had a full muster, Blakely, Marchington, Belford, Robertson, Congdon and Dobbie. Bert Bockett, secretary of the Department of Labour and twin brother of Arthur Bockett from the Waterfront Commission, was present as their adviser.

Sullivan stated that the government was anxious to hear the case from both sides. Blakely obliged on behalf of the shipowners, taking exactly one minute. He claimed their offer was both generous and final. Secure in the knowledge that the government would do their dirty work, shipowners saw no point in trying to justify their indefensible offer. Why keep a dog and bark too?

On behalf of our negotiating committee I endeavoured to submit a considered case. This dispute had its origin in the employers refusing to honour the agreement made the previous September before Mr Gilmour. Bereft of any argument against long-overdue and reasonable wage increases, employers had fallen back on Dalglish and the Arbitration Court as a cover for the paltry increases we had obtained. Now they would not even agree to the minimum of 15 per cent awarded by the court, had offered us less than 9 per cent, refused to negotiate, and stated that their offer was final.

We argued that the issue before the government was simple. The meeting before Mr Gilmour was a directive of the government, and the government should order shipowners to honour their undertaking and enter into genuine negotiations.

This was accompanied by a volley of interjections, followed by Sullivan and Webb submitting us to the usual wild and lying accusations disseminated by politicians and press for so long. Holyoake's contribution was brief. He admitted he did not know much about industrial matters and asked us to take our case before the Waterfront Industry Authority. We informed him that this had not existed since September when shipowners' representatives had agreed with us to have direct negotiations. Now, endeavouring to justify their repudiation, they were conjuring up a non-existent body.

At this stage Holyoake asked the employers to retire. We were then asked to suggest an alternative to the Waterfront Authority which, with another change of front, they conceded did not exist. We pointed out that such a proposition was premature and that the question of the employers honouring our agreement was the immediate problem. We suggested that the September meeting be reconvened with Mr Gilmour again acting as chairman. Given a settlement there, and in the event of a disagreement between the parties, we would accept Mr Gilmour's decision. Once this was settled, we could then discuss an alternative to the Waterfront Authority.

Holyoake then asked us to retire and stated he would get in touch with us later. At 8pm we were advised that the acting Prime Minister would like to meet us again. This took place at 10pm and, apart from our negotiating committee, the only others present were Holyoake, Sullivan and Bockett. Obviously the shipowners were confident that the government was going to put their case and saw no reason for either attending or perpetuating the farce of negotiations.

Holyoake stated that the employers would not budge and gave us an ultimatum: compulsory overtime on Monday, put your case before the non-existent Waterfront Authority—or else! We replied that we would refer their ultimatum to our membership and when we were advised of their decision we would advise the government. Our union members had a noble history of fighting for their rights and were veterans of many past struggles with no illusions about the fight ahead. They knew the choice: submissively file into their industrial gas chambers and see trade unionism in New Zealand destroyed, or fight back.

By 10am on Monday 19 February we had received replies from most branches—Dunedin's was the first. Their meeting took three minutes. By 11.30am all branches had replied, unanimously rejecting the ultimatum and firmly resolving to fight for justice and their fundamental rights.

Holland and his government, as well as the sinister forces behind them, were going to find that the New Zealand Waterside Workers' Union was no two-man band.

But even before any branch meeting took place, before any government reaction was known, men prepared to work a 40-hour week were confronted with large notices: 'Work is offered subject to the acceptance of normal hours of work including overtime.' Shipowners had unilaterally wiped clause 47b of the Order of the Waterfront Commission, which allowed any individual man or men to refuse overtime and return to the same job the following morning.

This open rejection of the Commission's Order was ignored by both press and government, while the press continued to thunder about waterside workers who never honoured agreements etc.

Waterside workers at all ports in New Zealand were locked out. The gloves were off. No more lying and fatuous allegations from government and shipowners but a declaration of war.

On 17 February Sid Holland returned from Washington, and Dulles was now in town. In the Prime Minister the Americans had a dimwitted lackey. In Washington, Holland had said he would 'lend every fibre of his being to the promotion of good relations between the United States and the Commonwealth' and, as his parting shot, 'tell me what else I can do and I will do it'. In shipowners, the Americans had a group who scented a

National Party Cabinet, 1951, assembles in Wellington. Clockwise from left: W.H. Fortune, J.R. Marshall, T.C. Webb, J.T. Watts, T.L. McDonald, K.J. Holyoake, ?, S.G. Holland, J.F. Dulles, W. Sullivan, E.B. Corbett, W.A. Bodkin, W.F. Doige, W.S. Gooseman (*NZ Herald*)

once-in-a-lifetime opportunity to sit on the sideline and watch others do their dirty work. We were determined to stand up to this Cold War offensive, not just for the rights of our union but for all democratic New Zealanders. This was not so much an expression of national independence as a recognition of the evil machinations of Dulles and his puppet Holland; recognition that this was a follow-up to Korea. That New Zealand was in grave danger of being involved in another engineered blood-bath.

The Anti-wharfie Offensive

For years we had been subjected to vicious press propaganda but we now witnessed a disgusting campaign unparalleled in the history of New Zealand. This was not misrepresentation, incorrect conclusions or the expression of one-eyed opinion. It was an orchestrated series of hate and deliberate lies, unsurpassed if ever equalled by Dr Goebbels at his best. The tone was set by the *Star* in its leader of 22 February. Its two inflammatory columns, containing not one factual or substantiated statement, were designed for one purpose only: to condition the public of New Zealand into accepting government dictatorship.

This gem was part of it:

Jobs are plentiful. The Government must counter that by forbidding other employers to give them work. It should be made as costly to employ a striking watersider as to retain an 18 year old not registered for military training.

The same day, its cousin the *Christchurch Star-Sun*, in a typical rabble-rousing article, wrote that 'the watersiders are being used as tools of the Cominform that is preparing the way for Soviet world domination'. This was a line that was taken up by all of the country's newspapers. The New Zealand press was demonstrating that regulations making it a criminal offence to present one word of our case were superfluous!

By this time Judge Dalglish had disappeared from the scene. He knew nothing of waterfront affairs and had done the job for which he was appointed—a yes man for the Minister of Labour. Bert Bockett, on the other hand, was well informed and was Sullivan's adviser. As it had been with McLagan, that advice was very much anti-wharfie.

On 21 February Holland declared a state of emergency. On the following day, the *Star* reported on Holland's speech:

> 'The enemy within works night and day. He gnaws away at our very vitals,' said Mr Holland. 'He works inside and he constantly weakens our preparations for defence which are so necessary for the peace of the world.
>
> The Government is alive to this menace and is determined to do its duty. The time has long since passed when soft and honeyed words will do. The situation calls for action. We must all pull together. We can marshall a great force for good, and peace will be preserved because we will demonstrate our strength.

A piece of hypocritical humbug and hocus-pocus seldom equalled anywhere, even in the ranks of politicians.

In Britain after World War One labour unrest was widespread. Faced with riots consequent on wholesale unemployment and a naval mutiny at Invergordon, the government passed the Emergency Powers Act 1920. Following the riots in New Zealand in 1932 the Public Safety Conservation Act was passed in this country. Prime Minister Forbes stated at the time that it followed the lines of the British Emergency Powers Act. This was blatantly false. Omitted from the New Zealand act were the clauses in the British act safeguarding the right to strike, the rights of fair trial, the calling of an immediate session of Parliament, and a guarantee that in proceedings against any person charged under the act, the ordinary laws were to be observed.

The power to declare a state of emergency in New Zealand is contained in section 2 of the Public Safety Conservation Act:

> If at any time it appears to the Governor-General that any action has been taken or is immediately threatened by any persons or body of persons of

such a nature and on so extensive a scale as to be calculated, by interfering with the supply and distribution of food, water, fuel or light or with the means of locomotion, *to deprive the community or any substantial portion of the community of the essentials of life* [emphasis added], or if at any time it appears to the Governor-General that any circumstances exist, or are likely to come into existence, whereby the public safety or public order is likely to be imperilled, the Governor-General may, by Proclamation, declare that a state of emergency exists.

As a 1913 scab on the Wellington waterfront, the Governor-General would have had no difficulty in agreeing that watersiders working a 40-hour week satisfied these provisions.

Sid Holland, however, who had offered the British Minister of Food, Maurice Webb, four shiploads of meat for free, could have had difficulty in reconciling this with the claim that a 40-hour week on the waterfronts of New Zealand would 'deprive the community of the essentials of life'!

But all camouflage had disappeared. On 21 February 1951 fascism reared its ugly head in New Zealand.

The power to act without sanction of Parliament is dealt with in section 2 of the act:

Where a Proclamation of Emergency has been made, the occasion shall forthwith be communicated to Parliament if Parliament is then in session, and if Parliament is not in session, shall be communicated to Parliament within fourteen days after the commencement of the next ensuing session.

The British act calls for immediate consideration by Parliament; it also states that 'no regulation shall make it an offence for any person or persons to strike or persuade any other person to take part in a strike'.

The provisions of New Zealand's section 3 are incredible:

Section 3(4)—Every person who commits, or attempts to commit, or does any act with intent to commit, or counsels, procures, aids, abets or incites any other person to commit, or conspires with any other person (whether in New Zealand or elsewhere) to commit any offence against any such regulation shall be liable on summary conviction before a magistrate to imprisonment for a term of three months or a fine of one hundred pounds, or both imprisonment and fine, together with the forfeiture of any goods or money in respect of which the offence has been committed. In any prosecution for any such offence the Court may admit such evidence as it thinks fit, whether such evidence would be admissible in other proceedings or not.

New Zealand school children are still told that the right to trial by jury is the right of every New Zealand citizen. Like hell it is!

In 1932, when the Public Safety Conservation Bill was being debated, Labour member H.G.R. Mason, then in opposition, said:

The Lockout Begins

> If a man cannot be convicted on ordinary evidence, why should he be convicted at all? It simply means the conviction of anyone who is obnoxious to the Government. Charges can be trumped up and put through with the utmost readiness.

Needless to say, in his many years as attorney-general in the first Labour government, Mason was silent on this frightful denial of justice.

The British act stated:

> Section 3(7)—No such regulation shall alter any existing procedure in criminal cases or confer any right to punish by fine or imprisonment without trial.

Any existing act of Parliament can be superseded by this. However, no such safeguard existed in New Zealand in 1951. To quote Mason in 1932 once more:

> We are under this Bill constituting absolute dictation with no responsibility of any description and no limit to the scope of their authority.

Waterfront Strike Emergency Regulations 1951

Under the provisions of this pernicious and indefensible act, Holland assembled his Cabinet and brought down regulations that made Draco's code of laws look like an advocacy for civil liberties. The regulations read as follows:

1. These Regulations may be cited as the Waterfront Strike Emergency Regulations 1951.
2. 'Declared Strike' means a strike declared by a notice under these regulations to be a strike to which these regulations apply.
   'Act' includes acts of omission as well as acts of commission.
   'Strike' means—
   (a) The act of any number of workers who are or have been in the employment of the same employer or different employers—
      (i) In discontinuing that employment, whether wholly or partially, and whether by refusing or failing to work overtime or otherwise; or
      (ii) In breaking their contracts of service; or
      (iii) In refusing or failing after any such continuance to resume or return to their employment; or
      (iv) In refusing or failing to accept engagement for any work in which they are usually employed.
   (b) Any reduction in the normal output of workers in their employment.
   (c) Any other transaction in the nature of a strike or combination, agreement, common understanding, or concerted action on the part of any workers—the said act, reduction, or other transaction being

> intended or having a tendency to interfere with the manufacture, production, output, supply, delivery or carriage of goods or articles or the carriage of persons in or in connection with any industry or undertaking or otherwise to interfere with the effective conduct of any industry or undertaking.

Once again, today's generation will find it incredible that such legislation could have ever been enacted in New Zealand. A strike had become anything that Holland and his gangsters so labelled. Workers' elementary rights were outlawed and they had no more than any African slave transported to work on the cotton fields of the southern United States. In fact, fewer. The slavemaster had to provide food and shelter. Holland and the *Star* aimed to starve watersiders and their families.

Deliberate lies and misrepresentation of our just claims were no longer needed. They had been the preparatory excuse for the exhibition of unashamed fascism. He was with the US, right or wrong. Tell me what else we can do and I will do it.

Regulation 3 authorised the Minister of Labour to apply the regulations against any union as he saw fit. Regulation 4 continued:

> Every person commits an offence against these regulations who—
> (a) Is a party to a declared strike; or
> (b) Encourages or procures a declared strike or the continuance of a declared strike; or
> (c) Incites any person or any class of persons in general to be or continue to be a party or parties to a declared strike; or
> (d) Prints or publishes any statement, advertisement, or other matter that constitutes an offence against these regulations, or that is intended or likely to encourage, procure, incite, aid, or abet a declared strike or the continuance of a declared strike, or that is a report of any such statement made by any other person.

It was therefore a crime for the press to print a word any of us might say. A superfluous provision really; there were no cries about freedom of the press.

Regulation 5 stipulated:

> If a member of any union or any branch of a union is a party to a declared strike, every officer of the union or of that branch shall be deemed to have encouraged or procured the continuance of the strike unless he proves that he counselled the members of the union or branch to discontinue the strike and that he did not encourage or procure the continuance of the strike or incite any person or any class of person or persons in general to be or continue to be a party or parties to the strike.

British justice reversed: guilty until proved innocent.

The Lockout Begins

If one union member exercised his right to refuse overtime or if one was not working hard enough to satisfy his master, every union officer was up for three months' jail, a fine of £100 or both.

Regulation 7 empowered a receiver to confiscate all union funds, books, records or documents of any kind. This effectively authorised the Public Trustee to act as Public Burglar!

Regulation 8 continued:

> Every person commits an offence against these regulations who—
> (a) Makes any payment or contribution to any union while any member of the union or of any branch of the union are parties to a declared strike.
> (b) Makes any payment or contribution to any branch of a union while any members of that branch are parties to a declared strike.
> (c) Makes any payment or contribution to or for the benefit of any workers who are parties to a declared strike.

A provision unequalled in the civilised world. Embarked on a deliberate policy of starving workers, their wives and children, the government now made it a criminal offence to give a loaf of bread to a starving child.

Regulations 9 and 10 empowered the Minister for Labour to suspend awards and to authorise the use of members of the armed forces as scabs.

Regulation 11 continued:

> (1) Any constable may direct any person not to enter or remain upon any wharf or loiter in the vicinity of any wharf . . .
> (3) Any constable may give such directions as he thinks fit to any person who enters or remains or is about to enter upon any wharf for regulating his conduct while on the wharf, whether in relation to anything that he has with him or otherwise.
> (4) Every person who acts in contravention of or fails to comply in any respect with any direction given under this regulation commits an offence against these regulations, and may be arrested without warrant by any constable.

A police state instituted by the defenders of the free world, with the dumbest copper on the beat able to act as official judge and jury.

Regulation 12:

> (1) Every person commits an offence against these regulations who—
> (b) Attends at or near any premises or place where any other person resides or works or proposes to work for the purpose of compelling, counselling, procuring, or inducing, or for the purpose of attempting to compel, counsel, procure, or induce, or in such a manner as would be likely to compel, procure, or induce that other person to do any act to which this regulation applies;
> (c) Is found by a constable attending at or near any premises or place

where any other person resides or works, and fails to satisfy that constable that his attendance is not an offence against this regulation.
(3) Every person who commits an offence under this regulation may be arrested without warrant by any constable.

This was New Zealand, 1951.
Regulation 13:

(1) Every person commits an offence against these regulations who uses, either orally or in writing, any threatening, intimidating, offensive, or insulting words to another person or to the wife, child or parent of another person for the purpose of procuring that other person to do any act to which regulation 12 applies or on account of that other person refusing or failing to do such act.
(2) Every person who commits an offence under this regulation may be arrested without warrant by any constable.

The most illiterate constable in the force was now an authority on words and their meaning and, once again, authorised to arrest without warrant.
Regulation 14:

(1) Where the presence of any person on any road or street, land, premises, or place is, in the opinion of a constable, intended or likely to influence any other person—
   (a) To do any act that would constitute an offence against these regulations; or
   (b) To refrain from or to cease working in any employment or doing any work—
that constable may give to the first mentioned person such oral directions as the constable considers necessary in the circumstances, including a direction to remove himself forthwith from the road or street, land, premises, or place where he then is or both a direction to so move himself and a direction to remain at such distance from the road or street, land, premises, or place as may be specified by the constable.
(2) In any prosecution for an offence under this regulation it is immaterial whether or not the evidence establishes that any particular person was intended or likely to be influenced as aforesaid.
(3) A constable may form an opinion as aforesaid from the circumstances of the case, and in any prosecution for failure to comply in any respect with the requirements of a direction given to him by reason of his having that opinion it is immaterial whether or not the evidence establishes that any particular person was interested or likely to be influenced.
(7) Every person who fails to comply in any respect with the requirements of a direction given to him under this regulation by a constable commits an offence against these regulations, and may be arrested without warrant by any constable.

The Lockout Begins

The remotest semblance to even their own concept of 'law and order' was abandoned. Established rules of evidence were abolished and guilt was determined on the opinion of any halfwit in uniform. An order to any person or person to depart for the Auckland Islands, if not obeyed, was a criminal offence. What was even more shocking was that the original provisions of the regulations were even more extensive and punitive and only toned down after widespread criticism from the press, the Law Society, the churches, the Federation of Labour, the universities and individual members of the public. How vicious were the original proposals? The mind boggles.

After commencing proceedings with prayers for heavenly guidance, Holland and his thugs continued to defame watersiders for conspiring to disrupt 'law and order'. Regulation 15:

(1) Every person commits an offence against these regulations who—
   (a) Carries or displays, or drives or causes to be driven any vehicle carrying or displaying, or affixes in any place where it is in sight of any other person, any banner, placard, sign or other thing which contains any words to which this regulation applies; or
   (b) Writes or prints or displays, or causes to be written or printed or displayed, on any vehicle, wall, fence, erection, road, street or footpath or otherwise within sight of any other person, any words to which this regulation applies.
(2) This regulation applies to—
   (a) Any words counselling, procuring, or inducing any person to do any act to which regulation 12 applies.
   (b) Any threatening, intimidating, offensive, or insulting words in relation to any person or persons or class or classes of persons in respect of his or their refusal or failure to do any act to which regulation 12 applies.
(3) Every person who commits an offence under this regulation may be arrested without warrant by any constable.
(4) Every vehicle, banner, placard, sign, or other thing or any written or printed matter in respect of which an offence under this regulation is committed may be seized by any constable.

Regulations 16 and 17 prohibited processions and meetings, whether in a public place or not, and authorised police to arrest without warrant any person failing to give his name and address to any law enforcer. Regulation 18 continued:

Any member of the police force who is of or above the rank of sergeant may enter at any time, using force if necessary, and with such assistance as he may deem necessary, into or upon any land, premises, or place—
(a) In the exercise of or for the purpose of exercising any power conferred

upon members of the police force by these regulations.

(b) When in his opinion an offence against those regulations has been, is being, or is about to be committed in or on that land, premises or place.

(c) When in his opinion any person who has committed an offence against these regulations may be found in or on that land, premises or place.

(d) For the purpose of searching for anything which may afford evidence of an offence against these regulations, or in respect of which there are reasonable grounds for believing that it is intended to be used for the purpose of committing any such offence.

Taking a Stand

We were faced with an ultimatum. Sullivan had 'declared' the lockout to be a strike. We were to agree that less than 9 per cent is equal to 15 per cent and to work all overtime at the pleasure of the boss—or else. The fact that this was a negation of our agreement was of no consequence. The issue now was the survival of the free world.

On Monday morning every branch in New Zealand met. The decision from the men was unanimous. All were still prepared to work a 40-hour week, all rejected the regulations, and all would fight back. Was it for this that so many of our members had fought and died on foreign fields? The answer was a resounding NO, and those who had returned, together with the rest of their comrades and their womenfolk, would fight fascism in New Zealand with the same strength and fortitude shown from 1939 to '45. Liberty and freedom would not be quietly surrendered. There would be no white flag and, long before it was over, our opponents would know they had been in a fight that they would never forget.

Monday's press featured a statement from Sullivan. Our just claims were ignored, as was any attempt to cover up for the shipowners' rejection of our agreement:

> The policy of the Waterside Workers' Union is undoubtedly the policy of the Communist-controlled World Federation of Trade Unions . . . The Government would show no mercy to those who used New Zealand trade unionism to sabotage and imperil the Dominion and the free world . . . The dispute was part of a Communist plot . . . The brow-beating Communist serving agitators will be crushed.

This was in the morning papers before any branch meetings had been held. If anything else was needed to solidify our ranks, it was this.

9 SUPPORT FLOODS IN

That we were not to stand alone was soon demonstrated. The enforcement of the regulations on Tuesday 27 February 1951 saw the first of thousands of union members make our fight their fight. The principle of an injury to one being an injury to all was fundamental. Waikato and King Country miners, Ngauranga and Gear freezing workers, hydro-electric workers in the Waikato, Portland and Golden Bay cement workers all struck, soon to be joined by thousands more.

Our Auckland branch, whose members amounted to nearly 30 per cent of our national union, had long been subjected to more attacks than the rest put together. The Ladies' Committee, press, relief and transport committees etc were well established and ready for action. The first of hundreds of illegal pamphlets was issued on Monday 26 February. Wellington, Lyttelton and Dunedin were to follow. As they were able, smaller branches followed suit. Despite constant harassment and intimidation by the forces of 'law and order', Auckland missed scarcely a day with its illegal bulletins. They were widely distributed and read, even in the British House of

NZ Waterside Workers' Union (Auckland Branch) Lockout Committee 1951 (*NZ Herald*)

Commons. At a later date barrister John Platts Mills QC, a good friend of the union, was to tell me that members of the British House continued to be amazed that we could do such a job in defiance of the fascist rule operating in our country.

With the issue now blowing up to national proportions, the FOL moved in to try to take over the dispute. They had tried to do the same during the lengthy strike by railway workers in 1950 but had been refused by that union. At the weekend I received this telegram from Baxter, addressed to me personally and delivered to my home:

> Unions affected by the watersiders' dispute directed the national executive of the Federation of Labour to approach the Prime Minister with the object of negotiating a settlement. Trust that your national executive will concur with the decision.
> (signed) Baxter

He got this reply:

> February 27, 1951
>
> Mr K. Baxter
> Secretary
> New Zealand Federation of Labour
>
> Dear Sir
> The New Zealand waterside workers have now been locked out by the shipowners' for 7 days and a State of Emergency has been declared against the New Zealand Trade Union Movement for 5 days, but we have yet to see a statement of protest from the Federation of Labour at the Holland Government's actions.
>
> Your telegram proposing to negotiate a settlement unilaterally was received on Saturday, but we are yet to see some sign of your Executive's *bona fides* in the dispute.
>
> As individual Federation of Labour officers were told yesterday, the Federation Executive must declare itself for or against the workers before the question of accepting or rejecting your proposal even arises.
>
> In this respect we cannot do better than recommend to your conscience the traditional trade union path already shown to you by the rank and file of your own affiliates.
>
> Yours faithfully
> H. Barnes, President
> T. Hill, Secretary

WWU Deregistered

By now we had the full support of the TUC, with all resolved that it would not be a bloodless coup for the Yankee dollar and its fascist puppets. We knew full well that we would be hurt, but so would they—and badly.

The last day of February saw Sullivan cancel the registration of our union and the Public Trustee seize any records he could find and confiscate any available funds. Wages due our two national office typists were seized. I had pleasure in advising the trustee that the two ladies were members of the Clerical Workers' Union and, on their behalf, I had called on Walsh as head of that union to take immediate action for their recovery. The money was soon returned!

With troops on the wharves and emergency regulations in place, decent unionists decided to take a stand. Seamen, harbour board workers, more drivers, freezing workers, miners and hydro-electric workers all struck in protest. The railway unions instructed their members to do no work that was rightfully watersiders'. Gas workers refused to handle scab coal and many were the individuals who, in refusing to do any work associated with scabs, joined the fight.

Over 25,000 union men and women gave Holland their answer: We will fight for free trade unionism, we will fight your draconian regulations, and you can tell Dulles that we will not be puppets of American imperialism.

Large numbers of police had by now been drafted to all our wharves. They were soon to become active in a manner perhaps only equalled during the 1981 Springbok rugby tour.

The *Star* of 1 March gave massive headlines to a statement from Baxter. Our letter of 27 February asking him and his national executive to declare themselves for or against workers had not been answered. The *Star* reported his decision to isolate us totally:

> The FOL contemplates no further action in the national waterfront dispute, the secretary, Mr K. McL. Baxter, said yesterday. The FOL has done everything it could be expected to do within reason, and the Waterside Workers' Union can blame only itself for its present position.

If Baxter, Walsh and the FOL executive had taken no further action, it would have been recorded as a disgrace to any organisation purporting to represent workers. But it would have been welcomed with the knowledge that this was one treacherous enemy we would not have to combat. However, running true to form, they were not just to isolate us but to work in alliance with the Holland government and to engineer a scab-herding campaign unparalleled in New Zealand history.

While Baxter could always be assured of cordial press coverage for his statements, the newspapers did their best to hide the level of our support. In small print the *Herald* carried this bald statement:

> The national council of the United Mine Workers' Federation has decided to instruct all Branches to cease work immediately.

Also in small print it said that 300 Patea freezing workers were out, and coolstore workers at the Farmers' Freezing Company had walked out after refusing to handle produce unloaded by servicemen.

The *Herald* also lamented the fact that sugar was in short supply, that the gas situation was serious due to the shortage of coal, and that the lack of cement was delaying building and construction work.

Auckland was one branch that stood rock solid. Its solidarity had been proven too often and, in the capable hands of old campaigners like Alec Drennan, Johnny Mitchell, Fred McNamara, Jack Armstrong and a host of others, it would stay that way.

As for Wellington, despite the fact that Tommy Wells and Eddie Napier, president and secretary of the Wellington branch, were represented on our union's negotiating committee, they were of little help during the lockout and Wellington's efforts were largely left to the rank and file. What great battlers emerged! Clarry Armstrong, Alf Kite, Ron Dore and others too numerous to mention.

Due to their great efforts, the first *Wellington Bulletin* appeared on 12 March. Considerable assistance was given by others such as Bob Adams, secretary of the Wellington Painters' Union and executive member of the TUC. He played a mighty role from start to finish. A feature of Wellington's bulletins was the cartoons by Max Bollinger, which brought screams of rage from Holland, Sullivan and the Walsh gang, and which are today collectors' items.

One of the features of the lockout was the emergence of younger members who were later to play such a significant role in the New Zealand trade union movement. These included Jim Knox, Bill Andersen and Frank Barnard who need no introduction, all graduates from the class of '51.

As well as issuing branch bulletins, we maintained close liaison with other unions, and thousands of solidarity leaflets were produced. The Auckland combined unions support committee published the following:

> Labour Minister tells the world that the Emergency is not directed 'against unionism in general', but against watersiders only.
>
> And the very next day, police ban a meeting of Wellington Painters.
>
> The meeting was cancelled, but still Bob Adams, their secretary, had to appear in Court on a charge in connection with it.
>
> In Christchurch, a leaflet signed by among others the Mayor and Labour MP McFarlane, is banned by police
>
> Despite cancellation of the meeting, A.B. Grant is charged in connection with it. Archie Grant is National Secretary of the TUC and Christchurch secretary of the ASRS [Amalgamated Society of Railway Servants] and Rubber Workers.
>
> Painters, railwaymen, rubberworkers . . . That's just a start, and Sullivan

still tells us the regulations are aimed only at watersiders.

The truth is clear for all to see. The regulations are aimed at all Trade Unions, designed to crush all Unionism, to reduce all workers to standards of slavery.

In the interests of solidarity and self protection, it is the duty of all Unions to protest against this thing that Holland calls freedom and we call the police state.

While active on the propaganda front, we also had to look after the material needs of our members and their families. Auckland's relief depot was first established in clubrooms in Customs Street but such was the support received that larger premises were taken in Grey Lynn. As early as bulletin No. 5, the relief committee reported that substantial supplies were on hand and more were constantly being donated. The Dalmatian community of Henderson area was particularly solid: fruit, vegetables, poultry, eggs etc continued to be delivered until the end. Many were the contributions from individual supporters. A pound or two and gifts of food and clothing. One, who remained anonymous, gave £100 per week for the duration.

The Auckland branch Ladies' Committee, now reconstituted as a Women's Auxiliary, was particularly helpful in looking after the needs of women and little ones. Clothing, baby layettes and help that only women could provide was always there.

Shoe repairers and a hairdresser were part of the system. One farmer donated a bullock, which was cut up by some of our men who had been butchers. Bread and the essentials of life were distributed every day. This was all under the eyes of police! While the depot and helpers were constantly subjected to police threats and harassment, no serious attempt was made to implement Sullivan's baby-starving regulations. They were well aware that if such was attempted, they would be biting off more than they could chew, and that the overwhelming mass of New Zealand men and women would rally to our side. They were finding, as countless dictators have before them, that legislating for fascism and enforcing it are different stories. Resistance movements are born that eventually will win.

The Lyttelton branch, too, was solid throughout the struggle. This branch produced many men and women whose names belong on any union roll of honour—Johnny Sargentina, Johnny Porter, Frank McNulty, Jim Burke (father of former MP Kerry) and many more. Later, as national secretary of the Freezing Workers' Union, Frank McNulty was to give politicians good cause to wish they had left him alone on the waterfront.

The Lyttelton comrades maintained close contact with West Coast miners and had a most competent relief system organised by the Women's Auxiliary, for whom no praise is too great. Vegetables and other produce were regularly exchanged for West Coast coal.

Gib Smith (Dunedin), Frank Vella (Bluff), Jack Harris (New Plymouth) and thousands more of like calibre made the New Zealand Waterside Workers' Union the threat it was to warmongers, corrupt politicians and big business.

Rank and File on the Move

Great men and women demonstrated that it was their fight, not that of Barnes and Hill alone, as some half-baked historians claim. Bassett and Roth, in particular, would have you believe it was mine alone. In flattering me, they fail to recognise the real strength of our union and of the unions that fought with us. In more than one case it was a fight of the rank and file, not only against fascism, but also against their renegade officials. The seamen and miners were prize examples.

More news of support was given in *Auckland Bulletin No. 5*:

Railwaymen
At a mass meeting of 500 at Otahuhu Workshops, these resolutions were carried with 3 dissentients:
(1) That the ASRS [Amalgamated Society of Railway Servants] gives no support to any policy of the FOL to sell out waterside workers to the National Government, as we were by the same body. We view with alarm any policy of the FOL that would sell out watersiders. We have noted that waterside workers have had to ask the FOL the same question as did the ASRS: 'Are you for us or against us?'
(2) Immediate action on wage claims of Railway Workers or a general strike.
(3) Complete co-operation with any Union fighting for wage increases.
When servicemen trucked wheat to the rail, railwaymen refused to handle it.

Storemen
A.B. Donald's men walked out when wheat arrived for service trucks.

Maori People
Speakers have been visiting North Island centres where our Maori people reside. Tribute must be paid to our Maori comrades for their work on behalf of our union. The response has been magnificent. We have received the following telegrams:
We pledge our unity and support in this fight for right in spite of adversities.
(signed) Whakatane Maoris,
R. Hudson secretary, Whakatane Branch
Kia Kaha Tatau Tatau (be strong we are all one).
(signed) Peneti

Freezing Workers
At a meeting of boners held at Hellaby's today, Thursday March 1, the

following resolution was carried unanimously:
> That this meeting reaffirms the District Executive's support of the watersiders. We congratulate the Kings Wharf men on their stand and condemn Sill's action in asking them to handle scab produce.

Bill Sill was their secretary. Yet another illustration of officials in the bag being wiped by their rank and file.

In their first few days we were already witnessing one of the features of the struggle. Meetings everywhere were being addressed by men who had never before spoken in public. They spoke as one worker to another; men convinced of the justice of their cause and defying the regulations every time they spoke. By their actions they clearly showed that this was indeed a union, not dupes led astray by their communist misleaders nor parties to a Cominform plot, but men and women fully conscious of the issues involved and, in their defence, fighting back.

Baxter had said in his press statement that the FOL contemplated no further action in the dispute. The facts are that Walsh and members of his national executive were meeting Cabinet members every day. The depths of his perfidy are to some extent revealed by Michael Bassett in his book *Confrontation '51*:

> During the debate on the Police Offences Amendment Bill 1960, J.T. Watts, who had been a junior minister in 1951, referred to a deputation led by Walsh in May 1951 which appealed for more intensive action against wreckers and law breakers who had been menacing the public.

On 1 and 2 March Walsh called a meeting of unions, some affected by the dispute, and others, such as the New Zealand Workers' Union, in no way concerned. Freezing workers' representatives moved a motion for the meeting to endorse our claim for a minimum wage rise of 15 per cent, which they as freezing workers had already received. The meeting broke down, however, when Walsh insisted we agree to binding arbitration as a way of resolving our dispute with the shipowners.

On 6 March the Miners' national council, officials of the Freezing Workers' Union and our negotiating committee met Sullivan and Bert Bockett with a view to resolving the dispute.

Sid Giles, national secretary of the Freezing Workers' Union, was spokesman of our group and made it abundantly clear that neither his members nor miners would tolerate the emergency regulations. However, the first thing to settle was the watersiders' wage claim. The government continued to accuse watersiders of refusing to conciliate, when the direct opposite was the case. It had been the shipowners' representatives who had refused. Sid argued that conciliation should take place and, if shipowners continued in their refusal to participate, it was the government's duty to call a compulsory conference of all interested parties. This was a restatement of our original proposition.

However, bereft of any contrary argument or reason for not complying, Sullivan retreated to more familiar ground with a litany of abuse directed at myself and Toby Hill. The government would no longer talk with these communist misleaders—this was a fight for the survival of the free world!

On 7 March we held another meeting with the Miners' and Freezing Workers' Unions. Prendiville, national president of the Miners' Union, read a reply from Sullivan, which indicated that he was now prepared to agree to conciliation as suggested by Sid Giles. It was agreed that the following formula be submitted:

(1) The New Zealand Waterside Workers' Union is prepared to allow its dispute to go to conciliation and, if necessary, arbitration for settlement.

(2) The New Zealand Waterside Workers' Union has agreed, and the United Mine Workers' Union and the New Zealand Freezing Workers' Union have agreed, that three representatives from the Miners' Union and three from the Freezing Workers' Union shall be their [watersiders'] representatives at conciliation, conditional on the shipowners doing the same.

Servicemen unloading on the Auckland wharf during the lockout
(News Media: *Auckland Star* collection)

Our position was that the two main parties concerned, ourselves and the shipowners, stand aside as observers in order to allow our representatives to attempt binding negotiations on our behalf. A refusal would expose Holland and his government as using a wage dispute as an excuse for a more sinister purpose. That is, to those who still had doubts.

Two days later, however, despite our conceding on the point of arbitration, Walsh made a vicious attack on the leaders of our union at a special conference of the FOL in the Wellington Town Hall. Walsh called on affiliates to scab, while sanctimoniously also claiming to be interested in 'saving' our union. The *Star* devoted two columns to this while the *Herald* editorial praised 'the lucid and clear sighted statement of Mr Walsh denouncing the waterfront strike as a communist plot'.

While Sullivan and his friends on the FOL executive were doing their best to undermine our case, solid support was coming from all quarters (see Appendix 4 for more cables of support). A bulletin of 7 March gave this information:

- Seamen are walking off their ships immediately scab labour attempts to work them.
- Drivers are refusing to drive to or from servicemen.
- Slaughtermen have refused to kill at Westfield and chamberhands have ceased work rather than load out to scabs.
- The majority of gasworkers in Auckland and Wellington have left their employment rather than work with servicemen.
- All mines in New Zealand except Southland are on strike against fascist regulations.
- Harbour board workers are refusing to drive cranes for ships being worked by servicemen.
- National officers of the Freezing Workers' Union have directed all members to cease work immediately troops enter the works.

International
- The Australian Waterside Workers' Federation has voted £1000 for immediate relief and called on all its branches for financial support. It has declared black all New Zealand ships worked by servicemen or non union labour.
- Queensland Labour Council sent the following cable:
    Special meeting Queensland Labour Council representing 34 trade unions and 100,000 trade unionists convey best wishes your Federation on magnificent fight to win your legitimate demands. Assuring you of our support.
    Healy, Secretary
    Dawson, President

- From Melbourne wharfies came the following:

    700 Melbourne wharfies at meeting this morning congratulated your Federation's courageous stand against Holland Government in the fight for increased wages and better living standards.

- And from their co-workers:

    Melbourne ship painters and dockers congratulate New Zealand wharfies and pledge full support.
    Doyle, Secretary

We were beginning to have an impact. The *Star*, now in hot competition with the *Herald* for the No. 1 spot in baiting wharfies, had headlines aplenty:

Railway Services Drastically Cut
Auckland Gas Co Only Enough Gas for 24 Hours
Nelson Growers Ordered to Leave Apples on Trees
Ferry Services Cut
Wellington Shops Without Meat
All Wool Sales Postponed Indefinitely

How such an effect could be caused by workers who never did any work was not explained. The *Star* also found space to announce that the Communist World Federation of Trade Unions was firmly behind New Zealand dockers. On 9 March the *Star* switched its attack to seamen:

Collier's Deckhands Cause Gas Crisis
Order to Open Hatches Defied
Deckhands of the collier *Kaitangata* maintained their defiance of an order from their national office to open the hatches so that coal could be discharged.

Both papers continued to print the lie that watersiders had rejected the 15 per cent given to all other workers.

On 12 March the *Herald* informed us that 95,000 tons of cargo was waiting to be discharged in Auckland. Seven ships were waiting to be loaded, eight were anchored in the stream, and four more were idle in the Hauraki Gulf beyond Rangitoto.

Other news was that goods and mixed trains had been cut by 51 a day in the Auckland railways district.

From Blenheim:

When airmen from Woodbourne arrived at Picton to load the refrigerated feeder vessel *Rannah* with frozen meat, the crew indicated they were not prepared to take the ship to sea with meat handled by servicemen.

A resolution by the Victor Plaster Workers demanded the repeal of the emergency regulations, levied themselves 10/- per week and offered all possible assistance. They also threatened to take strike action if the regulations were not repealed by the next time they met.

Industry everywhere grinding to a halt presented press and politicians with problems.

Walsh, Baxter and their clique in the FOL were now openly engaged as scab-herders and defenders of the emergency regulations. From Invercargill it was reported that 'the executive of the Southland Trades Council discussed a confidential report from the executive of the FOL concerning a meeting between the president, A.W. Croskery, and a member of the national executive, P.M. Butler'. Following this, the executive of the Southland Trades Council offered to assist in the formation of a scab union at Bluff. However, workers, *en masse* and as individuals, continued to walk off contaminated jobs. The number of vermin offering their services had been reduced to a trickle and service personnel were not making a decent dent in the problems.

On 13 March the *Star* and most New Zealand dailies were back in the business of headlines:

> **18 Year Olds to be Sent Home and Warships Recalled**
> **Instructors Freed for Wharf Work**
>
> The Government is suspending the compulsory military training of 18 year olds so that regular service instructors can be used to augment manpower on the waterfront.
>
> The cruiser *Bellona* and a frigate are under immediate recall from exercises with the Australian Navy to release more naval men to work on the wharfs.

This was a real problem for Dulles. On the one hand he had thousands of New Zealanders in training for the preservation of the free world, and on the other, thousands more were needed to work our waterfronts! There could be but one decision—first priority must be the destruction of the New Zealand Waterside Workers' Union.

Sullivan was now exhorting the public to pay no heed to the 'spate of propaganda aimed critically at the Government'. He stated: 'The Government has no intentions of showing other than consideration and respect for members of the Free Trade Unions not affected by the present holdup'.

The Government's 'Seven Points'

Meanwhile, it had taken the minister a full week to reply to the peace formula advanced by miners, freezing workers and our negotiating committee on 7 March. In his reply he advanced seven points as the basis of a settlement to the dispute. A week later, following meetings of our negotiating committee, we responded to each of these points in turn. The seven points and our replies were as follows:

1. The basis of all negotiations shall be that agreements and obligations are honourably observed by all parties.

Union's reply: This is agreed.

2. To devise ways and means of increasing substantially efficiency in the industry and of speeding up the turnaround of ships.

Union's reply: There can be no objection to this provided that at the same time positive steps are taken to give waterside workers such amenities and facilities as other workers enjoy as of right.

3. To devise ways and means for the quick and just investigation and settlement of disputes within the framework of conciliation and arbitration.

Union's reply: This is agreed. However, it must be clearly understood this is not tying the Union to the Arbitration Court.

4. To ensure that secret ballots are always taken on strike issues.

Union's reply: This is a matter that could well be raised when workers in New Zealand have a legal right to strike. We would point out they have not that right today.

5. To make the waterfront industry one that workers who seek to enter that employment may do so the same as in any other industry.

Union's reply: On this matter we would point that the opposition to admitting new members comes from the employers and the commission. We have no objection, provided an adequate guaranteed wage is given to the complete membership of the Union. In this respect we would point to the guaranteed weekly wage agreed upon in Conciliation for Wellington District Abattoirs of £8.9/2.

6. To place the industry as far as practicable on a basis of full-time permanent employment the same as other industries.

Union's reply: This is agreed.

7. To establish a method or system that will ensure to watersiders a just reward for their labours comparable with that obtaining in other industries.

Union's reply: This is agreed.

Prendiville, national president of the Miners' Union, said that in his opinion the government was prepared to accept our reply, but that the Bockett brothers were adamant that our response to clause 5 should be rejected and that the employers should be given the right to hire, fire and admit members to the union. The brothers were united in their desire to smash our union.

In reply, we insisted that union coverage must be maintained: to have done otherwise would have led to the destruction of our union and its replacement by a shipowners' one. While the press had been eagerly anticipating a break in our ranks, this was not to be. Our stance on this issue was endorsed by a mass meeting of the Wellington branch and also in a telegram from Frank Vella, national council representative from Bluff.

On 21 March the state of emergency was extended for another month, accompanied by a government instruction to the police commissioner to take immediate action against any person asking for or giving contributions for the benefit of watersiders. For good measure, the Post and Telegraph Department was empowered to open mail containing *or suspected to contain* material in support of watersiders and an order was issued that £70,000 in bonus payments overdue to waterside workers not be paid.

Meanwhile the FOL continued to back the government. On 23 March the *Herald* reported:

> All workers have been called upon to resume work by the executive of the Federation of Labour. The executive says this direction carries with it the obligation to handle goods at present being loaded and discharged on the waterfronts . . . This dispute has since become more than a wages issue, and has developed into a challenge to the state. It has become a political issue and can succeed only by overthrowing the democratic system of Government.

'Rank and file vote to continue fight at Wellington branch meeting'
(Jock Barnes)

That the emergency regulations, which were the subject of worldwide condemnation, were not mentioned surprised few; but that they had the gall to call Holland's government democratic was worthy of Botha and Pinochet at their best.

That Walsh and his fellow renegades continued to prosper within the FOL demonstrated the value of compulsory unionism to both government and employers. Within their ranks of unwilling conscripts, the ratio of unionists to licensed ticket-holders would have been about one to 20. With the odd exception, any union worthy of the name was in the TUC; and with Pat Potter, chairman, and Archie Grant, secretary, it continued to fight in the best traditions of the New Zealand trade union movement.

At the 1946 elections the National Party had published a pamphlet called *Russianizing New Zealand*. It said that freedom was gone, homes could be searched, arrests made without warrants, and instead of calling Parliament, the Labour government was ruling by Orders in Council. How ironic that five years later the Holland government had now become the agent of Moscow!

Friends and Enemies

We also heard at the time of the cancellation by the Minister of Labour of the registration of the Wellington, Nelson, Marlborough and Taranaki Freezing Workers' Unions, and this was followed by the entire staff of chamberhands at R. & W. Hellaby's Otahuhu works refusing to load out for servicemen.

More drastic railway cuts to conserve coal and further rationing of gas were announced, but there was no suggestion of deregistering miners. The government was relying on the enemy from within and in Prendiville, national president of the Miners' Union, it had a firm ally. The Miners' national council had instructed all members to strike in protest against the regulations, but alone in Southland they continued to work. This was the home territory of Prendiville and his secretary W. Crook. As Baxter was to Walsh, so Crook was to Prendiville.

Now in the second month of emergency regulations, a police state, and government by Order in Council, the Labour Party remained silent. But at long last Nash, who had taken over from Fraser on the latter's death in 1950, spoke out. An article from the *Star* of 30 March:

Mr Nash Would Use Emergency Powers

The Leader of the Opposition, Mr Nash, told a public meeting in Hamilton last night that he did not favour the repeal of the regulations, which were essential if the economy of the country and the welfare of the public was to be protected. Both Mr Nash and Mr K. McL. Baxter, secretary of the

Federation of Labour, were given attentive hearings.

At question time Mr Nash admitted that if the Labour Party was in power it would have no hesitation in using the necessary powers to ensure that essential supplies were delivered to all the people and that the economy of the country was not wrecked.

Mr Nash said the authority to open correspondence should not be taken in peacetime, while it was not Christian to refuse to give necessary food to wives and children of men who happened to be on strike.

This from the leader of the Labour Party on regulations condemned throughout the civilised world! This good Christian also forgot to mention that the men were not on strike, but were locked out. He also had no comment to make on the shipowners who had provoked the lockout.

That a considered policy of starving watersiders' families was not mere talk is instanced by this letter dated 24 March from our Opotiki branch, which was one of our smallest, with its members only employed part time and, of necessity, having other jobs.

The National Secretary

Dear Sir

I thought I would write and let you know that this Branch and its members are still standing solidly behind the National Union and have no intention of letting down our National Officers or our Union on Holland's orders.

Things are pretty tough here; the members have been discharged from their other employment and no one here will give a wharfie any work. The business people are stopping credit too. They are trying to starve the members into forming a new union. Opotiki butter is being loaded at Whakatane by scabs.

Yours fraternally
(signed)   C. Sherman
Secretary

As an instance of solidarity, this would take some beating. The heat from the local community, inflamed by propaganda from the newspapers, can be imagined. While Auckland branch did its best to supply relief to such outlying posts, this was very limited due to police harassment.

Other figures from the Establishment also mobilised against our men. In a letter dated 2 April and sent to all members of the deregistered branch, the Mayor of Nelson, J.A. Harley, decided to have a go at scab herding:

Dear Sir
I have been requested by many citizens to call a public meeting of those men who are willing to form a new Waterside Workers' Union and work

cargo at the Port of Nelson under the seven point policy as enumerated by the Prime Minister . . .

I feel very sorry for you and your fellow workers who I am convinced find yourselves in an unenviable position through the misconceived policy of your leaders on the National Executive. In other words and to put the position bluntly I feel you have been sold a 'pup'.

I am satisfied that men who have earned a high reputation for honest and willing work and who have previously been prepared to negotiate with their employers, cannot now be so foolish to lose everything they have striven for and earned over forty years by becoming at loggerheads with the people of New Zealand, and being looked upon as disruptive people who are unworthy of further consideration. I write to you in an endeavour to assist you to avoid this condemnation by your fellow citizens . . .

This mixture of humbug, flattery and threats continued for a page and a half. Harley had obtained police permission to meet at the Municipal Chambers on Wednesday 4 April at 7.30pm. Our men were not swayed, and Harley's meeting drew an attendance of three.

For seven weeks we had been subjected to a ruthless campaign that only succeeded in hardening the determination to resist. On 3 April we called a meeting of our national council, which unanimously moved to instruct the negotiating committee to again offer to meet the employers on the issue of wages, and to immediately lodge with the government the following claims:

1. Repeal of the Emergency Regulations.
2. Re-registration of the National Union.
3. Recognition of Messrs Barnes and Hill as the chosen representatives of the Union.
4. Reinstatement of all striking workers involved.

This list of claims was met with the expected reply— a flat refusal.

We were by now receiving support from all around the world. Messages of solidarity were pouring in from waterside workers and seamen from London, Queensland, New South Wales and San Francisco. Our stand was also supported in telegrams from unions representing NSW hospital workers, Adelaide, Melbourne and Port Kembla iron workers, Australian engineering tradesmen, Sydney and Wellington railway workshops, NSW southern districts coalminers, NSW postal workers, Australian building workers, as well as the Newcastle Trades Hall Council. We even received a copy of a telegram sent by Australian author Frank Hardy, which read:

Holland
Prime Minister
Wellington, New Zealand

> If history ever records your name it will be on the same page as Adolf Hitler.
> Frank Hardy, Author

Rationing of gas, industries closing and working short time, cancelled trains and ferries, congested ports, shortages of goods and the solidarity of those fighting the emergency regulations showed Holland and Sullivan that increased activity from the Walsh fifth column was essential to survival. More borer bugs were forced to emerge from the woodwork. Two of these were Prendiville and Crook from the Miners' Union, who consistently refused to hold a meeting of the union's national council despite being urged to do so by the union's membership. In the face of their leadership's inaction, members set up an emergency strike committee at a meeting on 5 April. The committee comprised delegates representing 3700 members of a total membership of approximately 4800. The meeting appointed Gerry Harrington of Runanga, West Coast, as president, and Bob Ross of Brunnerton, West Coast, as secretary and was attended by representatives of the West Coast district, Buller and the Waikato district, all of whom were members of the national council. In addition there were representatives from Roa, Blackball, Brunner, Grey Valley, Runanga State, Runanga Co-op, Ngakawau, Millerton, Buller Gorge and Northern Miners.

This strike committee elected representatives to form a new negotiating committee to act in conjunction with the Freezing Workers' Union in order to make overtures to the government for a settlement of the dispute. It further decided that 'all coal including present production and storage (with the exception of hospital requirements) be declared black on a national basis'.

In openly violating a decision of their national council, Prendiville and Crook had followed the Walsh–Baxter pattern. In their own territory of Southland, the directive to strike had never been obeyed. Now they had abandoned all camouflage and had joined the unholy alliance of Walsh and Holland.

From the start, Prendiville had agreed with the justice of our wage claim and was united with the rest of the national council in condemnation of the regulations. This stand he now abandoned in favour of the holy crusade against communism. Largely instrumental in getting a section of miners to scab on their mates, his efforts were of vital importance to the great conspiracy and he was suitably rewarded by the US government for his services in this critical period with an all-expenses-paid trip to the United States courtesy of the State Department in October 1951.

Prendiville and Crook were not alone, however, and more termites continued to emerge. Kilpatrick, secretary of the Canterbury Freezing Workers' Union, joined their ranks, and he too was disowned by his members. Miners and freezing workers, as with seamen, cooks and stewards, Wellington drivers, Mangakino hydro workers and all others on strike were out in protest against regulations unparalleled in our country and equalled in few others. For these rats to desert their comrades was an unforgivable crime, but to join forces with the government made them even lower than the legislative baby-starvers.

- Dynamite strikers threaten to blow up Ministers' homes
- Colliery in flames after big underground explosion

REIGN OF TERROR GRIPS THE WHOLE OF NEW ZEALAND

From WILLIAM GREEN   *Wellington, Saturday.*

A REIGN of terror grips New Zealand tonight. In the eleventh week of a Communist-inspired wages strike, dock workers have begun a campaign of unrestricted violence, dynamiting railway installations, threatening to blow up the homes of Cabinet Ministers, and battering into insensibility men who have gone back to work.

With 20,000 New Zealand volunteers enrolled in a citizen's army to keep open vital communications and assist the police and military, a state bordering on civil war is approaching.

Down come

Last night came a new sensation. A terrific

10   BOTH SIDES DIG IN

Since the lockout, Auckland watersiders and supporting strikers had been meeting daily in Trades Hall. However, on the morning of 9 April we found the hall occupied by police. Delegations of Waikato miners and Mangakino hydro workers had come through for this meeting, which resulted in a gathering of well over 2000.

Inspector Jack Southworth, who was in charge, invited Alec Drennan, Ron Jones and me inside and advised us that he had instructions from Wellington that we were to be stopped from holding any more meetings in the hall. However, he had no instructions to stop one outside the hall so we took out a table and chairs and for about two hours addressed a crowd of thousands. Hobson Street was blocked off, traffic was stopped and trams had to be diverted. It was a great opportunity to tell our story to the public and, for what it was worth, to police. Later that day we were advised there would be no more objections to our holding meetings inside the hall!

For weeks the public had been regaled with tales of the fantastic rates of cargo handling being achieved by servicemen. The claims were so absurd that they were no more than a bad joke. The *Herald*, however, blew this racket to pieces with its story of 9 April:

> **Waterfront Strike Now in 8th Week**
>
> As the strike nears the end of its eighth week the majority of watersiders are still idle. The Government's next step is expected to be announced in the next few days.
>
> Meantime the port of Auckland is choked with 42 overseas, intercolonial and large coastal ships. Fifteen of them are riding at anchor in the great queue stretching beyond the harbour limits. In the holds and on the decks of these ships lie 278,094 tons of cargo.

With the huge queues clearly visible to Auckland citizens, they were starting to ask the inevitable question. Why, if watersiders never worked, did we not see sights like this before?

Sullivan announced his latest plan the next day. A letter was to be sent to every individual watersider in New Zealand, inviting him to register with the Labour Department for a return to work.

The combination of lockout and fascist regulations was proving to be neither a bloodless coup nor the Walsh-predicted Blitzkrieg. It was hurting the government and the shipowners, and the pain was great indeed. New tactics had to be employed and we now witnessed a complete somersault: unlimited praise for the thousands Sullivan had seen fit to lock out and deregister. They were decent patriotic New Zealanders and good workers who had been misled by Barnes and Hill, who now stood exposed as key figures in Moscow's plans to subjugate the free world. He appealed to them to think for themselves. No mention was made of his fascist regulations, and the men's reply was akin to that received by the Mayor of Nelson!

Peaceful Protesters Bashed by Police

Left with no alternative but to create scab unions, Walsh, Baxter, Prendiville and the rest of the fifth column, together with police, were called upon to intensify their actions as Wellington drivers joined the honourable ranks of deregistered trade unions. A peaceful protest march in Wellington by wharfies and our supporters to Parliament was stopped and bashed by baton-happy police in Cuba Street. Con Doyle, president of the deregistered Freezing Workers, led the way and was the first to get the treatment.

Following the Cuba Street bashings, Tommy Armstrong, Labour MP for Napier, addressed a meeting of Wellington watersiders and supporters. A grand fighter, he showed he hadn't left it behind in the boxing ring as he attacked police thuggery, fascist regulations and the international pirates that called themselves shipowners. However, he was almost alone among the gutless wonders that made up the Labour Party opposition. He was therefore a marked man and lost his seat in the following election after being deserted by the Labour Party hierarchy.

While not one New Zealand seaman scabbed from start to finish, on 10 April, Wellington seamen decided it was time to give their secretary, F.P. Walsh, the message loud and clear, resolving not to accept engagement on *any* ship, even if it had not been worked or manned by scab labour. For good measure Wellington drivers, after secret ballots in Wellington, Palmerston North, Masterton, Martinborough and Petone, determined to stay on strike. The same day the 280 members of the Auckland Shipwrights' Union reaffirmed their previous decision not to work on any ship the subject of scab labour.

The following day saw the Union Steam Ship Company announce that the liner *Monowai*, which was to have taken 400 passengers from Wellington to Sydney, had been withdrawn from service indefinitely. 'The withdrawal of the *Monowai* is regretted,' said the company, 'but because of the crew's refusal to man the ship, it cannot be helped.'

The shipowners had long refused our claims for increased regular employment on the waterfront; they preferred an army of non-union labour at their beck and call and subject to no guarantees. The government now tried to break our union by declaring the waterfront open to non-union

Cuba St march, Wellington, shortly before being broken up by police
(News Media: *Auckland Star* collection)

labour. This was in clear breach of the preference clause, whose rationale had been spelled out by Justice J. Fraser from the Arbitration Court back in 1924:

> The most important change we have made in the award is the preference clause. The Court has always maintained the policy of an open union, but it recognises that the waterfront is the place to which the unemployed of all trades gravitate. The Waterside Workers' Unions accordingly have to carry more than their fair share of the unemployed, and the consequent increase in their membership reduces the earning capacity of the greater number of their members. We have endeavoured to decasualise waterside work as far as possible by providing for a system of limitation of membership of the unions, based on the labour requirements of the different ports. This will not prevent the employment of non-union labour in rush times, but it is hoped that it will diminish the number of the so called fringe of men who frequent the wharves on the chance of fishing up occasional jobs. This principle of limitation has been decided upon after very full consideration, and the Court has drafted the clause in such a way as to keep the matter under its own control, and it retains full power to delete or vary the provision if it thinks it wise to do so. If, however, the clause works out in operation as it is intended to do, the result will be to provide more constant work and larger earnings for the regular waterside worker.

We knew that to talk of an open union and at the same time of permanent and guaranteed wages was ludicrous. An open union on the lines proposed by the Holland would have meant a return to the auction block and the corruption that were part and parcel of those days. The law and order brigade now overrode Justice Fraser's wise judgment: nothing now was to get in their way!

Meanwhile the provocations continued. Thornley William Calcott, president of the Tatu state mine, Ohura, was arrested at the mine by Senior Sergeant Procter, accompanied by a number of other police. He was charged under the emergency regulations in the prelude to a police reign of terror in this isolated community. It was too much for miners at Kamo, the only underground mine in the North Island still working, and they voted to strike.

In a two-column headline on 19 April the *Herald* praised the national radio broadcast by James Freeman, vice-president of the Timber Workers' Union, who denounced our union and red-baited us to boot. This contemptible act was to earn for him a reputation exceeded only by that of Walsh. Hot on the heels of Freeman, Walsh lined up another one, S.V. Glading of the Engineers' Union who went on national radio with this gem:

> Today the word 'scab' is being used by Communists and their stooges in a desperate attempt to prolong the waterfront strike and to paralyze the country. In this dispute no trade unionist who returns to work or carries on normal work can be called a scab. The real scabs are those who are deliberately trying to destroy trade unionism in New Zealand.
>
> Now is the time for all decent watersiders to show that they have the courage to defy these efforts to intimidate them by the scurrilous and unjustified use of the word scab.

Glading was not prosecuted for breaking the regulations by using the word scab, and by now the FOL was defining scab labour as normal work!

The FOL now had strange friends, as the *Herald* reported on 22 April:

> After paying a tribute to the Prime Minister, Mr Holland, and to the Minister of Labour, Mr Sullivan, the Taihape branch of Federated Farmers, on the motion of the president, Mr A.J. Michelson, passed the following resolution:
>> That this annual meeting unanimously endorses statements by the Federation of Labour in the present dispute between the Government and the watersiders, and sincerely congratulates the Federation on the stand it has taken in defence of our democratic principles.

In the further defence of our democratic principles, Sullivan instructed the Public Trustee to seize the funds of the Wellington District Freezing Workers, Wellington District Drivers, Portland Cement Workers and

Golden Bay Cement Workers. With the 1951 FOL conference beginning the following day this was, no doubt, timed as a further assurance of the government's determination to destroy resistance. By contrast, neither the Seamen's Union nor the Miners' Union was deregistered, and nor were their funds seized. To have done so would have undermined the power base of Walsh, Prendiville and Crook and thereby destroyed the government's fifth column inside the labour movement.

FOL Conference Resolves on 'No Action'

The only surprise at the FOL conference itself was the number of votes cast against Walsh and his national executive's policy. Walsh was returned as vice-president by 172:61, and the policy pursued by the national executive supported by 167:41. Our union was subjected to the long, scurrilous and lying statement that was expected, and an application by the Seamen's Union to have Toby Hill and I address the conference was rejected. Baxter was reported as saying that no action was to be taken over the emergency regulations, and Nash, in an hour-long address, declared that no-one had worked harder than the president and secretary of the Miners' Union, Prendiville and Crook, and the vice-president of the FOL, Walsh, to effect a satisfactory settlement and the resumption of normal work. In deciding to take no action against the emergency regulations, the FOL had effectively endorsed them. Sullivan was thereby given the green light to register 'normal' unions, which were to be welcomed and given red-carpet treatment by the FOL.

For the seamen, the FOL conference was the last straw. Rank and filers took over and speakers from our union, the freezing workers and the miners addressed their meetings. At one such meeting in Wellington they rejected the request of Walsh and his national council to obey the FOL call for scabs, and by 262:2 resolved to strike 'till the finish'. They were writing another chapter in the proud history of their union and well was it done. Miners, freezing workers and Wellington drivers had done the same.

After 12 weeks of lockout and a campaign by press, radio, politicians and union traitors unique in the history of our country, our ranks remained solidly united. With the exception of Timaru, whose stand had been undermined from the start by its own leadership, the government had not got enough scabs from our ranks to stage a football match.

Now, despite the FOL blessing, all talk of 'normal' work was nonsense and the baby-starvers were forced to campaign for scab unions that no words could disguise. This would be coupled with increased intimidation and violence.

On 1 May our national executive met, primarily to approve registration under the Trades Union Act and also to receive branch reports. The

Wellington Drivers' Union had been successful in re-registering under the act. But while we were in session the government cancelled their registration and by regulation proclaimed that registration could take place only with the minister's approval. Another longstanding act wiped by the defenders of law and order and another step towards the fascist state. Government by Parliament was a thing of the past.

For some considerable time the FOL executive had been endeavouring to register a scab watersiders' union at Bluff. At a public meeting called by the Labour Department, all not prepared to join a new union were ordered to leave. Fifteen remained and from this bunch a scab union was formed. The membership of our Bluff branch, by contrast, was 270. It was at this time that we also learned with deep regret of the death of Frank Vella, secretary of the Bluff branch. He was a great unionist and worker in the labour movement and it was a tribute to him that after 12 weeks, only 11 of the 15 scabs were ex-members and four of these for only a few weeks. Even at Timaru, where 75 members had voted to scab, 33 men had voted not to. Shipowners rewarded the Timaru branch with a reduction in the number of men working in freezer gangs.

From Napier, Jim Black reported to the executive that the branch had not been able to hold many meetings. Police had been present at the meetings, and he was subject to police persecution both at his house and in town. Not one member of the Napier branch had joined the scab union.

Similar reports were received from all branches, with Auckland as usual taking most of the heat. Alec Drennan reported that out of a membership in Auckland of 2370, the massive nationwide scabbing campaign had resulted in only six members scabbing. Relief depots and all auxiliaries were flat out. All food was purchased in bulk, meat killed on the hoof and the hides sold. Gangs were out cutting firewood and all were being continually harassed by police. The Women's

Locked-out unionists watch scab wharfies going to work from behind a police cordon (*NZ Herald*)

Auxiliary was doing a great job. Public meetings were held at Myers Park and a very successful concert had been held in the town hall.

At the conclusion of the executive meeting, the following resolution, moved Archie Dellaway and seconded Eddie Napier, was carried unanimously:

> That this national executive reaffirms the policy of this union to continue the struggle together with miners, freezing workers, drivers, seamen, cooks and stewards and all other New Zealand workers who are fighting fascism.

In Auckland, the *Herald* reported that the Labour Department had sent 500 telegrams to prospective members of the new scab union but despite all attempts at secrecy, the news leaked out and outside the meeting organised for them in the town hall, 5000 wharfies and their supporters staged a demonstration. In scenes repeated 30 years later during the Springbok tour, there was chaos and disorder outside the town hall and police were forced to draw batons to protect the 70 degenerates who were cowering within. Trams were barred from Upper Queen Street, Cook Street was blocked off, and large cordons of police surrounded the town hall. So are scabs given the full protection of the state.

The government's three-month-old campaign of lies and infamy had achieved one result never anticipated by Dulles or the baby-starvers. Waterfronts were being worked at less than half the normal pace and then only by the use of armed forces personnel. Holland's promise to send the Americans another battalion of men for Korea was now impossible. How many New Zealand soldiers owe their lives to this backdown is anyone's guess.

Meanwhile, scabs were being hailed for working both Saturday and Sunday. The urgent and essential work that once again necessitated wartime hours was loading wool for the US. As with New Zealand, so had the Dulles gang underestimated Korean resistance to American bullying. Uniforms and blankets were urgently needed for the prolonged war.

Increased Police Repression

Things were not going according to plan, and Dulles was compelled to order his boy to step up the action. In announcing the formation of a volunteer emergency organisation to assist in the preservation of 'law and order', Holland called on 'every able-bodied man who is prepared to serve his country in the present crisis'. The police force in Auckland was to be strengthened by drafting men from other areas and police were instructed to take 'still stricter methods in dealing with strikers and their supporters'.

Clearly this vindictive campaign was no longer primarily about our claim for a wage rise. Rather, the government and its stooges in the FOL were turning New Zealand into an appendage of Washington's war machine and, to that end, destroying *bona fide* trade unionism. For 11 weeks our members, supporters and families had been subjected to phone-tapping, letter-opening, dawn raids, jail and constant police harassment. In obedience to Holland's latest orders, this campaign was intensified. The following is from *Auckland Watersiders' Information Bulletin* on the 77th day of the lockout:

> Auckland today is an armed camp. Any New Zealander who had any doubts of our statements that fascism had come to this country would have these removed after observing the situation here today. It has taken the police force, plus the army, plus the navy and armed marines to protect about 150 scabs who were driven to the wharves. It is estimated that for every scab there were six 'protectors'. What an indictment of Government plans to institute a new order on the waterfronts. The scabs were directed by telegrams to various police stations. They were then driven down to the Western Wharf in army trucks and along the viaduct, entering Princes Wharf through a guard of marines with fixed bayonets. A fire hose was stretched along the fairway as an added precaution. The scabs were mustered and then their names read out. Only eight members of our Union were present and of these, three changed their minds and walked off.

Auckland branch members and supporters hold meeting outside Auckland Trades Hall (News Media: *Auckland Star* collection)

We now ask Holland a question. If it is true that his plans have the approval of the broad mass of workers, why are there not thousands taking advantage of his offer? Why is it necessary to place Auckland City on a war footing in order to protect a handful of unclean workers misguided enough to be influenced by the lying and treacherous statements of him and his baby-starving colleague, Sullivan?

We know that the Government planned to make Auckland a battleground. Police have been brought in far removed from Auckland. Army and Navy personnel have also been transferred from other centres. It is obvious that a deliberate and cold-blooded plan has been prepared in an endeavour to break the spirit of our Auckland members by intimidation, police action and all the other measures symbolic of the Fascist State.

What has been the result? We can record with pride that there has been no flinching on our part—nor on the part of Seamen and those other staunch Unionists who are determined to see this through to the finish. We are not being stampeded by police or anybody else. We have emphasised again and again that we are a legitimate, organised, disciplined and peaceful body of workers. We do not condone violence nor do we encourage it; but we are not a collection of jellyfish. We would not be fitted to be called New Zealanders if we submitted to what has now become a reign of terror on the part of a Government which has used every act in the Nazi textbook, short

Scab wharfies going to work in covered wagons, protected by large police contingent (News Media: *Auckland Star* collection)

of firing squads and gas chambers. In our ranks we have members who have been decorated for gallantry on the battlefield, fighting for the very things that are being filched from them today. We would betray the whole of the New Zealand people if we did not remain steadfast to the principles of Free Trade Unionism, Peace and Democracy. It is not us who are the betrayers—it is the Holland Government and those who are its willing tools in this dastardly attempt to crush Trade Unionism in New Zealand.

In an editorial entitled 'Preparing for the Worst' on 2 May, the *Star* continued its incitement against watersiders and supporting unionists:

> The police are trained for the job and so far there is no evidence to suggest that, *if properly armed*, they will be unable to counter any foreseeable challenge to their authority.

The police, of course, were already armed with truncheons and had demonstrated their willingness to use them. A logical conclusion from the *Star*'s advice would be that the police should be armed with guns. With the powers vested in them by the emergency regulations they would then be authorised to shoot anyone who challenged their authority.

From a newspaper that had advocated a policy of starving the families of waterside workers and other unionists fighting fascism, and of making it a criminal offence to employ a locked-out watersider, such comment came as no surprise.

By now all talk of industrial issues was long gone. All loyal citizens were being urged to enrol and fight the deadly communist threat to our free and democratic country. This became quite comical at times. The Auckland Law Society informed its members that should their practice suffer as a result of service in the civil emergency organisation, they would receive assistance from the society's council. The *Herald* of 3 May reported an even better one:

> The Devonport Borough Council has offered to provide guards and patrols to protect military and naval installations in the borough. Yesterday, the Mayor, Mr C.F. Woodall, sent a telegram to the Prime Minister offering to take over the responsibility during the absence of army and navy men from the bases on special duties.

Perhaps the threat to big business interests stopped the resurrection of the Home Guard and a wartime blackout!

When deeds of gallantry and heroism were told, how Horatius kept the bridge was left for dead by the heroic fight of Holland, the Auckland Law Society and the Devonport Borough Council to save New Zealand!

In another leader headed 'Time for Action', the *Star* (1 May) made its attitude abundantly clear:

> The Government should announce that crowds on the waterfront will be dispersed without hesitation, and that in view of what has already happened the police will be armed. And the Government should make it known, before any further incidents occur, that should individuals or groups defy the ban and challenge the authority of the police, the police will shoot.

No; this was not Nazi Germany; the *Star* was not a right-wing South African publication; nor was it one of Pinochet's. This was New Zealand, 1951.

On 10 March the *Herald* had reported that 'Cornelius Patrick Murphy, union waterside worker, was fined £5 for using insulting language—the word scab'. Con pleaded guilty, saying this was the ultimate in insulting language and he had used it. In the same column the *Herald* reported that a 53-year-old hospital worker was also fined £5 for the same crime. Two months later Con Murphy was sentenced to one month's imprisonment with hard labour for the same offence. So reported the *Star* of 15 May.

On 19 May the *Star* reported that, while a collection was being taken for deregistered waterside workers at the Mangakino hydro works, police moved in and seized money, subscription lists and a quantity of literature.

Tom Magee, secretary of the deregistered Wellington Drivers' Union and Sid Giles, secretary of the deregistered Freezing Workers' Union, were charged under regulation 7 of the emergency regulations that they failed to deliver to the Public Trustee funds, books, accounts, vouchers and records under their control. In a reserved decision, Mr J. Hessell SM fined the two of them £50 each. The magistrate said that in fixing the penalty he took into account the fact that the defendants had been acting under legal advice. Presumably, acting without legal advice would have meant jail as prescribed by the regulations.

One deregistered waterside worker who, with his family, had been a tenant of a council house for 18 years and who had fallen five weeks behind in his rent, was given, by the Auckland City Council, seven days to get out.

Through all of this we continued to win support from other workers. The annual meeting of the Wellington branch of the New Zealand Journalists' Association unanimously passed the following resolution:

> That the Union urge the New Zealand Journalists' Association to write to the Prime Minister and the Newspaper Proprietors' Association strongly expressing the opinion that the general restrictions on the press under the Emergency Regulations are wrong in principle and harmful in practice.

A similar resolution was passed by the Christchurch branch of the association. While appreciating their resolutions, one wondered if they were naive enough to believe that the removal of restrictions would have made

Sid Giles, secretary of Freezing Workers' Union, counts the cost of an overnight police raid (News Media: *Auckland Star* collection)

any difference to New Zealand's scurrilous propaganda rags, of which the *Star* was typical.

Sometimes we found support in the most unlikely quarters. On 18 June a 2ZB radio announcer who interpolated his own remark after reading an advertisement calling for labour on the Wellington waterfront was suspended. This fact was reported, but not his remark—'I've had enough of advertising for bloody scabs.'

However, we could always rely on opposition from the FOL. Alex Croskery, nominally president of the FOL but in reality little more than a mouthpiece for Walsh, shed his undercover role and in a national broadcast appealed for more scabs, assuring them of the FOL's full support. We gave as good as we got. One of our members targeted Walsh in a poem that we printed in our *Wellington Bulletin*, with apologies to the Ayshire Bard:

> Ye see you birkie F.P. Walsh
> Wha stamps and shouts an a' that?
> Though hundreds worship at his belch
> He's but a scab for a' that.
> For a' that and a' that,
> His stocks and shares and a' that
> True union men a' know this truth,
> A scab's a scab for a' that.

Daylight Robbery by the Shipowners

It was the shipowners, however, who supplied the real news and it was a beauty! From London, the international brotherhood of pirates announced a 50 per cent increase in freight charges to New Zealand, supposedly to reflect the increased costs associated with the New Zealand waterfront stoppage. This was on top of a 7.5 per cent increase the year before. This was a stand-and-deliver job if there ever was one! Given the fantastic rates of cargo handling attributed to scabs, the community could reasonably have expected a reduction in the charges. It shocked even the business community but received little press publicity. This was not a question of another penny or two on our wages, or whether a shipowner's wand could change a 9 per cent wage rise to 15 per cent. Exploiters who had always regarded New Zealand as a cow to be milked dry were in for their chop. We were being held to ransom to the extent of many millions of pounds a year and the pirates had Holland over a barrel. They knew that an attack on their charges would have meant implicit support for our campaign, and well did they know that would not happen.

This was a major part of the communist plot ignored by Holland and Dulles; it evoked no national broadcasts by the Baxters, Croskerys and Freemans, and Walsh lost the power of speech.

On the 82nd day of the lockout New Plymouth produced another 'believe it or not'. The scabs who were working the port were presented with a sample of the tactics of benevolent shipowners who never broke an agreement. The number of men in a freezer gang was reduced from 12 to eight, a cheese gang from 16 to 12 and in almost every other case gangs were shortened. Even the scabs had had enough. They held a secret ballot and voted to strike. Needless to say, this further dastardly escalation of the Cominform plot against the free world escaped the attention of both press and radio. Faced with the disastrous possibility of deregistering the scab union, Sullivan called on his major strike force—the FOL. Baxter duly obliged, travelling to New Plymouth in a government Chrysler with a police escort. After a four-hour meeting, at which he assured them of full FOL support, they resumed work. At all costs the 'new unions' had to be stopped from striking. What Sullivan could not do, the scab-herding FOL could and would.

Nash 'Neither For Nor Against'

Such was the pressure of public opinion that even the Labour Party had to voice its grievances. Its leader, Walter Nash, as well as MPs Bill Anderton and Ritchie McDonald, had been denied the right to speak at public assemblies in Auckland by police. Nash released a press statement, which was reported as follows:

'The acts of past months completely violate the principles upon which British law and freedom have been built.' For more than two months, [Nash said] the Press had presented only one side of the case. Statements issued by himself and on behalf of members of the Labour Party had been published, but they had consistently been followed up by leading articles attacking the principles expounded and those who advocated them.

'Immediately before a meeting I was advertised to address in Hamilton, I was warned by an inspector of police that I was not to refer to the Emergency Regulations. On three occasions I have made representations to the Prime Minister to call Parliament together so that the 34 representatives of those electors who voted Labour could be heard. Each request has been refused.' [Nash said] the radio had been consistently used by Mr Holland and Mr Sullivan to state one side of the case only and, at the same time, to abuse those who have been making efforts to solve the problem.

'The Government refuses to convene Parliament. The Prime Minister has refused in writing to allow myself, or any member of the Parliamentary Labour Party, to speak over the air. And now efforts are being made to prevent Labour members of Parliament from addressing public meetings.'

The advice of the police to Mr W.T. Anderton, MP for Auckland Central, that a permit would not be granted him for a meeting in his electorate, and that no permit would be granted to himself [Nash] as leader of the Opposition, to speak in Auckland, was a startling reminder of the conditions into which the country was plunging.

Allegedly to prevent the introduction of a form of Government repugnant to the British way of life, the Holland Government was acting in exactly the same way as other Governments which had ended in dictatorships.

This statement produced an immediate reaction. People were starting to question a government that refused to call Parliament and denied opposition members the right to speak. Even the *Dominion* and the *Star* wrote critical editorials. The government had gone too far. Backed by some of the FOL unions, the TUC organised a public meeting at the Auckland Domain for Sunday 13 May, which drew a crowd of about 8000. Pat Potter was chairman and Nash the invited speaker. It was at this meeting that he uttered his historic remark that he was 'neither for nor against' the wharfies. By being neither for nor against, he was tacitly accepting every action of the baby-starvers, and Holland flogged it to death.

But the crowd was not there to hear Nash apologise for the Holland government, and called out for me to have a go. Pat Potter called me forward to speak but Nash, with police in attendance, put up his hands and said, 'No, no, he is not going to speak.' The *Herald* reported:

> Nash's words were drowned with cries of: 'Let Jock have a go. You just advocated freedom of speech so let him have a go. Where is the freedom of speech you talked about?'

I did not make an issue of it; I was speaking in the town hall the following Sunday. But Nash's performance was indicative of the spineless and despicable attitude of the Labour Party. With the exception of Tommy Armstrong, and to a lesser degree two others, the Labour seat-warmers didn't have the guts of a disembowelled whitebait.

Reports that members of the armed forces who had refused to scab were being given outrageous sentences had been consistently denied. However, we were now hearing reports from the Press Association that this was indeed the case. On 10 May the association reported that a rating off the naval frigate *Taupo* had been taken to hospital at Westport after a nine-day hunger strike. The seaman had been on hunger strike in protest at being locked up in the frigate for refusing duty. He was supported by the ship's ratings, who sent a letter to a newspaper reporting that he had been locked up in an eight-foot by five-foot lavatory compartment.

Similarly we heard from a Greymouth man who had just completed national service in the air force that two men from the Te Rapa air force station had been placed in Ardmore detention camp for seven days and then transferred to Devonport naval base for more detention for refusing work on the waterfront, and that six army men in Papakura Camp had been given six months' detention for refusing wharf work. The overseas press had their own representatives in New Zealand and from them we

Wellington branch secretary, Tommy Wells, addresses a rally of waterside workers and their supporters outside parliament (News Media: *Auckland Star* collection)

heard still more. The *Melbourne Argus* published the following dispatch from John Boland:

> A serviceman claimed today that he had been arrested and then dishonourably discharged for refusing to work on the wharves. He said he was at first to have been sent to a detention camp, but the camp was overcrowded with other servicemen who had refused wharf duty. Possibly 200 servicemen had been put under detention and hundreds more were dodging the issue by parading and having themselves sent to sick bay for treatment.

There were constant attempts to break our solidarity. No scab union had been registered in Wellington and great was the scheming to get them to go back in a body. In an attempt to break our ranks in the larger ports Sullivan submitted peace proposals that aimed to introduce 'open' employment on the waterfront in return for 'due consideration' of our claims. These were unanimously rejected at a meeting of 1500 members in Auckland. Instead, the men unanimously endorsed the following demands:

1. Repeal of the Waterfront Emergency Regulations.
2. No victimisation.
3. Recognition of our democratically elected leaders and the re-registration of our national union.
4. Calling a compulsory conference with a view to settlement of the dispute by conciliation and arbitration.

Further Police Bashings

Friday 18 May saw more police bashings in Auckland. To give the lie to claims from both press and Holland that our members had drifted away, we organised a large lunchtime march of watersiders and seamen, who paraded at the foot of Queen Street. It was orderly and, with police adopting the role of spectator, there were no disturbances. Later that day we were to witness a vastly different scene.

In response to public demand the TUC had booked the Auckland Town Hall for a meeting on Sunday evening, 20 May. A delegation from Wellington was coming up, with Bob Adams, TUC executive member and secretary of Wellington Painters' Union, one of the speakers. We arranged to meet them about 5pm on Friday 18 May, outside the Chief Post Office. Whereas hundreds had attended at lunchtime, this evening there were only about 30 or 40 of us. While we were peacefully talking, the SS charged with batons flying. Some of the older police acted moderately and fairly, but many of the younger ones relished their unbridled power and acted like the legalised thugs they were. Those of us still standing were kicked, bashed and punched from the Central Post Office to Milne and Choyce. Alec Drennan had been viciously bashed and then thrown into Fort Street.

Shoppers or anybody in the way went down or were knocked aside. An 81-year-old man, walking with the aid of a stick, was bashed and kicked for good measure. His legalised basher, as with others of his kind, had gone berserk. I was to deal with this one at the town hall meeting.

The police charge ended outside Milne and Choyce, when hundreds of men and women knocking off work or shopping surrounded the police in open hostility. Trams and other traffic were stopped. The odds for the police were not so good so the retreat was sounded. All that were missing from the scene were the jackboots and swastika armbands. One man, shopping hundreds of yards away, was arrested for insisting on his right to enter the shop. Guilty of obstructing a constable was the charge. Nine were arrested altogether, including three seamen. When bailed later that night, most were still covered in blood. Those who arranged bail were, in their turn, assaulted in Albert Park. Two of those arrested were jailed for six weeks, and on fining the others, the magistrate assured them they were not being harshly treated.

Sunday night, as might be expected at that time of the year, was wet and cold; but thousands of Auckland citizens had gathered at the town hall well before opening time. With both main hall and concert chamber full, loudspeakers were placed in Queen Street and Greys Avenue. The *Herald*'s estimate of 4000 would have been about half the real attendance.

As Pat Potter rose to declare the meeting open, in rushed the police. About 70 to 80 strong, they didn't walk—they ran, in true SS manner. The crowd erupted into the most spontaneous booing, hooting and counting-out I have ever seen. As one, the whole town hall rose and let them have it. Any other ideas they may have had stayed with them as they lined along one wall and remained motionless for the duration of the meeting. A repetition of Friday's violence would have incurred the same fate as that meted out to their predecessors outside the same hall in 1932.

Bob Adams, Mrs Esther Freeman of our Women's Auxiliary and Alan Baxter, president of Rotowaro Miners' Union and former Labour MP, received rousing receptions from the crowd, most of whom were hearing the truth for the first time.

I spoke for 70 minutes and as well as outlining the whole dispute, gave details of Friday's bashings. Johnny Mitchell had also noted the number of the bully boy who had knocked over the old man and put in the boot. I gave his number—326. An undercover policewoman, falsely claiming to be a press reporter, was given a seat at the press table.

At the conclusion of the meeting, three resolutions were carried practically unanimously. From the *Herald*:

> The first demanded that the Government immediately repeal the Emergency Regulations and call a compulsory conference of the principal parties in order

to resolve the present deadlock.

The second asked that Mr Barnes be given the right to state his case over the radio.

The third accused the police of provocation and brutality, and asserted that the Mayor, Sir John Allum, had misused his public office. It demanded an immediate public inquiry into the behaviour of the police, and the impeachment of the Mayor for seditious intention and seditious conspiracy.

A collection to buy food for women and children realised £240.

In those days £240 was a lot of money. This vast audience were not Mangakino hydro workers, from whom police had felt free to seize funds, and while those donating money consciously and deliberately flouted the

John Allum (mayor of Auckland) and Sid Holland (Prime Minister), 1952
(News Media: *Auckland Star* collection)

regulations, the police decided that discretion was the better part of valour and did nothing.

That same afternoon in the Wellington Town Hall, at an overflow meeting at which Toby Hill was the main speaker, the speakers were given outstanding receptions. The Press Association reported cheering and stamping, few hostile interjections and that women had formed a considerable proportion of the audience.

On 24 May the *Star* reported:

> For assaulting Alfred Farr [a leader of the new scab Cargo Workers' Union] outside the Town Hall on April 28, after a meeting at which the new waterfront union was formed, Patrick Kevin Michael Kirwin (34) a member of the deregistered watersiders' union, was sentenced to 14 days imprisonment with hard labour by Mr W.S. Spence SM.
>
> Counsel for Kirwin said he was married, had one child and owned his own home. He served in the Royal Navy and was in a destroyer doing convoy work. In 1944 he came to the Royal New Zealand Navy and served in the Pacific until 1945. Later he got his discharge in New Zealand and remained her. In 1948 Kirwin joined the Waterside Workers' Union. This was the first time he had appeared in any Court.

Pat Kirwin was typical of thousands of other watersiders, seamen, miners, drivers and freezing workers who had fought in two world wars and were now branded as part of a sinister communist plot to destroy the free world.

In contrast to men such as Pat, we can see the type of material from which the scabs were made from this report in the *Star* of 16 June:

> A charge of making a written statement to Constable D.H. Williams, alleging contrary to fact and without belief in the truth of the statement, that the crime of assault and robbery had been committed, was admitted by a member of the Auckland Cargo Workers' Union, Max Noble, aged 28, when he appeared before Mr L.G.H. Sinclair SM in the Magistrate's Court. He was convicted and fined £10.
>
> Sub Inspector H. Coddington said that the accused, soon after midnight on May 4, approached Constable Williams in Parnell, and complained that he had been assaulted and robbed of £15 by five or six members of the deregistered union. Subsequent inquiries revealed there was no truth in the statement. He had been drinking and engaged in a fight with another Maori, but had not been robbed.

Magistrates such as Spence were jailing watersiders, seamen and others fighting fascism for simply bestowing on vermin like Noble their correct epithet.

Throughout this time the underground miners were solid. The *Star* reported on 16 June that a meeting of about 400 miners and members of the United Mine Workers in Huntly had endorsed the stand of their national council and carried a motion to remain on strike by a big majority.

The mining community at Ohura was, by contrast, subject to police terrorism from the beginning. Under orders from Holland, it was now intensified. Men and women were continuously harassed at home and on the street. Houses were turned over at any time the police felt like it, and the lies and scab-herding efforts of Prendiville and Crook were the only communications allowed. Executive members were placed under house arrest.

We decided to break the blockade and organised a meeting in Ohura, together with Benneydale and Waikato miners, to restore some semblance of free speech. Police again decided that discretion was the better part of valour. We were represented by an Auckland waterside worker—Jim Knox—who later went on to great things in the FOL. The men and women of Ohura pledged their support and were solid till the end.

Solidarity was still coming from overseas. The *Otago Daily Times* reported that the government had received 2155 overseas cablegrams up until 10 May protesting against its handling of the waterfront dispute. Now we received news that a mass meeting of Melbourne watersiders on 23 May had decided to support a ban on all New Zealand ships coming to Australian ports. The meeting also decided to impose a strike levy of £1 a head on the 5400 Melbourne members to assist New Zealand watersiders. From Sydney, it was reported in early June that the crew had refused to sail with the *Aorangi* and it had been tied up indefinitely.

Disgust with the role of the Labour Party was widespread and so we were not surprised to read tucked away in the *Herald* that the Railway Tradesmen's Association of 2600 members had decided in a secret ballot to disaffiliate from the Federation of Labour. Nor were there headlines reporting on a Wellington meeting of 300 seamen that had recommended a general strike in support of our cause.

Grocers complained about irate customers abusing them over the continued shortage of goods, and chambers of commerce and kindred bodies now did an about-turn. Abuse of watersiders ran second to their hostile criticism of the shipowners for increasing freight rates by 50 per cent. It was generally accepted that this was an unjustifiable action by an unprincipled foreign monopoly, whose sole interest in New Zealand was holding it to ransom. Appeals to Holland were ignored.

Even the *Star*, now as biased and as vicious as the *Herald*, carried an article by its financial editor which read:

> Under the 50% freight surcharge imposed on New Zealand imports and exports by British shipowners, there is a widespread feeling in the Dominion

Both Sides Dig In

John Allum (mayor of Auckland) and Sid Holland (Prime Minister), 1952 (News Media: *Auckland Star* collection)

that an attempt at exploitation is being made by shipping interests.

Already, farmers' groups are comparing the action of the shipping companies with the sacrifices New Zealand has made, to the extent of many millions, in selling dairy produce and meat to Britain below world price levels over the past decade.

In the same issue a typically stupid statement by Sullivan to the effect that cargo handling had improved by 60 per cent did nothing to assuage the criticism.

Bloody Friday, 1 June

The night of 24 May was not one likely to tempt people from their fireside, least of all in Dunedin. However, it was at the Dunedin Town Hall that I again spoke to a packed house of over 2000 with Bill Richards, stalwart and respected trade unionist and president of the New Zealand Tramways Union, presiding. Dunedin Town Hall is massive but, for the first time in many years, it was necessary to open the top gallery. Apart from the fact that the large police contingent walked in, in contrast to the charge of their Auckland confreres, it was a replica of the Auckland meeting. The average New Zealander had had a gutful of lies and propaganda and wanted the truth. Once again, the regulations were openly defied and a relief collection of approximately £200 was taken while police watched silently.

I was scheduled to speak in the Wellington Town Hall on the afternoon of Sunday 3 June and in Christchurch the following Wednesday. In Auckland, meanwhile, a combined trade union committee had organised a meeting for Sunday afternoon in the domain to be addressed by Toby Hill and other speakers.

Due to the pressure of public opinion, the Auckland City Council had reversed its previous attitude and permission had been granted for the meeting. In order to publicise it, the committee decided to hold a march on Friday 1 June, which assembled at about 11am below the town hall to march up Queen Street. With some 600 or 700 assembled, members of our Women's Auxiliary led the way, carrying banners advertising the meeting. It was a peaceful demonstration but had gone only about 400 yards when, by Myers Park, they found Queen Street blocked off by police cars and massed rows of police. These unarmed and peaceful men and women halted and looked at the serried ranks of baton-wielding thugs. Not the slightest move was made to continue. Then it was on. Bloody Friday, 1 June 1951, Queen Street, Auckland. That women were in the forefront was of no concern to those uniformed bastards. Row after row charged; batons rising and falling on defenceless men and women.

A great victory for the forces of law and order, as claimed by Holland and his sycophantic press? I think few would agree. It was an exhibition of wanton brutality that will, for all time, remain an indelible and filthy stain on the escutcheon of the New Zealand police force. The injuries were dreadful and involved severe cuts and bruises to the scalp, face, eyebrow and forehead, concussion, and bruising to the shoulders, ribs and legs.

Next morning's *Herald* reported:

> ... There was a great deal of violence and resistance. The first police line was attacked and broken, but it sealed and the second line helped to drive them back. Bottles were thrown at the police and at least one constable received injuries through having been struck by a bottle. A sergeant had his face laid open.

National secretary Toby Hill speaking at the Auckland Domain during the lockout (Jock Barnes)

Even for the *Herald*, this evil, lying distortion of an unprovoked and brutal attack represented an all-time low.

Public Resistance Grows

While the police had their way on the Friday, they could not stop the massive protest on Sunday 3 June when 17,000 people assembled at the Auckland Domain. This was more than a trade union meeting. This was a gathering of Auckland citizens, meeting in condemnation of the Holland government and of police brutality two days before. As well as Toby Hill, speakers were Alan Baxter from the miners, Mrs A.M. Cassie from the combined women's committee, D. Armstrong from the Democratic Rights Council, Alec Drennan from our union, Miss L. Watene, our Maori speaker, and Charlie Horton from the Freezing Workers' Union. Pat Potter from the Labourers' Union was chairman. Miss Watene, 18 years of age, was on strike against the emergency regulations. Her ancestors, so noted for their oratory, would have been proud of this girl. She was brilliant. But this was not just oratory, it was a cry from the heart—an appeal to all New Zealanders to unite in the fight to restore freedom and democracy to our country. Great was the response.

'It was an orderly gathering,' said the *Herald*, 'but any reference to the police was received with prolonged booing.' Their goon squad of about 100 was kept well away. In SS formation, they stayed under the trees. A pity, really.

Meanwhile in Wellington, where I was speaking, the town hall was again filled to overflowing. Once more, we had it clearly demonstrated that the New Zealand public had had a surfeit of Holland's lying propaganda and wanted to hear our story. Once again, a collection of just on £200 was taken up while police looked on.

Wednesday night in Christchurch was very cold, but again the people turned out. I spoke for more than an hour to an audience of 1800 people and six policemen. The press reported the enthusiastic reception for our case, and my criticisms of the Prime Minister and the government for their handling of the waterfront dispute were loudly applauded. Near-unanimous resolutions demanded the repeal of the emergency regulations, permission for officials of the deregistered union to broadcast, and a compulsory conference of workers and employers involved in the dispute, and recorded strenuous objection to the use of state force against working-class people. George Orman, Buller member of the national council of United Mine Workers, and Archie Grant, secretary of the Trade Union Congress, also spoke, and a collection was taken to continue the campaign and also for the wives and children of striking miners.

This was how it was reported by the *Star*:

Mr Barnes addressed an audience of about 2,500 for 70 minutes. A motion called on the Government to repeal the Emergency Regulations and call a compulsory conference of parties to the dispute, failing which it should resign and place itself before the country. It was declared carried on a show of hands.

No longer could Holland prohibit public meetings and we were holding them left, right and centre. A crowd of 1100 in Wanganui were addressed by Tommy Wells and Jim Napier from the Wellington branch. Toby Hill spoke to 1500 at the Lower Hutt Recreation Ground. There were enthusiastic receptions and substantial collections at both.

Rank and file members were getting their baptism in public speaking. Many such as Jim Knox, Frank McNulty, Bill Andersen and Frank Barnard, who were later to invigorate the trade union movement and cleanse it of the Walsh machine, were at the forefront.

Auckland, for so long the target, had no shortage of experienced speakers, such as Alec Drennan and Johnny Mitchell. Meetings were held throughout most of the North Island. Especially with the farming community, the 50 per cent freight increase guaranteed attentive audiences. Protest cables from overseas flooded Holland's desk.

It was now 16 weeks, and 7600 out of 8100 watersiders were just as solid and united as they were at the start, the only branch defecting being Timaru, which had been rotten from the start. The two-week Blitzkrieg promised by Walsh was proving to be a disaster. Dulles now put the squeeze on Holland's mate Menzies. The assistance we were getting now from our Australian fellow workers had to be stopped. Pig Iron Menzies needed no urging, and democracy, as in New Zealand, was thrown out of Australian windows.

From a Sydney paper:

> Federal investigation officers today raided the Sydney and Melbourne offices of the Communist-dominated Waterside Workers' Federation and the Seamen's Union. They thoroughly searched the premises, turned out drawers, lockers and cabinets, but made no arrests.
>
> The deputy Prime Minister, Mr Fadden, told a Country Party conference that the raids were the first step to rid Australia of a menace she could not afford to harbour.
>
> 'The sooner we find out who are against us and kick them out, the sooner we will discharge our responsibility to ourselves, our children and the generations that follow,' he said.
>
> The Melbourne *Herald's* Canberra correspondent says the raids are the first direct result of a Cabinet decision to force a show-down with Communist wharfies.
>
> The correspondent adds that the Government already possesses a good deal of information, and the main purpose of the raids was to obtain

supplementary material upon which prosecutions against union leaders could be launched under the Crimes Act.

A number of books, ledgers and other documents were taken from the offices after a search lasting three hours.

In immediate retaliation 4000 Sydney watersiders walked off 57 ships this afternoon and a number of seamen left their vessels.

Labour's Failure

With the ever-growing shortages of goods and services and general public reaction, we had reached a critical stage. With miners, seamen, freezing workers, cooks and stewards, Wellington drivers and many others, our members had been harassed, persecuted, jailed, fined and bashed by Holland's SS for nearly four months. Worse, they had seen their wives and families suffer. While we had dealt the forces of fascism some mighty blows, cost them many millions of pounds, given Dulles and his Washington warmongers an unexpected reverse and exposed the shipowners, there had to be an end. A determined onslaught from the Labour opposition would have destroyed Holland and his fascists. However, when put to the test, the Labour Party did nothing—or worse.

Although the efforts of Nash were weak, he was at least mounting some protest, and when his list of colleagues was surveyed, it would be unfair to be too critical. In the main, they were a collection of timeservers and no-hopers who could not have managed a peanut stall, but immeasurably worse were renegades like Semple and Walsh. Nash's deputy, C.F. Skinner, had already attacked our union and defended Holland and his emergency regulations, but that was nothing to the vitriolic attack mounted on our union in general and myself in particular by that renegade and repentant sinner Bob Semple. Needless to say, it received maximum publicity from press and radio.

Semple's tirade was followed by one from Noel Donaldson, who had been expelled from the Auckland branch for his anti-union activities and was now in his rightful place—the scab union. In the *Herald* of 8 June he criticised Nash and endorsed every sentiment expressed by Semple. The rat and the snake lay down together.

However, after Nash's next effort, it was hard to make out a case for him. The *Star* of 8 June said:

> Speaking to an audience of about 500 in the Huntly Town Hall, the leader of the Opposition, Mr Nash, said he had never defended the actions of the watersiders . . . 'The police have done a good job. Whether they have been right or wrong in some incidents I do not want to comment.' . . . He believed the Government had been justified in issuing the emergency proclamation.

What a pack of imposters! The Labour Party parliamentary opposition, there to safeguard the rights and freedoms of all New Zealand citizens, acquiescing in the face of open fascism.

The Holland government also did its best to prevent news leaking out overseas. The New Zealand government official news bulletin, which is disseminated to the British press and to a number of New Zealand organisations and New Zealanders in London, was to all intents and purposes absolutely useless to anybody wanting to become even reasonably well informed about the strike. Only the *Economist* and the *New Statesman* carried articles explaining the background and the promulgation of the emergency regulations. The latter commented that there was no precedent for these regulations in the history of any British dominion. They gave the government unlimited powers to override any existing law without any reference whatsoever to Parliament. The *New Statesman* also commented on the absence of any provision in the regulations for the calling together of Parliament within a stipulated time following the proclamation of a state of emergency. The absence of this safeguard was exploited to the hilt by the Holland government.

If the Labour Party had remained silent while fascism strode New Zealand it would have been bad enough; but for them to endorse the emergency regulations, praise police brutality and attack our union exposed them for the gutless fakers they were. This was the great betrayal. Their years as the government of New Zealand had seen many conflicts with us. Scrap iron for Japan, the *Mountpark, Barnhill, Rangitoto*, lampblack and a host of others had seen them side with big business and employers.

The Labour Party annual conference in Christchurch on 13 June presented rank and file members with the opportunity to stage an all-out offensive against Holland, US imperialism and the demise of freedom in New Zealand. However, with scab-herders such as Baxter, Freeman and Glading on the platform, together with politicians who supported emergency regulations, the result was as expected. Nash and his colleagues were congratulated and their actions endorsed. An amendment moved by John Roberts, secretary of the Canterbury Clothing Trades Union, to send congratulations to all those who had fought for working-class rights and for democracy was defeated.

'What's in a name?' A wealth of wisdom in one phrase. If there has ever been a word more foully abused that 'Labour', I have yet to hear it. The 'Labour Party' had allied itself with Holland in his attempt to snuff out the lights of freedom and democracy.

The scabs did not have to wait long to experience the gratitude of the shipowners. Marchington and Belford addressed them in Auckland and Wellington, with proposals that would reduce their hourly rate from 4/7½ to 4/3. An early introduction to the type of individuals to whom they had prostituted themselves!

My Wife Prosecuted

On 15 June the *Star* ran the following:

Mrs H. Barnes Accused of Inciting Disorder

It is with some reluctance that we prosecute a woman in these matters, said Senior Detective J.B. Finlay in the police court today, in outlining information against Freda Ellen Barnes.

Mrs Barnes, wife of Harold Barnes, president of the deregistered waterside workers' union, was charged that on June 1 at Auckland she did incite disorder.

Mr P.C.P. McGavin, of Wellington, pleaded not guilty for Mrs Barnes . . .

It was alleged that Mrs Barnes said twice, 'Don't you kick me.' These words it was suggested could incite disorder.

Few of the general public would have accepted that the words 'don't you kick me' constituted inciting disorder. Evidently, that was also the opinion of Magistrate L.G.H. Sinclair, for he allowed the information to be amended by adding: 'Come back you yellow bastards and get these cops.'

My wife never uttered those words and said so, adding that she knew who the yellow bastards were, and they were not watersiders or their wives.

Pat McGavin ripped the prosecution to pieces and called many witnesses who gave the lie to the police story. Mrs Dorothy Eyre, who was standing by my wife at the time, gave evidence that she had been punched in the face by a policeman and that Detective Packman had said, 'You are a pack of prostitutes and you are only here to cause trouble.'

In reply to Pat McGavin, Inspector Southworth said there were about 10 women in the front of the procession and he did not take any steps to protect them.

The prosecution had taken such a hiding that Sinclair thought it advisable to reserve his decision. We had no doubts about the outcome. An active Justice of the Peace for some years, my wife wrote to the Minister of Justice, resigning. She told him that she refused to be associated in any way with the administration of 'justice' in New Zealand, 1951-style.

When Sinclair finally announced his verdict on the charge against my wife on 22 June, he showed complete disregard for all witnesses for the defence, and accepted the evidence of Packman and his mate Russell. He voiced no criticism of Packman calling the women a pack of prostitutes. And nor were charges pressed against Mrs Dorothy Eyre, who was sister-in-law of Dean Eyre, National MP. No doubt it was felt prudent not to charge Dorothy with any manufactured offence! In fining my wife £10 and costs, Sinclair stated that with a male, this 'offence' would have been met by a term of imprisonment. As it was, his fellow dispenser of 'justice', Judge Luxford, was doing just that to Dick Johnson in a nearby court. Dick, an Auckland watersider, was sentenced to one month's hard labour after being charged with using the words, 'Come on, let's get them, don't take this lying down' at the police riot on 1 June. Dick was convicted on the sole testimony of Constable D.A. Rowe, despite a wealth of contrary evidence.

Again, on 15 June, we read of a demand by the Federation of Labour for stronger police methods. The flood of illegal pamphlets distressed them no end. Holland duly obliged and announced the strict prohibition of street marches and demonstrations and sterner action to be taken against incitement. After the green light given by the Labour Party conference, this was as expected.

This new regulation was soon put into action when Terry Flynn and Mrs Eileen Deniston were refused a permit for the Women's Auxiliary to hold a meeting in the concert chamber to outline the waterside workers' case to the women of Wellington. The chosen speakers, Mrs M. Heptinstall, Mrs K. Bollinger and Mrs F. Barnes, were rejected, the first two on the grounds that they were the wives of a seaman and a freezing worker respectively, and the last-named for no reason. Inspector McLennan also informed our representatives that I myself would not be allowed to speak again at a public meeting anywhere in New Zealand, and that the only reason I was not arrested at the last town hall meeting was the possibility of innocent persons being hurt.

Our national executive met on 12 June. We had now lost a third port, Port Chalmers, which had joined Timaru and New Plymouth in scabbing on their former comrades. However, reports from all other branches were unanimous in that they were solid and united.

A meeting with representatives of seamen, miners, freezing workers, drivers and labourers was scheduled for the following day.

The past few months had seen some great work by rank and file members of Wellington branch. Two of these, Eddie Manson and Terry Flynn, had addressed a Dunedin branch meeting where the members gave them an outstanding reception. Gib Smith, the Dunedin secretary, was doing a great job there. Eddie and Terry were denied a meeting at Port Chalmers, however. The secretary of the scab union said that if his men were to hear from them, more than half would walk off the wharf! We also heard from Wanganui that Labour MP Mrs Ratana was actively engaged in recruiting scabs.

On 13 June the combined conference of all unions involved carried this resolution unanimously:

That this conference pledges its determination to fight until an honourable settlement is obtained, based on the principles of no victimisation to any worker involved and the repeal of the Emergency Regulations.

While close liaison had been maintained at all times, the combined meeting now decided to form a national strike committee.

Meanwhile, the lamentable exhibition at the Labour Party conference encouraged Holland to greater efforts. I had been asked to address a meeting of Wellington seamen—not a public meeting—and when I arrived I was faced with half the police force in Wellington and denied admission.

On 21 June the annual conference of the New Zealand Drivers' Federation, which represented 11,420 members, passed a resolution condemning the actions and press statements of the national executive of the Federation of Labour concerning the waterfront dispute. The conference recorded its unqualified disapproval of the action of the FOL national executive in joining forces with the Tory government in its attempt to smash militant trade unionism and, in particular, the New Zealand Waterside Workers' Union. The resolution also declared that the space accorded by the newspapers to statements by leaders of the FOL was a further indication of the leader of the FOL's alliance with the labour movement's enemies.

11   TO THE BITTER END, AND A NEW BEGINNING

The key to our continued fight was the solidarity within our ranks. Under constant pressure from the Minister of Labour, the underground miners had put up a magnificent fight, and on 22 June a mass meeting of 900 Waikato miners unanimously rejected Sullivan's terms for a return to work. In a statement after the meeting, R. Dodds, secretary of the Waikato Central Committee of Miners' Unions, said:

> The Minister, by his letter, would like us to believe that there is no intended victimisation within the mining industry, but then plainly states that those open cast workers who have been on strike cannot return to their previous employment.
>
> Very definitely a new phase of the strike has emerged and a greater spirit of consolidated resistance has developed. It would seem apparent that the Minister believes the prolongation of the strike has beaten the workers. In actual fact, his statement has administered a spinal injection to those who were weakening and who had favoured a return to work.
>
> His terms for resumption of work would give dictatorial powers to the employers and trade unions would only be a mockery to the men they represent.

Waikato miners threatened to declare black all Waikato mines and render Huntly a ghost town. Drunk with power, Sullivan had now bought a fight with the mayor and business community of Huntly. He and his fellow fascists would be hard put to label them as parties to the communist plot! A Wellington branch bulletin informed us that Sullivan's proposals were also rejected by members there, and national union policy was unanimously endorsed.

However, despite the good news from Waikato, there were growing problems evident in the Miners' Union. A combined meeting involving freezing workers, miners, drivers, seamen, waterside workers and Auckland labourers heard reports of victimisation amongst some miners who had returned to work at Ohura and King Country. Often living in isolated communities and continually stabbed in the back by Prendiville and Crook, their condition was not good. George Lawson reported that some in the Waikato had been urging a return to work, but victimisation had effectively stopped that. This was something miners would never accept and while that threat remained, there would be no return to work. It was unanimously resolved that the national strike committee meet on 26 June to discuss the situation further.

Of chief concern at the national strike committee meeting of that day was the miners' position. In isolated communities, as most of them were, they were suffering the most. Wives of other union men could obtain employment to some extent; with miners' wives this was almost impossible.

Sold out by the FOL, and for good measure by Prendiville and Crook, they were still determined to go back only as a united body and with no victimisation.

Greatly appreciated by the miners was that, at a meeting of 1500 Auckland watersiders addressed by Arthur McGougan and me, our members raised £111 for miners' relief. What greater tribute could be paid to the superb rank and file of the Auckland branch—locked out to a man for 20 weeks?

Sid Giles and Arthur McGougan also reported on a meeting with the general secretary of the Auckland Railway Workers' Union. The response from this union, which six months before had the support of all now involved in the fight against fascism, was not to its credit.

The following day Hill and I reported on our meeting with the national council of Seamen. They were of the opinion that the time had arrived for watersiders to go back and capture control of the scab unions and assured us we would have both their active and financial assistance in doing so.

Amongst drivers, however, Alan Melville advised that he had met Bert Bockett, secretary of the Department of Labour, who was very concerned that drivers were refusing to go to the wharves and at the poor quality and number of scabs. Clearly the situation was uneven.

Strange allies were also starting to emerge. The arrogance of the shipowners in raising their charges by 50 per cent brought forth this beauty in the Auckland press—regrettably not just five months but years overdue:

> New Zealand is at the mercy of a shipping ring and something should be done by the Government to break it, in the opinion of several speakers at the annual conference of the Meat and Wool Section of the Federated Farmers. The conference will seek the opinion of the statutory producer boards on an Auckland remit proposing that the Government should be pressed to charter at least two refrigerated vessels for the overseas trade in an attempt to cut freight rates and break the present shipping monopoly.

Shades of the Royal Commission!

There was now widespread criticism of the shipowners, and even the

Star was now questioning the emergency regulations. Perhaps comment from Australian papers on the 'gutless New Zealand press' was having some effect. Many New Zealanders were being forced to accept that the shipping monopoly had created a new brand of robber barons.

Stranger still was the navy. Speaking at a Navy League function on 3 July, Commodore F.A. Ballance, Chief of Naval Staff, made it abundantly clear that the navy had had more than enough. He was reported as saying:

> The dispute had been going on for so long that people were taking for granted the fact that servicemen were still working on the wharves. For more than four months they had worked on the wharves and people were accepting it as part of the normal waterfront routine that servicemen should do part of the work.
>
> 'I read in a newspaper recently that there were 1000 men working on the Wellington waterfront but when I investigated I found that 750 of them were servicemen.' [He said] 18 or 20 coastal vessels were now being manned by naval men and naval men were also working coal on the West Coast. It was not the Navy's job to handle bales of wool and the longer they did it the longer it would be before they could get back to their real job of preparing for a possible war.

Clearly this was a grave breach of emergency regulations, but no proceedings were brought against the commodore, nor did Sullivan threaten to deregister the navy! Labelling Barnes and Hill as the Lenin and Trotsky of New Zealand was one thing, but citing Federated Farmers and Commodore Ballance as Cominform agents decidedly another!

Voting to Return to Work

While this pressure on the shipowners was welcome, it did not remove that bearing down on us. Miners' solidarity forced Sullivan to back off from his threats of victimisation. Where work no longer existed for open-cast workers, other suitable work would be found. He spoke no more of victimisation and his assurances were now accepted by a majority of miners. King Country had voted to continue the strike, but as a united body they had come out and as a united body they would go back. From 4 July, men who for 20 long weeks had fought fascism and treachery from the top, began again to work the mines. Their fight with that of their wives and families added another proud chapter to the history of New Zealand's working people. I pay homage to the miners and their womenfolk who fought fascism in '51.

It was at the same time, the first week of July, that the pressure became too much even for our members. We were by now faced with a grim situation as the situation in the different ports varied quite strongly. Timaru and Port Chalmers had returned to work, and on 4 July they were joined by Lyttelton where for some time there had been efforts by some of those in the branch leadership to undermine the fighting spirit of the large number of militant and well-informed rank and file members from that port. Elsewhere persistent government efforts to get scabbing under way failed dismally. Greymouth and Westport had none, with the only work on the West Coast being done by the armed forces. The same was true in Wellington, where the number of scabs was negligible, with the armed forces again responsible for the only work being carried out. However, in Wellington we faced problems of a different kind. Despite the tireless activities of fine individuals such as Ron Dore, Alf Kite, Archie Dellaway, Terry Flynn and Eddie Manson, leading branch officials had been conducting private negotiations with the Minister of Labour and leaders of the scab union for some weeks. In all other ports, our men stood solid by the union. Auckland branch was a special case in its own right. It had been the main target of the government which was determined to destroy it for good. The Holland government, the press, the shipowners and the FOL had expended millions of pounds and months of ceaseless efforts in organising police, propaganda and scabs on the Auckland waterfront. They had succeeded in recruiting large numbers of scabs from outside our ranks, to the extent that the employers had by now reached their manning target, even if many of the scabs quit soon after discovering what waterfront life was really like.

It was in these circumstances that we met the National Council of Seamen on 4 July who argued that we should now try to get as many of our men as possible back to the waterfront. The seamen resolved to recommend a return to work on Monday 8 July. We asked them to hold this over until after the national strike committee meeting the same day. They agreed. To return piecemeal would have been disastrous; but to return as a united front would serve notice to Holland and his masters that all that was over was round one and when the gong sounded for round two—we would again come out fighting.

The national strike committee met on 8 July. The following were present:
    Seamen's Union: F.P. Walsh and D. McLeod
    Freezing Workers' Union: Con Doyle and Sid Giles
    Drivers' Union: Tom Magee and Jack Drury
    Waterside Workers' Union: Jock Barnes and Toby Hill
    Miners' Union: Charlie Kemp
    Auckland Labourers' Union: Pat Potter

In opening the meeting, Sid Giles stated that the time had come to review the position, in view of the fact that the national council of Seamen had met and that the Waterside Workers' national council was meeting next day. What with the decision of the miners to return to work, it was clear that a full discussion was now warranted. I moved the following resolution, seconded Con Doyle:

> After 22 weeks of the greatest industrial struggle in New Zealand's history in which 20,000 workers have stood alone against the most vicious employers' Government seen outside fascism, the locked-out workers and strikers hold to the principles of Unionism more tenaciously and consciously than ever.
>
> After squandering tens of millions of money and their last remaining moral assets to smash at the heart of the New Zealand trade union movement, the employing class has failed. Only the abandonment of Union policy by the rank and file and their repudiation of their fighting leadership would represent victory to the employers.
>
> But despite their heroic stand in the face of sacrifice, hardship and persecution for themselves and families, the workers would have victory only if an aroused people had joined them to wipe out the Emergency Regulations and compelled the shipowners and shipowners' Government to negotiate.
>
> Neither capital nor labour can claim victory. The issue is yet to be decided.
>
> In this situation the maritime unions could turn their backs to the sea and leave the employers to the chaos of their own making—and to the scabs. But the ships and the wharves are the seamen's and the watersiders' own work places. They are the ground, together with mines, freezing works and other industries, where the battle for trade union rights must be won.
>
> Now is the time for that battle to be joined. Now is the time to consolidate the magnificent fighting unity developed during this epic struggle.
>
> Supremely confident of the conscious discipline of our ranks we call upon every individual member to return to work and hold up the banner of his Union on the job.
>
> We call upon watersiders, seamen, miners, freezing workers, drivers and all other unionists to stand by their fellow workers in a positive fighting programme to overcome screening, hold conditions and clean out scabbery root and branch.
>
> To this end the organisation of the Combined Unions resolves to join in a mutual assistance pact and pledge financial and moral support to any of the Unions requiring it to re-establish themselves.
>
> In unity we have fought, and in unity we return to fight again.
>
> In twelve months' time it will be time to say whose is the victory. We are confident in our strength.

After very full discussion, the motion was carried unanimously and it was further resolved that where possible, members resume work on Wednesday 11 July.

Toby Hill then moved and Tom Magee seconded:

> That this Committee continue to function in order that reports from the Unions involved be received and policy determined accordingly.

Bitter End, New Beginning

This too, was unanimously endorsed.

Our national council was meeting next day. In the meantime, Walsh had reported back to the seamen. They refused to accept his report and I had to attend and give them the story.

On the following day 31 delegates from the various ports attended our national council meeting, together with the following accredited visitors: Pat Potter, Charlie Kemp, Sid Giles, Con Doyle and Bob Adams.

In opening the meeting, and on behalf of our negotiating committee, I gave a comprehensive report of happenings since the last council meeting. This was unanimously approved. My next task was to move the adoption of the national strike committee's recommendations. This was seconded by Toby Hill.

I stated that if it was a matter affecting our union alone, I would not be moving it, but it was not. For five months we had received the magnificent support of other unions and individual workers who made it their quarrel because of their devotion to basic trade union principles and their resolute opposition to fascism. A resolution maintaining that amazing display of solidarity was of primary importance. To have had division in the ranks of those who had fought and suffered for five months would have been a trade union disaster and a fascist victory. This resolution maintained the unparalleled unity we had developed and laid the foundation for round two.

There had been a few disquieting features in our own ranks, mainly in Timaru and Port Chalmers. Their actions stank to high heaven. They not only scabbed on their own, but what was worse, on seamen, miners, freezing workers, drivers and all others who stood with us. The actions of some Wellington officials was also cause for concern and their explanation would be welcomed.

All 31 delegates spoke, with only one against—Archie Dellaway. Archie, an ex-miner, would not accept victimisation in any shape or form. We all knew that members from the Auckland branch would be targeted and barred from returning to their former jobs. Archie was in favour of declaring the waterfronts black and turning our members loose on other industries. He believed this would be to the entire benefit of the trade union movement. Looking back, there was a good deal of validity in his argument.

Alec Drennan also moved:

> That this Council condemns the National Executive of the Federation of Labour for its actions in this dispute. We declare that for all time they will stand as scab herders who have openly and actively collaborated with the shipowners and the Holland Government against the working class of New Zealand.

This too was carried unanimously. It was further unanimously resolved that our national office be retained.

We now turned to the issue of the Wellington branch and its role in conducting separate negotiations with the scab union. Johnny Mitchell, who had visited the branch, said that it would be hard to explain the officials' behaviour to Auckland members, some of whom were still in jail for union activities. Eddie Napier's explanation was not too well received in some quarters, with Johnny Mitchell and John Connor, also of Auckland, recording their names against it. That our concern was well founded was shown by subsequent actions of the same officials.

Addresses were given by Charlie Kemp, Con Doyle, Sid Giles, Bob Adams and Pat Potter. Valiant fighters all, and proven in the biggest industrial dispute ever before or since in New Zealand. Yet it was more than an industrial dispute—it was a fight against fascism, a fight against US imperialism, and a fight for peace.

Early Election Called

Meanwhile, with Parliament having at last been assembled on 26 June, the customary farce was being performed by a cast that would have been booed at a kindergarten party.

Typical of the hysteria was this effort by National MP Dean Eyre:

> New Zealand troops in Korea were engaged in a shooting war against the Communists. There was a Communist war in New Zealand too. In Korea Communists were being shot—but in New Zealand they were given the freedom of the country. Both the Korean and New Zealand Communists were working for the same master. The Soviet was aiming at world domination, either through a hot war or a cold war.

John Foster Dulles would have been proud of him!

Nash did a bit of shadow-sparring, but after his 'neither for nor against' and his admission that Labour too would have used the regulations, a boxing referee would have declared it a no contest. Even worse were the rest of them. With the exception of Tommy Armstrong, it appeared that most of Nash's colleagues disapproved of even Nash's few expressions of mild displeasure.

However, 5 July saw Nash move a motion of no confidence in the government. He concentrated chiefly on its financial policy and the rate of construction of state housing. However, due to his own public statements and those of C.F. Skinner and other Labour members, a comprehensive attack on the emergency regulations had been hopelessly prejudiced.

As the debate meandered on, government comment was largely confined to the communist menace and praise for the FOL, while those of the opposition not in the parliamentary bar might as well have been.

On 12 July Holland announced an early dissolution of Parliament to contest a general election on the issue of the waterfront lockout, or 'strike' as he called it.

That had looked inevitable following the Labour Party's efforts outside and inside Parliament, and its full support of the FOL, and the one-way radio and press coverage to which we had been subjected. Our public meetings had shown that a full-scale attack on Holland and his emergency regulations could have brought about a change of government. However, with the timeservers and renegades that made up most of the opposition, this was never a possibility.

The *Star* of 19 July reported remarks of Dr A.M. Finlay that were to be the pattern of most Labour Party speakers in the election campaign. At a public meeting in Devonport Dr Finlay sought to explain the party's disgraceful policy of being 'neither for nor against' the deregistered watersiders:

> Their previous history of abuses and disputes made it impossible for the Party to sympathise with them. They had refused arbitration at the outset and wanted to be their own counsel, judge and jury.

As a lawyer, Finlay knew full well that he could produce no evidence to support his claims, but that was of secondary importance to the policy of most of his colleagues—to abuse waterside workers. The next few weeks were to see a contest between Labour candidates and the Holland gang as to who could hurl the most abuse at watersiders. Comment on the fascist regulations or the causes of the dispute were conspicuous by their absence. Shipowners were everybody's friends, as was John Foster Dulles. After all, a Labour government would have done the same. For either party to mention that the 'strike' was in fact a lockout would have made blackballing from the club a distinct possibility.

A week later the scab Auckland cargo workers submitted a claim for an increase in the hourly rate from 4/7½ to 5/3—a rate we had previously claimed and justified. If there had been any genuine opposition from the Labour Party, this would have been the last straw for the Holland government. What a break! However, the Labour Party ignored it—joining the hate campaign against watersiders offered more political advantage.

Wellington next day produced another gem. Here we had 1200 deregistered men back at work, as against 200 scabs. At a stopwork meeting a no-confidence motion was passed against scab union president A.K. Bell and scab secretary A.D. Ayr. Officers and executive from the deregistered branch were then provisionally elected and conducted the rest of the meeting, which concluded at 9.25am. On returning to their jobs the men found employers had decided to lock them out for two days. For years similar tactics had evoked but one comment from press and politicians—watersiders were to blame. Now it was on again. Holland and his gang agreed that this move by the shipowners could be a fatal blow to their election prospects and, for the first time in living memory, a New Zealand prime minister attacked the shipowners. Headlines in the *Evening Post* of 27 July proclaimed:

> **Suspension of Wellington Unionists**
> **Mr Holland Condemns Action of Employers**
>
> 'I think the action on the part of the employers was precipitate and in view of the circumstances obtaining cannot be too strongly condemned,' said the Prime Minister this afternoon, after conferring with shipping companies' representatives . . .
>
> 'I appeal to the men to try to avoid irritation, and other causes that lead to these troubles. Surely New Zealand has had enough industrial strife to last it for years . . .
>
> 'We will never get anywhere if employers use their power to threaten people with mass dismissal. The Government will be glad to co-operate with employers and employees to smooth out any difficulties.'

The ultimate volte-face! A majority of deregistered watersiders were now back on the waterfronts of New Zealand outside Auckland, and Holland was pleading for co-operation! One shipowner's action had destroyed their vicious campaign.

To the Labour Party it was a gift from the gods, but the gift was rejected. Too many were committed to their odious election plan—abuse waterside workers more than Holland. 'We are neither for nor against' meant neither for watersiders nor against the shipowners. Typical was the following:

> Addressing a meeting at Hillsborough School, P.T. Curran said, 'The National Party has for years maintained a very close liaison with Mr Barnes. Mr Barnes actively co-operated with the National Party.' . . . [Curran said] he had confidence in the people on the wharf at present. He did not want the votes of deregistered watersiders.

He was not to be disappointed—he didn't get them!

Similar sentiments were expressed by A.G. Osborne in Onehunga, Nordmeyer in Newmarket, Christchurch member Macfarlane in Grey Lynn and all too many others. The question might well have been asked—why were they standing against Holland?

As a change from me, Nash decided to throw in Pat Potter and accused him too of co-operating with Sid Holland. McLagan also did not disappoint. His effort to remove the Holland government was his customary tirade of vilification and abuse of me. How he must have regretted not being there to do Sullivan's job! Further claims by National candidates that the emergency regulations had been taken from Labour pigeon-holes were not denied.

Two Months' Hard Labour

Perhaps the greatest tribute paid to me as a workers' representative was the hatred I inspired in politicians and the press. On 7 July, application for leave to begin proceedings alleging criminal defamation against myself were filed in the Auckland Magistrate's Court by the Crown Prosecutor, Mr V.R. Meredith, on behalf of an Auckland police constable, Robert James Edwards. The application, which referred to a statement allegedly made by me when addressing a meeting in the Auckland Town Hall on 20 May, said that the words I had used were 'likely to injure the reputation of the said Robert James Edwards, of Auckland, Constable No. 326, by exposing him to hatred or contempt or to injure him in his profession, and did thereby commit the offence of criminal defamation'. Anything said of Edwards had been passing comment and, rather than injuring him in his profession, was more likely to enhance his prospects in the Auckland police force!

An application to proceed against me under section 11 of the Law of Libel Amendment Act 1910 was heard by Judge Luxford on 13 July. In legal argument, Pat McGavin said this was the first prosecution to be brought under the act since it came into force in 1910, and it seemed it was the first

Outside the Supreme Court, (from left) Alec Drennan, Jock Barnes, Clarry Armstrong, Bob Adams and Johnny Mitchell consider legal tactics (Freda Barnes in background) (Jock Barnes)

in the long history of British justice. Luxford reserved his decision, but not for long, as leave was granted next day.

It is of historical interest to recall the circumstances under which this act became law. The Law of Libel Amendment Bill had a rough passage through the Parliament of 1910. The bill was sharply challenged by, amongst others, Mr Herdman (Wellington North), who opposed the removal of trial by jury. In Hansard, volume 153, it is reported:

> Mr Herdman said that the proposal law placed in the hands of a Magistrate the absolute right to find a man guilty of criminal libel. He had not a great deal of confidence in some Magistrates. No doubt there were some excellent ones but there were also others who made grave mistakes and he was not sure if it were wise to extend the scope of the law so as to enable a Magistrate to deal with cases of such gravity. It was a very serious matter to deprive a citizen of his ordinary rights of trial by jury . . .

Massey (then Leader of the Opposition and later to find fame in the 1913 waterfront dispute) said that if the object of the clause was what he understood it to be, he sympathised with it, but he agreed that too much power was being placed in the hands of magistrates. The 'object of the clause' that evinced Massey's sympathy was basically one of preventing cartoonists and satirists from lampooning judges and politicians.

I had no illusions about the class nature of capitalist law and, of course,

Outside the Supreme Court, (from left) Pat McGavin, John Platts-Mills, Jock Barnes (Jock Barnes)

in '51 any semblance of justice that might ever have existed had been abandoned. We knew I was already convicted; the only question was, how long would I get?

The case was heard before H. Jenner Wily on 2 and 3 August. Pat McGavin appeared for me and gave his usual outstanding performance. V. Meredith, Crown Prosecutor, appeared for Edwards. Their case was a family affair—Constable Robert Edwards was supported by his father, Senior Sergeant F.W. Edwards.

Under normal circumstances the fact that only one other police witness was called would have been of considerable significance, but such details meant nothing when 'justice' 1951-style was being dispensed. Jenner Wily faithfully obeyed the rules—Edwards father and son were paragons of virtue and all our witnesses liars.

The verdict: two months' hard labour.

After four days in Mount Eden I was visited by Johnny Mitchell and John Platts-Mills. John was a former Labour MP in the British House of Commons, a New Zealand Rhodes Scholar, and was recognised as being in the top bracket of barristers in Britain.

Johnny Mitchell told me that Auckland members had carried a resolution that I should appeal. John Platts-Mills said events in New Zealand had been the cause of deep concern to many in Britain and, while he was here for a holiday, he would like to handle my appeal. Needless to say I agreed and was released pending the appeal.

My wife Freda was also caught up in legal battles. At an election meeting in Mount Eden on 15 August the *Star* reported Bill Fortune, Minister of Police, as follows:

> 'Who is the Combined Women's Committee?' An interjector replied, 'Working men's wives' and Fortune replied, 'No, the Communist Party, it is a Communist organisation.'

By his remarks, the minister exposed the Women's Committee to the hatred and contempt of the peoples of New Zealand and the 'free world'. For six months Fortune and his gang had been proclaiming that Communism was a dire threat not only to New Zealand but to the whole of the 'free world'. Every crime, alleged or otherwise, was laid at the door of the Communist Party. The Communist Party was the black beast, evil incarnate. By the government's own rules, unless it were true, this had to be criminal libel most dastardly. It was not true, and well did they know it. My wife, as chairperson of the Women's Committee, applied for leave to prosecute Fortune for criminal libel. However, application was refused by Justice L.G.H. Sinclair, the same magistrate who had earlier fined Freda £10 and costs for allegedly 'inciting disorder' on Bloody Friday 1 June.

On 5 September my wife appealed against Sinclair's earlier decision at the Supreme Court. By coincidence this was the day when I too had my appeal heard, also at this court. While I was in the lower court, Freda's appeal against her fine was being heard in an upstairs court. However, in her case it was a repetition of the first hearing. Officers Packman and Russell told the truth and all witnesses for the defence were liars. Pat McGavin called evidence to prove beyond all doubt that Packman had called them a pack of prostitutes. Nothing could have been more conducive to creating disorder, but on this Justice Stanton was silent, and Freda's appeal was dismissed.

My own appeal lasted for two days, with most of the courtroom occupied by lawyers eager to hear John Platts-Mills. They were not disappointed. They saw and heard a master craftsman calmly and deliberately massacre backward beginners. Alec Drennan, Clarry Armstrong, Johnny Mitchell, Gordon McKay and Dick Richards all gave supportive evidence that the crown prosecutor could not refute. He was not a decent workout for the master.

Father Edwards opined that if the charge against son Edwards was upheld, he would be dismissed from the police force. If such was the case, we were left wondering why a hundred or more had not been dismissed after the Queen Street bashings on 1 June!

Mr Justice Finlay said he would deliver an oral judgment later.

My wife and I, together with John Platts-Mills, Pat McGavin and friends, returned to our home in Kelmarna Avenue. That evening we got a phone call from the judge's registrar, the late Eric Mosely. Freda had gone to law school with him and they were friends. He said he had good news. The judge had said that there was no way he could send me back to jail, but there would be a fine and it would not be a big one. The judge had also said that in all his years he had never heard such a brilliant exhibition as he had been privileged to hear from John Platts-Mills.

However, Eric had not reckoned with the politics of the case. On 12 September the final figures for the return of the Holland government were announced. On the same day, Justice Finlay handed down his decision—appeal dismissed. The judge was evidently carrying out riding orders from Wellington. So it was back to my Mount Eden dungeon.

I think it was correctly summarised by the *Auckland Watersiders' Bulletin* of 4 August.

> If ever there was a political sentence in New Zealand's history this is it. The Holland Government recognises the danger of Barnes, not as a person, but as a symbol of a policy that stands directly in the path of the plans of the Tories with all its warmongering, its Union smashing, its frame ups and brutality. That is why they want him out of the way.

Bitter End, New Beginning

Fresh Fields for Sowing

Little by little, as is generally the case, elements of truth leaked out. The *Star* of 30 November reported that:

> Shipowners gave £1500 to help establish the Auckland Cargo Workers' Union and guaranteed £500 to the president, Mr W.F. McMullen, to enable him to meet publishing bills for his newspaper, *The New Waterfront*.

Holland's Royal Commission had now begun to meet, and this blatant bribe was revealed when shipowners' representatives were questioning value received. The honeymoon was over. Now, to the scabs' dismay, the shipowners abandoned all camouflage and again hoisted the Jolly Roger.

By now, although weekly meetings of members were still being held, illegal bulletins were still being distributed, and the relief depot was still functioning, many hundreds of victimised Auckland watersiders were out preaching the gospel of unionism in a wide variety of industries. Labour was in demand, jobs were plentiful, and fresh fields were ripe for the seeds of freedom, truth and justice. A bumper harvest was there for the taking. Individuals such as Frank McNulty in Lyttelton, Gib Smith in Dunedin, Jack Harris in New Plymouth, Jack O'Connor in Portland and Frank Hill in Whangarei were ensuring that no pastures were without seed. Not only watersiders but giants like Con Doyle and Sid Giles. That they had been

Jock Barnes, Ossie Osman, Ernie Delaney, Bill Andersen and Frank Barnard at the Auckland wharf gates on the 40th anniversary of the lockout, 1991 (*NZ Herald*)

driven out of the freezing works made their ability and integrity effective over still wider fields.

At a later date Sullivan was to admit that in barring all Auckland wharfies, the government had made a grievous error. Over 2000 missionaries were to make their presence felt in industries nationwide, building genuine unionism where none existed before and preparing the ground for a clean and honest trade union movement. As an illustration of the strength of their influence, here are but a few—all from Auckland.

> Previously mentioned:
> Jim Knox (FOL), Bill Andersen (Auckland Drivers), Frank Barnard (Freezing Workers)

> Others:
> Johnny Mitchell (Auckland and national president, Engine Drivers' Union)
> Tom Spiller (Auckland and national president, Tramways' Union)
> Ken Fabris (president, Northern Drivers' Union)
> Charlie Read (president, Auckland General Labourers' Union)
> Ernie Delaney (organiser, Dairy Workers' Union and Drivers' Union)
> Albert Whowell (executive member and negotiating committee, Dairy Workers' Union)

With the exception of Johnny Mitchell, none had held office in the

Jim Knox and Jock Barnes at the Auckland May Day rally, 1991 (*NZ Herald*)

Bitter End, New Beginning

Auckland branch and all were typical of a great rank and file that exemplified the strength of our union.

A meeting of our national executive was held on 3 October. I was still in jail. It was here that the suspicions we had harboured in Auckland about certain Wellington officials were turned into proof. First, Wellington had taken no action in protest at my jail sentence and now, while I was still incarcerated, they made their move. The executive resolved to close down the national office, to cease all branch activity, and to terminate production of the *Transport Worker*. In other words, they not only had made no attempt to implement national union policy to rebuild our union, but now actively campaigned against it. We now understood why Wellington had experienced only a fraction of the heat directed at Auckland. Tommy Wells and the Napier brothers were acceptable to Holland, Sullivan and the shipowners. Not so the Auckland and national leadership.

Many deregistered Wellington men left the waterfront in disgust. To return for the purpose of 'cleaning out scabbery root and branch', as was the policy of the combined unions, was one thing, but to stay there when that policy had been abandoned was quite another. These men comprised the shock troops of Wellington watersiders. Ron Dore, Clarry Armstrong, Alf Kite were examples, and Archie Dellaway another. The merit in his opposition to our resolution to return to work on the waterfront was now being demonstrated. The passage of time has shown that the real issue was not to return to the waterfronts, it was cleaning out scabbery throughout the entire trade union movement.

If vindication of our stand was needed, we got it in 1968 when the Federation of Labour made application to the Arbitration Court for a general wage order. The answer from the court was for no increase whatsoever. Direct action by unions throughout the country caused the FOL to have second thoughts. This thoroughly discredited body now proclaimed: 'Trade unionists are becoming increasingly aware that compulsory arbitration protects the interests of the employers.' The wheel had come full circle.

Life After the Waterfront

As for myself, I was to be faced by a total employer blacklisting the length and breadth of the country. I was released from Mount Eden on 10 November, but Christmas came and went with no job and no prospect of one. I then spotted a small carrying business at Taniwha, near Te Kauwhata, which was for sale. We arranged to sell our home in Grey Lynn and borrowed enough money to buy it. However, even here we faced an immediate boycott and, with little or no capital, we could not survive. I was forced to sell it, and with the money we had left we bought an old villa in Robert Street,

Ellerslie. It was more than somewhat neglected and run down but my son Bill and I worked on it. Bill was a carpenter by trade and had been involved in both the 1949 carpenters' lockout and our own in '51.

All the while I was looking for work and chanced upon an advertisement for labour by the Railway Department. While their advertisements were still in the daily papers, I got this reply:

> New Zealand Railways
> Works Manager's Office
> Otahuhu: 30th July 1952
>
> Memorandum:
>
> Mr H. Barnes
> 13 Robert Street
> Ellerslie
>
> Dear Sir
> I am in receipt of your application for employment dated 29th instant.
> In reply I have to advise you that there are no suitable vacancies available.
>
> Yours faithfully
> Works Manager

Over a year after the lockout, it seemed I was on a permanent 'not wanted' board.

This blacklisting also had its funny side and was sometimes unevenly applied. While in jail, I got a few letters and this one I have kept:

> Auckland Workingmen's Club and Mechanics' Institute
> Kitchener Street
> Auckland, C1
> 24th October 1951
>
> Mr Harold Barnes
> 28 Kelmarna Avenue
> Herne Bay
>
> Dear Sir
> The General Committee of the Club at a meeting held last evening instructed me to inform you that in terms of Rule 56 of the Club Rules your membership has ceased as from the 23rd October 1951.
>
>   You may however be re-elected after a period of twelve months from that date provided that a three-fifths majority of the General Committee then in office vote in favour of your re-election.
>
> Yours faithfully
> Secretary

Bitter End, New Beginning

Rule 56 barred members carrying criminal convictions from further membership in the Workingmen's Club, but as was generally acknowledged, I was a political prisoner. The rule had only ever been used once before, and that was against a member who in no way could claim his conviction to be political.

While I was clearly *persona non grata* with the Workingmen's Club, the racing industry was not so vindictive. I was a member of the Avondale Jockey Club and, with Freda, often enjoyed a day at the races. All cares vanished when watching those magnificent animals and trying to pick the next winner. As compared with the Workingmen's Club, the rules governing admission to racecourses were not only strict but strictly administered. However, there had never been a suggestion of my expulsion from the Avondale 'club, and by chance a meeting was scheduled for the Saturday following my release. However, because the police had the final say on these matters, Freda rang Inspector Jack Southworth, who said that the rule barring undesirable persons was only for criminals. 'But Jock is a criminal,' my wife said. 'Don't rub it in, Mrs Barnes,' was the reply. 'Jock can go on

Jock Barnes and *Buland Star*, 1950s
(Jock Barnes)

any racecourse in New Zealand, he will never be questioned, and he goes with my blessing.'

Next Saturday, with longtime friends Angus and Eve Cobb, Freda and I went to Avondale. Angus was also a deregistered watersider. As we walked in we were met by Inspector Southworth and Inspector Munro. They were in full uniform, shook hands, wished us luck, and for the benefit of the public, walked the length of the stand with us. For six months we had been opponents with no holds barred, yet they had a respect for me that was missing from the Auckland Workingmen's Club. It remains the only such body in New Zealand that has enjoyed the dubious honour of expelling or barring me for my 'criminal' conviction!

Some months later a deputation from the club waited on me with a petition asking me to apply for readmission. I thanked them and told them I had no job and no money, but there was not enough money in the world to cause me to even consider it!

I was still out of work and something had to be done. One day I called in to see Mrs Cassie, a stalwart in the labour movement. Her son Jock, a drainage contractor, was also there and gave me a job as a drainlayer's labourer. At a later date I obtained my drainlayer's ticket and, after a year with Jock, started to work for myself together with my son Bill.

Construction work was going on everywhere and there was strong demand for men with both drainlaying and surveying experience. Our services were in constant demand and by the late 1960s we had quite a prosperous little business. We worked on the university library block and halls of residence as well as a variety of city council and commercial buildings, including the Newtown Old People's Home and the Shortland Street carpark as well as buildings for the Bank of New South Wales, Norwich Union and the Waihou dairy factory. I served 14 years as president of the Master Drainlayers' Association and in that capacity served as representative on the Plumbers, Gasfitters and Drainlayers Board, setting and marking the qualifying exams for the trade. With the money I was making from this business I was able for some years to indulge my passion for the horses. I leased *Buland Star* and *Amber Star* for a few years in the late 1960s and won a little back and had great pleasure living just a few doors down from the Ellerslie Racecourse. I finally retired from the business in 1980 at the age of 73.

Reviving Old Memories

However, it was my years on the waterfront that are central to my life's story. In July 1976, Auckland branch deregistered Waterside Workers' Union (never dissolved) held a reunion. Some 25 years had come and gone and our ranks were thinning. Had memories of those left dimmed with the

Johnny Mitchell, 1980s (News Media: *Auckland Star* collection)

passage of time? How many would attend? Organiser Johnny Mitchell did a magnificent job. Preliminary enquiries showed we would have a large attendance, and we did. Over 1000 packed the hall. A delegate from Australia, Bill Richards from Dunedin, Waikato miners, several seamen and overseas cables all demonstrated to the full that we had not fought in vain.

July 1981 saw a repeat performance. This time 30 years had gone, the ranks were thinner, but again it was magnificent.

By July 1986 some 35 years had elapsed. How many this time? It was incredible. Jim Knox and Ken Douglas (who had been a deregistered Wellington driver in '51), Con and Enid Doyle with some of their family from Wairoa, and children and grandchildren of some who had passed away. A gathering of 800.

Here indeed was the proof. Children and grandchildren were there to pay homage to their fathers and mothers and to all who had fought back 35 long years ago. The memory of our struggle will never die, and the Loyalty Card that we produced for all those who had stood firm is a passport to trade union circles throughout the world.

We met again in 1991, smaller again this time, but still about 300 came to the celebrations of life and comradeship in Auckland. Jim Knox, Frank

Barnard, Bill Andersen are perhaps the best-known names amongst them, but most of the surviving wharfies from those days showed up together with their families. Tragically, Johnny Mitchell had passed away in 1990 but his family came in his place.

But if there was solidarity and comradeship within the veterans of '51, relations with the FOL and its successor, the Council of Trade Unions (CTU), were as rocky as ever. Then as now, the big wheels in the union movement didn't want to hear from the veterans of that struggle. The year 1987 was particularly busy in that respect. In May I was invited to the 50th anniversary conference of the FOL, and the issue of endorsing the Labour Party came up. Lange and Douglas had been in power for three years and the unions seemed hell-bent on giving them another three. I got up on my feet and gave the Labour government curry. I told the delegates that the Labour government was a bunch of renegades. I certainly got more cheers from the floor for that than did Lange and Geoffrey Palmer, who had spoken to what the *Herald* described as a 'painfully polite reception' the day before. At the end of the conference a group of us veterans were given a chance to have our say about the 50 years of the FOL. Alongside the rubbish from those such as Peter Butler (the leader of the Labourers' Union and a right-wing Catholic faction in the FOL in the 1950s and 1960s), some true words were spoken. They gave me a go and I lashed F.P. Walsh as a traitor of the worst type.

WWU members on the 25th anniversary of the lockout (Jock Barnes)

Bitter End, New Beginning

Later in 1987 I was invited to take part in a video about the events leading up to the '51 lockout, called *Shattered Dreams*. This was part-funded by the Trade Union History Project and turned out to be a fine documentary of events. And it was also in 1987 that I finished the first draft of what you

Jock Barnes addresses a meeting of the Young Socialists' Club at Auckland University, 1981 (*NZ Herald*)

are reading now. Within a couple of years, copies of the draft were circulating around the traps, and before long you could hear the squeals of protest from Wellington. The Labour government wasn't happy. The CTU was furious. And I also found out the cost of offending some of those in power: publishers refused to consider the manuscript for fear of defamation charges. I was happy to take the risk of being sued: then the whole sordid record of the FOL and both Labour and National governments could be exposed in the courts. But no publisher would touch it.

But that hasn't stemmed interest in the events of '51 and my role in it. I am constantly invited to speak at rallies and public forums. I have spoken at several May Day rallies in Auckland and got a warm reception. The younger people want an 'old hand' to come and tell them what it was like. They also want someone who isn't prepared to toe the Labour Party line but to give them the unvarnished truth.

In 1989 I received one of the biggest honours of my life. The socialist publisher Pathfinder Press was opening a new head office in New York City and wanted to cover one of its walls with a huge mural of all those from around the world who had fought for equality, freedom and against injustice. And so in a big office building in New York City, tourists can see my picture alongside that of Harry Holland, the Labour Party's only genuine socialist, and Te Kooti, the famous Maori resistance fighter, as well as Nelson Mandela and Karl Marx!

Looking back at the great battles on the waterfront culminating in the 1951 lockout, it is important for today's readers to understand that it was not just an industrial struggle. In fighting the evil schemes of US imperialism and John Foster Dulles, I think some seeds were dropped that have been of value in recent battles for peace, freedom and human rights. In the years that have gone, we have seen the Americans intervene in Korea, Vietnam, Nicaragua and Chile—in fact anywhere where working people have struggled to free themselves from the chains of imperialism and build a better life. There is only one way that this can be achieved—fight back and never surrender.

The same is true in New Zealand. At the anniversary celebrations of the veterans of '51, as I mingled with those mighty people, the years fell away and I was young and strong again. But, old as most of us were, we knew full well that if called upon again, we would fight again and there would be never a white flag.

Appendix 1: History of the Waterfront Commission

DURATION	CONSTITUTION AND PERSONNEL	REMARKS
9 April 1940–30 June 1946	**Waterfront Control Commission** R.E. Price; H.A. McLeod (to 1941); T.H. Bowling; Jim Roberts	No elected employer or union representation.
1 July 1946–13 February 1947	**Waterfront Industry Commission** Chairman: Judge Ongley Employers: K.A. Belford; G.L. Almond Union: H. Barnes; J. Flood	Part-time body. Chairman resigned.
14 February 1947–9 November 1947	**Waterfront Industry Commission** A.E. Bockett	Sole commissioner.
10 November 1947–5 December 1948	**Waterfront Industry Commission** Chairman: Judge Dalglish Government rep: J.O. Johnson Employers: G.L. Almond; J.A. Anderson Union: J. Flood; R.J. O'Donnell	Full-time body. Union reps resigned on 25 June 1948 over *Mountpark* dispute. Provision then made for quorum of three.
6 December 1948–31 October 1951	**Waterfront Industry Commission** Chairman: A.E. Bockett Employers: L.F. Malcouronne Union: R.J. O'Donnell *and* **Waterfront Industry Authority** Chairman: Judge Dalglish Employers: K.A. Belford; T.S. Marchington Union: H. Barnes; T. Hill until September 1949, replaced by A. Dellaway and J. Flood April 1950	Full-time body. Part-time. Judicial functions.

Source: Green (1996, Appendix B), see also Gordon (1951: 8).

Appendix 2: Key Information on the Waterside Workers' Union (Auckland branch), 1935–51

OFFICE-HOLDERS

President
1935–36:	W.J. Cuthbert
1936–38:	T.H. Solomon
1938–39:	R.G. Jones
1939–41:	T.H. Solomon
1941–50:	H. Barnes
1950–51:	A. Drennan

Secretary
1917–39:	H. Hillier
1939–40:	W.J. Cuthbert
1940–45:	E.A. Girven
1945–51:	R. Jones

MEMBERSHIP

1935:	1200
1940:	1444
1945:	1812
1951:	2198
1956:	1748

Source: Roth (1993: 201)

Appendix 3: Our Union is Attacked, 1949

Our Union faces a Fascist-like threat to its rights. This report gives the facts, warns of the dangers ahead, and sounds the call for every member to stand alert.

Here Are Their Crimes

In the four months since the Commission and the Authority were set up Jock Barnes and Toby Hill have gained:

★ Guaranteed wage increased to £5/10/-.
★ All special cargo rates improved.
★ Meal money raised to 2/6.
★ Improved relieving deckmen agreement.

★ Guaranteed wage increased at Awanui, Whakatane, Opotiki, Tokomaru Bay—established at Motueka, Tauranga.
★ All attempts by employers to worsen conditions successfully opposed.

THE ABOVE GAINS, PREVIOUS GAINS, THE FIXED INTENTION OF GOING ON TO GAIN A 1/- AN HOUR INCREASE—THESE ARE THE "CRIMES" OF BARNES, HILL AND DRENNAN!

All Branches stand firm. Auckland says "thanks for the gains made," Wellington says "take action to get the 1/- an hour," Lyttelton says "full confidence in the national leadership."

OUR UNION ATTACKED

★

Members will recall that in July of last year a tribunal, presided over by the Chief Justice, Sir Humphrey O'Leary, was set up by the Government to arbitrate on the "Mountpark" dispute. The Chief Justice found that the members of the Auckland Branch were justified in refusing to lift the Mountpark hatches. Compensatory payments were awarded and, finally, the N.Z. General Harbour Regulations were amended, giving the Union full satisfaction of its original grievance and ensuring greater safety for the lives and limbs of our members.

At this stage, the main matter of concern is not that the Waterfront Industry Commission was proved wrong but that the Union demonstrated the Commission to be acting as judge and jury in its own case. This, of course, was a fundamental breach of all the principles of common justice. The Union also alleged that the Chairman of the W.I.C. was merely a rubber stamp for the real Waterfront Controller—the Minister of Labour.

After the successful ending of this dispute, negotiations were held between your National Executive and the Minister of Labour on September 22nd. You have already been advised of these negotiations by an 11-page circular sent to all Branches on the 19th October, 1948. During these negotiations it was stated by the Minister of Labour that "in view of the criticism of the Commission being judge and jury in its own case, **and much of the criticism being valid,** the Government was of the opinion that the Commission should be in two parts:—(1.) Administrative and (2). Judicial."

The Government was desirous of continuing Commission control and he hoped

REPORT TO MEMBERS

that agreement would be reached with the Union and the employers. He stated that Judge Dalglish had been working on the principle of the Commission, and the following suggestions were for the Union to consider: (1) That a Judicial Tribunal be set up to deal with terms and conditions of employment for waterside work, **including wage rates** and other matters covered by the main order of the Commission and (2) that an Administrative Commission deal with levies for administrative and other purposes.

Authority to Fix
Wage Rates

Your National Executive was in agreement with these proposals and, consequently, the form of Waterfront Control was re-constituted, giving us the Waterfront Industry Commission on the one hand as an administrative body and the Waterfront Industry Authority on the other hand as a judicial and legislative body and a final Court of Appeal **completely independent and subject to no outside influence.**

Sittings of the Waterfront Authority were held on the 6th December, 1948, and your representatives have already reported to you of the gains achieved for members. We refer you to circulars dated 15th December, 1948 and 24th February, 1949, where these are dealt with at some length. Again, members have been fully advised of the Union's efforts to secure an adequate increase in wages and you will know from circulars sent to you on the 14th February and 22nd February, the result of negotiations on this matter.

Authority Evades
Giving Wage Increase

In the circular of 22nd February, it was stated by your representatives in summarising the facts that:

1. "The Waterfront Authority is not the body that determines the wages of waterside workers, and

2. The Employers' representatives on the Waterfront Authority are not empowered to make any offer on wages notwithstanding the merits of the claim. They both admitted that we were entitled to a substantial increase in wages but the New Zealand Employers' Federation was the body to determine wages."

We also pointed out in the circular of 22nd February that it was abundantly clear that the real body determining our wage case was not the Waterfront Industry Authority, but the Arbitration Court.

We protested most strongly at the attitude adopted by the Chairman of the Waterfront Industry Authority and the Employers' Representatives. On these facts you have already been advised. Following on this a meeting of the National Executive was held on the 22nd and 23rd February.

Resolutions were received from several Branches requesting the National Executive to implement a policy of action in order to achieve satisfaction on our wage claim.

National Executive
Calls for Patience

However, the National Executive was anxious to take no precipitate action for which we might be condemned as disrupters and your National Executive passed the following Resolution:—

"That in considering the demands of the Branches of the National Executive to adopt a policy of direct action on the wage question, the Executive points out to the Union membership that the decision of Judge Dalglish granting 2½d per hour is an interim decision to be finalised on the 28th March, 1949. In those circumstances the National Executive adjourns discussion on the aforementioned Resolutions of the Branches until the Judge makes his final decision when, if necesary, the National Executive will convene a National Council Meeting to determine policy."

Your National Executive was acting at all times in a manner that could not be considered provocative by any stretch of imagination. Its actions were also in absolute line with the policy of our Union as laid down by the National Council. A circular was sent to all Branches on the 24th February and we are satisfied that members appreciate these facts.

OUR UNION ATTACKED

On the 28th March a further meeting of the Waterfront Industry Authority was held, this being the day on which our final wage decision was to be given. However, the Arbitration Court had not yet brought down its decision on the general wage increase and Judge Dalglish, Chairman of the Waterfront Authority, together with Messrs. T. Marchington and K. Belford, made it crystal clear that the decision of the Arbitration Court would be the decision of the Waterfront Industry Authority.

Union Reps Protest
At Authority's Action

Your representatives protested vigorously against such conduct. We claimed that the Waterfront Industry Authority was supposed to be a judicial body. We pointed out that it was not even bound by the Economic Stabilisation Regulations and we said that its duty was to hear the facts argued and presented by both sides and then to give it a fair and impartial decision.

We protested in the strongest possible terms about this situation—a situation in which the Arbitration Court, a body that had never heard our case and never would, was determining the decision.

Our protests were of no avail and we did all we could do under the Regulations, i.e., dissent from the decision.

Intense Provocation
Begins

In the week following the 28th March, your representatives were subjected to extreme provocation in an obvious attempt to get them to walk off the Waterfront Industry Authority. We refused to be stampeded by this disruption and continued in our task of arguing on behalf of the members of our Union.

It is interesting to note that arising out of a short stopwork meeting held by the Wellington Branch, on Tuesday, 29th March, Mr. K. Belford, one of the employers' representatives, threatened to walk off the Waterfront Authority. We suggest, in passing, that if this had been the attitude of either of your representatives, it would have been headline news and Messrs. Barnes and Hill would have been accused of disrupting another Waterfront Commission.

The Authority adjourned on Thursday, 31st March until Monday, 4th April. However, on the 1st April at 10.45 a.m., a letter from the Minister of Labour was delivered to the National Secretary. At the same time and before the Union had had any opportunity of considering the letter, a copy was made available by the Minister to the press. In passing, we think that all members will condemn this action. If the Minister of Labour and the Government wished to discuss any matters with the Union, their duty was clear and your National Executive, as on all previous occasions, would have been happy to discuss any matters with them.

The fact that the letter was published makes it quite clear that the letter's primary purpose was to be an attack on the Union.

This letter has been published in every newspaper in New Zealand and we will not reprint it in full. However, the salient features at this stage must be emphasised. We are accused:—

> 1. By the Minister of Labour of perpetuating gross and flagrant breaches of our previous undertakings.
>
> 2. The Government says it will take the necessary steps to ensure that at any Port where an unauthorised stoppage of work occurs, the guaranteed daily and weekly payments will be cancelled and such other disciplinary action taken as may be necessary. and
>
> 3. The Government requests two issues to be put before our members per medium of the secret ballot before April 21st.

This provocative letter was of such a serious nature that your National Executive was immediately summoned.

Point One
Serious Trouble Expected.

With regard to point 1, we think that the number of stoppages in industry has been very small and it has been admitted by Messrs. Marchington and Belford that when the decision of 2½d was brought down they

REPORT TO MEMBERS

expected trouble of a very serious character.

We wish to make it clear that we are in no way criticising the affairs of another Union when we say that for every stoppage on a waterfront in New Zealand there have been many more in a New Zealand mine. We believe that any time our comrades in the mines or any other section of workers cease work, they have very good and sound reasons, but we point out to our members that there has been no suggestion from the Minister that miners should have a secret ballot on the question of the abolition or continuance of the Coal Mines' Council. In fact these stoppages seem to have entirely escaped even the notice of the Minister. Can it be that he regards us as poorer unionists than the miners or are they next?

Point Two
Minister Exposes Himself

With regard to point 2, we think none of our members will dispute the fact that the Minister, by his ill-considered letter of 31st March, makes it perfectly clear that the Union's charge made before the "Mountpark" Tribunal as to Ministerial dictation is completely and wholly sustained.

Point Three
No Room for Dr. Ley.

With regard to point 3, we feel that all our members will agree with us when we say that any issues to be put before our members by secret ballot will be determined by the proper authorities, as defined in our democratic and registered rules.

These rules, being democratic, make no provision for dictation by a prototype of Germany's Dr. Ley.

On Monday, 4th April, the Waterfront Industry Authority resumed its adjourned meeting, and the following motion was moved by your representatives:—

> This Waterfront Authority resents the statement by the Minister of Labour with reference to the Government's interference in the conduct and control of the waterfronts of New Zealand. We point out that this is the prerogative of the Waterfront Industry Commission and the Waterfront Industry Authority. As members of the Waterfront Industry Authority, a body supposed to be a judicial character and subject to no outside pressure groups, political or otherwise, we advise the Minister of Labour that we strongly resent the attempts of him and his Government to override our Constitutional Authority. Knowing that State control of the Trade Union Movement was a prerequisite to Fascism in Italy and Nazism in Germany, we view the matter most seriously. We make it abundantly clear to the Government that we will carry out our duties as defined by the Waterfront Industry Regulations, that we are not political puppets, and that we will accept no outside dictation. We will decide what will be done on the subject of guaranteed wages or any other condition of employment — not the Government.

AUCKLAND SAYS "THANKS A MILLION"

16th March, 1949

"That this Branch expresses full confidence in the National Executive and the National Officers of the Union for the benefits that have been gained for the members of the Union."

Judge Dalglish said that he had been concerned about the letter from the Minister of Labour, but that he had since discovered a Regulation, known as the "Waterfront Industry Emergency Regulations 1946" Amendment No. 1. This says:

> "The Minister may from time to time, by Order in writing, suspend in whole or in part all or any of the provisions of the principal regulations or of any order, direction or decision made by the Commission or by any Port Committee under the principal regulations in respect of the application to all or any of the Ports in New Zealand and may at any time or from time to time revoke or vary any such Order."

This Regulation was brought down on the 16th December, 1946, when the Ongley Commission had been disbanded and its validity to-day, with the re-constituted body, might well be challenged. However, with that aspect we are not greatly concerned.

Authority Meekly Submits
to Ministerial Dictation

The matter that concerned us and must concern all members is that while Judge Dalglish and Messrs. Marchington and Belford had constantly adopted the attitude that the Waterfront Industry Authority was a final Court of Appeal, subject to no outside

Appendices

OUR UNION ATTACKED

influence or pressure, and that waterside workers must unquestionably obey all its decisions, **yet they were prepared to accept the fact that the Minister of Labour could override, suspend or vary any of its decisions at any time he had the particular whim.**

This is a matter that must receive the most serious consideration of all members. In fact Mr. Belford threw aside all pretence and said he welcomed this dictation by the Minister of Labour. A peculiar attitude, we think you will agree, from one who is supposed to be sitting in a completely judicial and independent capacity, subject to no outside pressure!

After further discussion, the Chairman of the Waterfront Industry Authority adjourned the Authority sine die.

These facts were considered by your National Executive and the following Resolution was unanimously carried.

> "That this National Executive of the New Zealand Union strongly resents the letter from the Minister of Labour dated the 31st March 1949. We consider it most improper interference in the affairs of the New Zealand Waterside Workers' Union and also a wilful attempt to usurp functions that rightfully should be those of that alleged independent judicial body—the Waterfront Industry Authority. While we regret the fact that the Chairman has seen fit to adjourn the Waterfront Industry Authority sine die, that body is still the governing body and the National Executive will be please to discuss any problem with the Authority at any time.
>
> At the same time we make it clear that any issues to be put before our members and any change of Union policy will be determined by no one but the proper authorities as defined in our democratic and registered rules. The policy of our Union, as determined by our National Council, is for a continuance of Commission Control. That policy will be continued unless and—or until our National Council decides otherwise.
>
> With regard to the second issue raised by the Minister of Labour we would be pleased to have advice of any decisions of the Waterfront Industry Authority (excepting the "Northumberland" dispute when our Union was loyally abiding by a direction of the National Council of the Federation of Labour and of the Auckland Trades Council) that our Union has refused to accept.
>
> "In accordance with its former undertaking the Union will continue to accept and abide by decisions of the Waterfront Industry Authority and not the decisions of any other body."

WELLINGTON SAYS "GET BUSY"
18th February, 1949

"That we, the members of the Wellington Branch, affirm our confidence in the National Officers and Executive and approve of their action in makeing the wage increase of 1/- per hour a priority question **and we request the National Executive to prepare a course of direct action to achieve a satisfactory decision.**

The next matter of importance was that on Tuesday, 5th April, your officials were subjected to an hysterical and vicious attack by the Prime Minister who charged them with violating lawful decisions of the Authority. The Prime Minister has been challenged to nominate one such occurrence. **We are still awaiting his answer.**

Union Condemns Minister's Interference

Following on this your National Executive passed a further resolution:

> That the National Executive, in view of the vicious and unwarranted attacks being made on our National President, Mr. Barnes, and our National Secretary, Mr. Hill, reaffirms its continued confidence in them. We place on record our thanks to these Officers for the substantial gains obtained by the Union over recent months, and we have to commend their restraint and patience in a situation of extreme provocation.
>
> These attacks upon the officials we acknowledge as a prelude to a general attack upon Union conditions and warn the members of the Union to refuse to be diverted by these attacks from their basic duty to defend the hard won conditions which have not been achieved without sacrifice and privation by the waterside workers throughout the years.
>
> In the face of this incitement against our officials and inspired to smash our Union, the National Executive calls upon the Union members to stand firm and unite the ranks and guard the unity of the Union as the first condition for further progress of waterside workers' interests.
>
> The National Executive, appreciative of the universal expressions of confidence contained in the resolutions of the Branches on the work of the National Officers and Executive, also records its fullest confidence in the members of the Union everywhere that they will respond as one man in face of attacks in defence of the Union.

OUR UNION ATTACKED

It was felt by your National Executive that a comprehensive circular, setting out the above facts should be sent to all Union members. Your Executive feels, as it says in the resolution, that attacks on your officials are merely the prelude to a general attack upon Union conditions.

Your Executive warns members to refuse to be diverted by these attacks, and in the face of the hysterical provocation that is being directed against us from the Prime Minister downwards, calls upon members to stand firm, to unite their ranks and to conduct themselves in accordance with the proud traditions of N.Z. Trade Unionism.

Executive Sounds Warning to Members

What action will be taken by the Government after April 21st, we do not know. In the meantime we ask members not to be provoked into taking local action and to advise the National Office of any situation which may arise.

If attacks are made after the 21st April, it will be clear that these attacks are not against individuals, but against the fundamental rights and hard-won conditions of every waterside worker in the country.

If this situation arises, your National Council will be summoned. And we are confident that the traditional solidarity the steadfastness and the honesty of purpose which prevails in our ranks will, as in the past, repel all attacks.

WE WILL NOT ONLY HOLD OUR GAINS—WE WILL MARCH FORWARD TO MAKE FURTHER GAINS AND TO TAKE THE HIGHER STANDARD OF LIVING WHICH IS OUR DUE.

"Jock" Barnes, President

Toby Hill, Secretary

For and on behalf of National Executive.

Universal Printing Products Ltd.

SUMMARY

July, 1948.
Union action upheld in "Mountpark" dispute and W.I.C. condemned as judge and jury in its own case.

September, 1948.
Minister of Labour agrees criticism of W.I.C. is valid and offers independent, judicial Authority to fix wage rates and other conditions.

December, 1948
Waterfront Authority sits and Union makes some gains.

February, 1949
Authority refuses wage increase despite merits of claim. Grants 2½d and promises to finalise on 28th March. Some Branches call for direct action but Executive anxious to give Authority a chance.

March, 1949
Authority meets and admits Arbitration Court—not evidence before it—will decide watersiders' wages. Union "reps" protest. Efforts made to provoke "reps" to walk out but they continue to sit on the Authority and put forward unanswerable case for immediate wage rise.

April 1st, 1949
Provocation having failed to divert Union from 1/- an hour wage claim Minister of Labour gives press letter before Union can consider it. Letter threatens Union and dictates to Authority.

April 2nd, 1949
Union refutes charges and tells Minister no dictation on internal affairs of Union will be tolerated.

April 4th, 1949
Union "reps" on Authority call for maintenance of judicial independence and condemn Minister for interference. Judge discovers old clause, accepts Ministerial dictation and suspends Authority. Union again declares willingness to participate in independent Authority and places onus for disruption on Minister.

April 5th, 1949.
Prime Minister makes hysterical, vicious attack. Union rebuts charges, reaffirms confidence in leadership and warns members to be prepared to resist attempts at smashing their organization.

Tomorrow
Personal vilification, provocation and diversions will intensify but the Union will continue to demand what no attacks and no amount of distortion and abuse can conceal—the justice of a 1/- an hour wage increase.

Appendix 4: Messages of Support from Australian and Other Unions During 1951

London
London Port workers acclaim stand of New Zealand brothers against Tory anti trade union set up. Extend hands across the sea in common struggle.
T. Mahoney

Mackay, Queensland
Mackay Branch Waterside Workers Federation congratulate your members on their solidarity. Sending through Healy approximately £800 weekly.
Massy Secretary

Sydney
Hospital Employees Association NSW assures full support your dispute.
McPhee General Secretary

Newcastle, NSW
Members of Australia No 2 Branch Newcastle endorse action of New Zealand waterside workers. Congratulate them on stand defence trade unionism. Pledge fullest support. Protest sent Holland.
Stewart Branch Secretary

Adelaide
Adelaide Branch Iron Workers monthly general meeting declared solidarity with your organisation in its struggle. Called on ACTU to declare solidarity. Protest forwarded to Holland.
McCaffrey—Secretary

San Francisco
Extend our support for your strike and stand by for whatever assistance we can give.
Marine Cooks and Stewards

Sydney
Commonwealth Council Amalgamated Engineering Union behalf 70,000 members assure support every way your splendid struggle have called Prime Minister protesting demanding settlement.
Devereux Secretary

Wollongong
On behalf 5000 iron workers Port Kembla NSW am directed to forward our congratulations and appreciation of heroic struggle waterside and other

workers against government repression including use of service personnel and police in present dispute have forwarded protest Holland government we pledge our full support.
Arrowsmith Secretary

Sydney
NSW firemen congratulate wharfies miners freezing workers and seamen on magnificent fight against fascist attack.
Lambert Secretary

Chullora, NSW
We the workers of the Electric Car Workshops condemn the repressive actions of the New Zealand government against the waterside workers of New Zealand. We pledge our full support for the Waterside Workers' Union in their fight against reactionary government.
Cable forwarded Prime Minister Holland, Parliament House

Wellington
One thousand workers in state railway workshops condemn government attack on trade unions and urge immediate return to normal conditions enabling just settlement dispute.

Wollongong
Southern District Miners Federation congratulate New Zealand waterside workers on their fighting stand full support guaranteed.
W Parkinson—President, M Fitzgibbon—Secretary

Melbourne
President Waterside Workers Trades Hall Auckland. Stick it out tremendous support for you in Victoria we will see you don't starve.
Jim Jones Shop Steward Iron Workers Union

Newcastle
Newcastle Trades Council make common cause with waterside workers in New Zealand in their fight against union busting Holland Government. Newcastle workers are with you in your great fight and send fraternal greetings.
Dowling, Secretary Trades Hall Newcastle Australia

Sydney
Holland
Prime Minister
Wellington New Zealand

NSW Postal Workers Union horrified at your government's action under emergency regulations. Considers your government grossly violating United Nations Charter. Urge immediate cessation hostilities to bona fide trade unions.
R.E. Wellard, Secretary

Sydney
Prime Minister Holland
Wellington New Zealand
Australian Seamen's Union crew Trans Tasman passenger ship Wanganella have legally quit job rather than continue trading to New Zealand where your government is endeavouring enforce repressive measures against locked out watersiders and supporting strikers. Australian Seamen's Union urges repressive measures be rescinded and government confer with workers' leaders to effect honourable settlement in interests of people.
Elliott, Federal Secretary

Sydney
The Secretary
New Zealand Waterside Workers' Union
Dear Comrade,
With thousands of other workers the BWIU of Australia is watching the epic struggle of your members, the miners, seamen, freezing workers and other trade unionists, against the Holland Government's attempts to destroy the powerful National Union in New Zealand.

Seeing the New Zealand scene as a repetition of the happenings in so many capitalist countries today, we cannot fail to realise the importance of the victory of the workers of New Zealand, knowing that your victory will be shared by all who fight for peace, freedom and security throughout the world.

This attack is part of the plan to eliminate all organised opposition to the war programme directed by Wall Street and agreed to by the recent meeting of Empire Prime Ministers.

Here in Australia all the usual propaganda tricks have been used to distort the news of your magnificent fight but news is filtering through of the remarkable steadfastness of those taking the brunt of the struggle.
E.W. Bulmer, Federal President
F Purse, Federal Secretary
Building Workers' Industrial Union of Australia
Federal Office
535 George Street, Sydney

Appendix 5: Other Works on the Waterfront, 1935–51

Other than the many pamphlets issued at the time by the WWU, government ministers and individual watersiders, personal dossiers compiled in the Barnes (Auckland University), Scott (Auckland Museum), Mitchell (Alexander Turnbull, Wellington) and Roth (Auckland University) collections, and reports on conferences and the Royal Commission (for a comprehensive listing of which see Roth, 1993), academic and other more substantial work on the New Zealand waterfront in Jock's time includes:

Bassett, M. (1972): *Confrontation 51: The Waterfront Dispute*, Wellington.
Fernandez, B. (1969): 'Trade union policy and practice in the New Zealand waterfront industry', thesis, Otago University.
Green, A. (1989): 'Battling on the Job: the struggle for control of the New Zealand waterfront, 1915-1951', PhD thesis, Auckland University.
―――― (1992): 'Spelling, go-slows, gliding away and theft: informal control over work on the New Zealand waterfront 1915-1951', *Labour History*, 63, 100–14.
―――― (1994): 'The unimportance of arbitration? The New Zealand waterfront 1915–1951', *New Zealand Journal of History*, 28 (2).
―――― (1996): 'British Capital, Antipodean Labour: The New Zealand Waterfront, 1915–1951', unpubliahed manuscript.
McDonald, R.N. (1955): 'An historical survey of the actions and policy of the New Zealand Watersiders' Union from 1937 to 1951: Being a critical account of their domestic and foreign policy', thesis, University of New Zealand (Wellington).
Meade, C.J. (1980): 'New Zealand waterfront unions, 1951-67', MA thesis, Otago University.
Parker, D. and Wevers, F. (1990): *Shattered Dreams*, video, Trade Union History Project, Auckland.
Parsons, K. (1991): 'The Women's Auxiliary of the Waterside Workers' Union', research essay, Waikato University.
Pettit, P.N. (1948): *History of Labour in the Wellington Waterfront to 1937*, Standard Press, Wellington.
Porzsolt, V.M. (1985): 'Rhetorical Smoke without Revolutionary Fire: a study of the consciousness of the New Zealand Waterside Workers' Federation, 1915-1937', MA thesis, Massey University.
Roth, B. (1993): *Wharfie: From Handbarrows to Straddles. Unionism on the Auckland Waterfront*, Waterside Workers' Union, Auckland.
Scott, D. (1952): *151 Days: Official History of the Great Waterfront Lockout and Supporting Strikes, February 15–July 15, 1951*, reprinted in 1977 by Labour Reprint Society, Christchurch.
Townsend, W.L. (1985): 'From Bureau to lockout: Lyttelton waterside workers 1920s to 1951', MA thesis, Canterbury University.
Turkington, D. (1976): *Industrial Conflict: A Study of Three New Zealand Industries*, Wellington.
Young, S. (1975): 'The activities and problems of the police in the 1951 waterfront dispute', research essay, Canterbury University.

INDEX

Acheson, Dean 157
Adams, Bob 152, 174, 204-5, 223-4, **227**
Allum, J.A. 37, 98, 206, **206**, **209**
Almond, G.L. 79, 81, 92, 105
Andersen, Bill 174, 212, **231**, 232, 238
Anderson, J.A. 37, 62, 65, 67, 73, 92, 100, 105
Armstrong, Clarry 174, **227**, 230, 233
Armstrong, Tommy 190, 203, 224
Auckland Star 34, 76, 78, 94, 96, 99, 111, 118, 120, 155, 162-3, 166, 173, 179-81, 184, 198-200, 202, 207-8, 211, 213, 215, 220, 225, 229, 231
Australian Waterside Workers' Federation 35, 120, 129-30, 179, 212

Barnard, Frank 174, 212, **231**, 232, 237-8
Barnes, Freda 35, 43, 44, 215-6, **227**, 229-30, 235-6
Bassett, Michael 17, 19, 25-6
Baxter, Alan 205, 211
Baxter, Ken 15, 18, 32-3, 37, 79, **81**, 84, 86 99, 105, 108, 111-2, 115, 124, 126, 129, 130-2, 137-8, 172-3, 177, 181, 184, 190, 193, 201, 214
Belford, K.A. 21, 32, 79, 81, 100, 103, 106, 111, 113, 122, 134, 136, 140, 144-5, 153, 155-6, 158, 160, 214
Belsham, R.S. 34
Berendsen, Carl 37, 78, **157**
Blakely, V. 32, 160
Bockett, A.E. 37, 75, **75**, 83-4, 87, 106, 135-6, 140-1, 149, 160, 182
Bockett, H.E. 33, 37, **75**, 160-1, 163, 177, 182, 219
Bowling, T.H. 62
Brockett, H. 75-6
Burke, Jim 175
Butler, P.M. 21, 181, 238

Canadian Seamen's Union 114-6
Carpenters' Union 21, 31, 85, 106-8, 110-2, 116, 128, 130, 138-9
Cassie, A.M. 211, 236
Cement Workers' Union 32, 34, 171, 192-3
Chelsea Sugar Refinery 45, 50
Christchurch Press 103, 118, 126
Cleary, T.P. 100, 102
Clerical Workers' Union 126, 137
Coates, J.G. 37, 44, **45**
Communist Party 20, 79, 85, 88, 106, 108, 120, 229
Congdon, Captain 32, 160
Crook, W. 24, 184, 187, 193, 208, 218-9

Croskery, Alexander 15, 37, 105, 107, 138, 181, 200-1
Cuthbert, Bill 30, 54-5, 61-2, 64-6, 68-9, 72-6, 91

Dalglish, D.J. 37, 87, 92-7, 105-6, 110-3, 115, 121-2, 134, 136, 140, 144-5, 147-9, 154, 160, 163
Delaney, Ernie **231**, 232
Dellaway, Archie 140, 195, 221, 223, 233
Dobbie, H. 32, 153, 155, 160
Dominion 88, 139, 141-2, 202
Donaldson, Noel 16, 21, 129, 213
Dore, Ron 174, 221, 233
Doyle, Con 87, 190, 221-4, 231, 237
Drennan, Alec 16, 83, 88, 100, 110, 129, 145-6, **147**, 174, 189, 194, 204, 211-2, 223, **227**, 230
Drivers' Federation 217
Drivers' Union 33-4, 137, 139, 149, 179, 190, 192-5, 199, 213, 219, 221-3, 232
Dulles, J.F. 32, 156, 161-2, **162**, 173, 181, 195, 201, 212-3, 224-5, 240

Edwards, Robert 36, **227**, 229-30
Employers' Federation 111, 116, 147
Engineers' Union 83, 149, 192
Evening Post 126, 139, 149-50, 152, 226
Eyre, Dean 215, 224
Eyre, Dorothy 215

Fabris, Ken 232
Fawcett, Bob 59, 92-6
Federation of Labour 13, 15-24, 26, 31-5, 37, 56, 79-81, 83-4, 88, 95-6, 105, 108-12, 114, 116, 126, 130-4, 137-9, 148-9, 153, 157, 169, 172-3, 179, 181, 183-5, 192-3, 195, 2002, 208, 216-7, 219, 221, 223-5, 232-3, 238, 240
Flood, Jack 30, 67, 79, 88, 92, 93, 96, 140
Flynn, Terry 216, 221
Forbes, G.W. 37, 44-5, 163
Fraser, J. 191-2
Fraser, Peter 15, 21, 37, 52-3, **53**, 56, 58-9, 62, 65, 67, 72, 74, 76-7, 79, 83-9, **87**, 94-6, 98-9, 102, 105, 107-8, 111-2, 121-3, 126-9, 184
Freeman, James 192, 201, 214
Freezing Workers' Union 32-4, 83, 86, 137, 139, 149, 171, 174, 177-9, 181, 184, 187-8, 190, 192-3, 195, 199, 211, 213, 221-3, 232
Freyburg, Bernard 80, 123

Giles, Sid 87, 138-9, 177-8, **200**, 219, 221, 223-4, 231
Gilmour, J.A. 55, 153, 155, 158, 160
Girven, E.A. 30
Glading, S.V. 192, 214
Grant, Archie 152, 158, 174, 184, 211

Hamer, C.A. 100, 102
Hanson, Percy 83, 139
Hardy, Frank 186-7
Harrington, Gerry 187
Harris, Jack 176, 231
Healy, Jim 20, 22, 129
Hill, Toby 12, 16, 19, 21, 25, 30, 33, 88, 92, 96, 99-100, 103, 106, 110-2, 123-5, 128-9, 132, 134, 136, 139-40, **142**, 147-9, **151**, 153, 159, 172, 176, 178, 186, 190, 193, 207, 210, **210**, 211-2, 219-21, 222-3
Holland, Harry 45, 240
Holland, Sid 9, 20-2, 36, 37, 78, **87**, 98, 108, 129, 148-9, 152-6, **157**, 161-6, **162**, 173-4, 179, 186-7, 192, 195-8, 201-2, 204, **206**, 208, **209**, 210-4, 216-7, 221, 225-6, 231, 233
Holm, Captain 140, 143-4, 147
Holyoake, Keith 24, 32, 160-1, **162**
Hotel Workers' Union 138, 149
Hydro-Electricity Workers' Union 32-3, 171, 188

Jacobs, Freda *see* Barnes, Freda
Journalists' Association 199

Kelly, Jack 30, 54-5, 62
Kemp, Charlie 221, 223-4
Kilpatrick, H. 139, 187
Kirwin, Pat 207
Kite, Alf 174, 221, 233
Knox, Jim 174, 208, 212, 232, **232**, 237

Labour Bureau 10, 51-2, 68-9, 74, 94, 146, 159
Labour Daily (Sydney) 44, 47
Labour Party 13, 15-6, 22, 24-6, 35, 37, 44-5, 48, 54, 56, 70, 84, 108, 126, 129, 184-5, 190, 201-3, 208, 213-4, 216-7, 225-6, 228, 240
Labourers' Union 21, 139, 149, 211, 221, 232, 238
Langley, Frank 108, 139
Langstone, Frank 13, 49, 128
Lee, J.A. 48-9, 108
Luxford, J.H. 37, 69-70, 73, 95, 99, 216, 227-8

McAra, Bill 85, 108
McGavin, Pat 150, 215, 227, **228**, 229-30

255

McLagen, Angus 15-6, 18-9, 31, 37, 56, 74, 79, 81, 83-8, 91, 93-100, 102-3, 105-6, 108, 110-2, 115, 118-9, 121-9, 134, 136, 152, 155, 163, 226
McMullen, W.F. 35, 231
McNulty, Frank 175, 212, 231
Magee, Tom 199, 221-2
Manson, Eddie 216, 221
Maritime Cargo Workers' Union (Auckland) 35, 207, 231
Marchington, T.A. 32, 106, 111, 122, 134, 136, 140, 144-5, 149, 150, 152-6, 158, 160, 214
Mason, H.G.R. 65, 164-5
Melville, Alan 139, 219
Menzies 156, 212
Meredith, V.R. 69, 227, 229
Millar, F. 47-8
Miners' Union *see* United Mine Workers' Federation
Minhinnick, G.E. 16, 38, **60**, 62, **63**, 68
Mitchell, Johnny **85**, 145, 174, 205, 212, 224, **227**, 229-30, 232, **237**, 237-8
Moohan, Michael 38, 56
Monk, Albert 18, 23
Murray, Joe 30, 54-5, 62
Myers, Michael 102-3

Napier, Eddie **142**, **151**, 153, 174, 195, 224, 233
Napier, Jim 88, **142**, 212, 233
Nash, Walter 19-20, 22, 25, 33-5, 38, 83, **87**, 89, 95, **95**, 104, 184-5, 193, 201-4, 224, 226
NZ Herald 15, 16, 62, 70, 73, 76-8, 91, 94, 96, 99-100, 102, 111, 118, 120-1, 139, 141, 143, 148, 150-2, 155-6, 173-4, 179-80, 183, 189, 192, 195, 198-9, 202, 205-6, 208, 210-1, 213, 238

O'Brien, Jim 30-1, 38, 74-6, 79, 81
O'Donnell, Reg 88, 93, 96-7, 106
O'Leary, H. 100-1, 132, 135
Olssen, E. 18, 24-5
Ongley, F.W. 38, 79-84, 93, 106

Packman 215, 230
Painters' Union (Wellington) 174, 204
Platts-Mills, John 172, **228**, 229-30
Port Employers' Association 31, 154, 156
Porter, Johnny 175
Potter, Pat 139, 184, 202, 205, 211, 221, 223-4, 226
Prendiville, A.V. 24, 178, 182, 184, 187, 190, 193, 208, 218-9
Press Association 203, 207
Price, R.E. 38, 54-5, 62, 64, 76
Public Service Association 24, 47-8

Railway Tradesmen's Association 208
Railway Workers' Union 33, 83, 149, 172-3, 219
Read, Charlie 232
Red Federation of Labour 13, 18, 130
Richards, Bill 83, 139, 209, 237
Roberts, Jim 30, 38, 54-6, 62, 75, 126
Roberts, John 138, 214
Robertson, D. 32, 153, 155, 160
Roth, Bert 17-19, 21, 23, 84, 176

Sargentina, Johnny 175
Savage, Michael 30, 48-9, 85
Scott, Dick 12, 17, 26
Scrimgeour, Colin (Scrim) 47
Seamen's International Union 114
Seamen's Union 126, 149, 176, 179, 188, 193, 195, 197, 213, 219, 221-3
Semple, Robert 15, 22, 38, 52, 56, **57**, 62, 79, 106, 108, 124, 213
Shell Company 116-8
Shipowners' Federation 10, 103
Shipping Company 10, 140, 145-7, 151, 153
Sill, Bill 177
Sinclair, L.G.H. 207, 215, 229-30
Skinner, C.F. 213, 224
Smith, Gib 176, 216, 231
Solomon, Tom 30, 54-5, 61-2, 65-6, 69
Southworth, Jack 61, 189, 215, 235-6
Spiller, Tom 232
Stanich, Captain 118, 145-6
Stanley, Roy 106, 108, 128
Star-Sun (Christchurch) 126, 163
Sullivan, W. (Bill) 21-2, 32-4, 38, 134-6, **135**, 140-1, 148-9, 152, 155, 160-1, **162**, 163, 170, 173-5, 177-9, 181, 187, 189, 197, 201-2, 204, 209, 218, 220, 227, 232-3

Timber Workers' Union 87, 192
Trade Union Congress 18-19, 23-4, 31-2, 35, 138-9, 147, 152, 157-8, 172, 174, 184, 202, 204, 211
Trades Councils: Auckland 50, 55, 58, 67, 72, 83, 88, 109, 111-2; Otago 79; Southland 181; Wellington 37
Tramways Union 139, 209, 232
Transport Worker 12-3, 17, 96, 133, 144, 233
Transport Workers' Federation 83, 99, 115, 147
Truman, H.S. 156-7, **157**

United Mine Workers' Federation 32-3, 37, 130, 137, 149, 171, 173, 176-9, 181-2, 184, 187-8, 192-3, 205, 213, 218-9, 221-3
United Steam Ship Company (USSCo) 10, 62, 65, 67-8, 72-3, 75, 79, 81, 89-93, 96, 98, 100-02, 116, 118, 127, 153, 190

Vella, Frank 176, 183, 194

Walsh, F.P. 13, 15-6, 18-19, 21, 24-5, 31, 33, 38, **78**, 79-80, 83-4, 86, 88, 105, 107-8, 111-2, 114-5, 124, 126, 129, 131-4, 137-9, 148-9, 157-8, 173-4, 179, 181, 184, 187, 189-90, 192-3, 200, 201, 212-3, 221, 223, 238
Waterfront Control Com-mission 9, 12-3, 20, 30-1, 37, 53-4, 58, 61-70, 72, 74-6, 79, 241
Waterside Employers' Association 100, 103
Waterfront Industry Authority 37, 106, 110, 112-3, 119, 122-5, 128, 134, 136, 139, 143-7, 150-5, 158, 160-1, 241
Waterfront Industry Commission 9, 12-13, 20, 37, 79-80, 82, 84, 87, 89-94, 96-103, 105-6, 117-9, 121, 127-8, 134-6, 140-3, 146-8, 150-2, 154-5, 158, 160, 241
Waterfront Workers' Union: national council 33, 83, 93, 99, 106, 110, 120, 125, 186, 223; national executive 20, 32, 36, 82, 84, 93, 105-6, 111, 121-2, 125, 129, 139, 141, 151-2, 158-9, 193, 195, 216, 233; women's auxiliary (ladies' committee) 14, 171, 175, 195, 205, 210, 216
Waterfront Workers' Union branches: Auckland 11-2, 15-6, 21, 30, 32, 50, 52, 54-5, 62, 67, 69, **70-1**, 71, 73, 77, 82, 93-4, 98-9, 118, 121, 124, 128-9, 130, 133, 135, 144-8, 159, 171, **171**, 174, 185, 194, 196, 212-3, 219, 221, 225, 230, 232-3, 236-7, 242; Bluff 125, 176, 183, 194; Dunedin 124, 161, 171, 176, 216, 231; Lyttelton 12, 36, 93, 125, 136, 171, 175, 220, 231; Napier 194; Nelson 124; New Plymouth 21, 159, 176, 216, 231; Oamaru 125; Onehunga 125; Opotiki 185; Picton 125; Port Chalmers 35, 124, 176, 220, 223; Portland 231; Timaru 34, 129, 193-4, 212, 216, 220, 223; Wanganui 125; Wellington 16, 33-6, **70**, 93, 114-5, 128, 135, 153, 159, 171, 174, 183, 212, 216, 218, 221, 224, 233; Whangarei 125, 134, 231
Webb, P.C. 15, 32, 38, 52, **53**, 64, 67, 69, 160
Wells, Tommy **142**, **151**, 153, 174, **203**, 212, 233
Whowell, Albert **147**, 232
Wiley, H. Jenner 36, 229
Working Men's Club (Auckland) 234-6
World Federation of Trade Unions 130, 132-3, 156, 170, 180